VOID

Library of
Davidson College

ESSAYS ON THE PHILOSOPHY OF W. V. QUINE

Willard V. Quine, Edgar Pierce Professor of Philosophy Emeritus, Harvard University. Portrait in oil by Pietro Pezzati, 1969.

ESSAYS ON THE PHILOSOPHY OF W. V. QUINE

EDITED BY
ROBERT W. SHAHAN
AND CHRIS SWOYER

UNIVERSITY OF OKLAHOMA PRESS : NORMAN

Edited by Robert W. Shahan

Bonaventure and Aquinas: Enduring Philosophers (with Francis J. Kovach; Norman, 1976)
David Hume: Many-sided Genius (with Kenneth R. Merrill; Norman, 1976)
American Philosophy: From Edwards to Quine (with Kenneth R. Merrill; Norman, 1977)
Spinoza: New Perspectives (with J. I. Biro; Norman, 1978)
Quine (with Chris Swoyer; Norman, 1978)

Library of Congress Cataloging in Publication Data

Main entry under title:
Essays on the philosophy of W. V. Quine
  "Publications of W. V. O. Quine": p.
  Includes index.

CONTENTS: Harman, G. Meaning and theory.—Mohanty, J. N. On the roots of reference.—Levin, M. E. Quine's view of logical truth. [etc.]
  1. Quine, Willard Van Orman—Addresses, essays, lectures. 2. Philosophy—Addresses, essays, lectures. I. Quine, Willard Van Orman. II. Shahan, Robert W., 1935-   III. Swoyer, Chris, 1949-
B945.Q54Q56   191   78-21365

Copyright 1979 by the University of Oklahoma Press, Norman, Publishing Division of the University. Manufactured in the U.S.A. First edition.

PREFACE

The occasion of this collection of essays is Willard Van Orman Quine's seventieth birthday in June, 1978. We are pleased to be able to pay tribute to him and to his achievements; his lucid and penetrating treatment of many issues in philosophy and logic has exercised an influence on his contemporaries that is unsurpassed by the work of any other living philosopher. This seems an especially appropriate time for an issue devoted to him, for it has now been nearly ten years since the appearance of *Words and Objections: Essays on the Philosophy of W. V. O. Quine*, the only previous collection of papers devoted to Quine's thought. Meanwhile, he has been hard at work, and his influence has continued to grow. This is clear from the number of papers published each year that explicitly discuss one aspect or another of his work. But an equally important measure of a philosopher's eminence is the extent to which his interests and pursuits become those of his generation. On this score, too, it is hard to think of any living philosopher whose influence matches Quine's.

This issue contains papers by philosophers from a wide range of backgrounds. We have made a special effort to include several essays by younger authors, and their enthusiastic response indicates that Quine's influence on the newest generation of philosophers is at least as strong as it was on previous ones. His work may therefore be expected to be at the forefront of philosophical discussion for a long time to come. The present papers thus furnish more than a retrospective evolution of the work of an esteemed philosopher; they also represent a vital chapter of contemporary philosophy.

The present essays range from examinations of specific aspects of Quine's work to independent treatments of Quinean themes. The issue ends with Quine's own paper "Facts of the Matter."

We are grateful to Professor Quine for his help and encouragement in the preparation of this collection of essays. The editors and board of the *Southwestern Journal of Philosophy* congratulate him on his seventieth birthday and wish him many more happy and productive years.

ROBERT W. SHAHAN
CHRIS SWOYER

Norman, Oklahoma

CONTENTS

Preface	5
1. *Meaning and Theory,* Gilbert Harman	9
2. *On the Roots of Reference: Quine, Piaget, and Husserl,* J. N. Mohanty	21
3. *Quine's View(s) of Logical Truth,* Michael E. Levin	45
4. *Ontology and Reduction,* Richard E. Grandy	69
5. *No Entity Without Identity,* Dale Gottlieb	79
6. *Quine on Properties and Meanings,* Stephen Leeds	97
7. *Can Epistemology Be Naturalized?* M. J. Cresswell	109
8. *Warrant and Meaning in Quine's Clothing,* Mark Pastin	119
9. *Quine and Mathematical Reduction,* Mark Steiner	133
10. *De Re Propositional Attitudes Toward Integers,* Diana Ackerman	145
11. *Facts of the Matter,* W. V. Quine	155
Publications of W. V. *Quine*	171
Contributors	189
Index	193

Meaning and Theory

GILBERT HARMAN
Princeton University

In "Two Dogmas of Empiricism," W. V. O. Quine argues against any sort of verification theory as a general account of the meaning of individual sentences. At the same time he argues in favor of a holistic verification theory, concluding that "the unit of empirical significance is the whole of science."[1] This holistic verificationism plays an important role in Quine's philosophy; in particular it is an essential assumption of his argument for the indeterminacy of translation. In "Epistemology Naturalized" he puts the connection this way:

> The Vienna Circle espoused a verification theory of meaning but did not take it seriously enough. If we recognize with Peirce that the meaning of a sentence turns purely on what would count as evidence for its truth, and if we recognize with Duhem that theoretical sentences have their evidence not as single sentences but as larger blocks of theory, then the indeterminacy of translation of theoretical sentences is the natural conclusion.[2]

Quine spells out an argument for indeterminacy of translation on these grounds in his paper "On the Reasons for Indeterminacy of Translation," appealing there also to the assumption that

> physical theory is under-determined even by all *possible* observations. . . . Physical theories can be at odds with each other and yet compatible with all possible data even in the broadest sense. In a word, they can be logically incompatible and empirically equivalent.[3]

Quine discusses this second assumption, of under-determination of theory, in his recent article "On Empirically Equivalent Systems of the World."[4] In this paper I will not try to add to the literature on indeterminacy of translation, but I will look more closely at these two key doctrines, holistic verificationism and under-determination of theory.

I

Holistic verificationism takes two theories to have the same content if they are empirically equivalent. More precisely, the idea is that two theory formulations have the same content, and are therefore formulations of the same theory, if they are empirically equivalent.[5] But what is it for two theory formulations to be empirically equivalent? In the passages quoted above, Quine speaks of two different relations between observations and theory: observations can be "evidence" for a theory, and observations can be "compatible" with a theory. Let us then in a preliminary way distinguish two notions of empirical equivalence:

(1) T and U are empirically equivalent if and only if supported equally by the same observational evidence.
(2) T and U are empirically equivalent if and only if compatible with the same observational evidence.

I am not sure whether Quine has explicitly considered the difference between (1) and (2). He does not seem to distinguish them. Thus he invokes Peirce in order to support (1) but is soon using (2) without, as far as I can see, any further argument. He seems to assume, at least implicitly, that (1) and (2) come to the same thing. Why think that?

One might think that (1) and (2) come to the same thing if one believes that there is no other objective way in which evidence can support a theory formulation except by being consistent with that theory formulation and inconsistent with competing theory formulations. Quine may believe something of the sort.

Some philosophers suppose that evidence that is compatible with a theory can confirm it to a greater or lesser degree, so that a theory might be more or less probable on the evidence. These philosophers might want to distinguish (1) and (2). Two theories might be compatible with the same observational evidence and therefore empirically equivalent according to (2) but not necessarily according to (1), because they might be supported to different degrees of probability by the evidence with which they were compatible. But Quine does not accept this use of probability.[6]

What about simplicity and other features that distinguish better from worse hypotheses? Two theory formulations might be compatible with the evidence, although one, being simpler, less ad hoc, etc., than the other, was much better supported by that evidence. Could not two such theory formulations be empirically equivalent according to (2) but not according to (1)?

Quine might deny this. He might deny that the evidence gives more support to the simpler of two theory formulations that are compatible with the same observational evidence. For he sees only two sorts of reason to prefer a simpler formulation. One is that, given two theory formulations compatible with the evidence collected so far, the simpler stands the better chance of being counted compatible with further evidence.[7] But this reason cannot apply if the two theory formulations are compatible with exactly the same possible observations. The other kind of benefit Quine envisions is that simpler theory formulations are more beautiful and convenient, but he explicitly contrasts this reason for taking a given theory formulation to be "desirable" with reasons for taking it to be "more probable."[8] So perhaps Quine holds that simplicity and related factors are irrelevant to the amount of objective support evidence can give theory formulations that are compatible with the same observations. And that might seem to be a reason for not distinguishing (1) and (2).

This leaves a problem. Suppose T and U are compatible with the same observations, or suppose that T is much simpler than U, so that we would naturally accept T rather than U if faced with that choice. This makes a significant difference in the way we would *use* these theory formulations. Why shouldn't such a difference count as a difference in the content of the theory formulations?

On the other hand, suppose that we count such a difference in content. Then there is this problem. If this T and this U have *different* empirical content, what is the difference? What is being claimed by the one theory formulation that is not being claimed by the other? If we cannot specify the difference, how can we suppose that there is a difference?

Actually, we have so far been ignoring a very important point. In order to bring out the point, let us consider a specific example based on a suggestion by Barbara Humphries[9] and discussed by Quine in "Empirically Equivalent Systems of the World"[10]:

> Take some theory formulation and select two of its terms, say 'electron' and 'molecule.' I am supposing that these do not figure essentially in any observation sentences; they are purely theoretical. Now let us transform our theory formulation merely by switching these terms throughout. The new theory formulation will be logically incompatible with the old: it will affirm things about so-called electrons that the other denies.... Clearly ... the two theory formulations are *empirically equivalent*—that is, they imply the same observation conditionals. [P. 319]

Let T be the original theory formulation, and let U be the formulation obtained by switching the terms 'molecule' and 'electron' in T. Now suppose we accept T. Then we reject U. T and U cannot have the same content—one is we suppose true; the other is we suppose false. They cannot be equivalent in any sense. The one is logically incompatible with the other. Two incompatible theory formulations can be equivalent only if each is itself inconsistent, which we may assume is not the case with T and U. Nevertheless, T and U imply the same observation conditionals, they are compatible with the same observation sentences. This example clearly refutes (2).

(2) T and U are empirically equivalent if and only if compatible with the same observational evidence.

Equally clearly, the example does not refute (1).

(1) T and U are empirically equivalent if and only if supported equally by the same observational evidence.

Indeed, we suppose that the evidence we now have is evidence in favor of T and against U. So T and U are not empirically equivalent according to (1).

Recall our worry: If T and U have different empirical content, what is the difference? If we cannot specify the difference, how can we suppose there is a difference? This question had apparent bite as long as it seemed that we must specify the difference as a difference in empirical consequences. But T and U are clearly different in content while having the same empirical consequences. If we are to specify the difference, it will have to be in some other way, e.g., as a difference in how T and U might be translated into another language.

Indeed, notice that if other people were to accept U rather than T we would not suppose that they were wrong. The fact that they accept U would lead us to interpret them as meaning by 'molecule' what we mean by 'electron' and vice versa. U in their dialect would have the content T has in our dialect. The content of a theory formulation will obviously vary from one dialect to another and depends in part on whether that theory formulation is accepted by speakers of that dialect. T in our dialect is not equivalent in content to U in our dialect; but T in our dialect is equivalent to U in the modified dialect whose speakers accept U.

Quine recognizes this point, indeed insists on it, but also oversimplifies it when in comparing T and U he says:

> Yet their only difference, the man in the street would say, is terminological; the one theory formulation uses the technical terms 'molecule' and 'electron' to name what the other formulation calls

'electron' and 'molecule'. The two formulations express, he would say, the same theory. Someone else might urge, however perversely, that they express very different theories: both of them treat of molecules in the same sense but disagree sharply regarding the behavior of molecules, and correspondingly for electrons.... I think... we should individuate theories in such a way as to agree with the man in the street: the two formulations formulate the same theory, despite their overt logical incompatibility. [P. 319]

This is oversimplified because it leaves out of consideration which dialect a theory formulation is in. It is not "perverse" but simply common sense to think that T and U express very different theories in the same dialect. And "the man in the street" would not say that T and U express the same theory in the same dialect. The point is rather that T in the dialect of someone who accepts T expresses the same theory as U does in the dialect of someone else who accepts U.

Next consider someone who accepts neither T nor U but does accept a theory formulation T' that approximates T. His dialect will be much more like our dialect (we accept T) than the dialect of someone who accepts U. Indeed it will be reasonable for us to use the "homophonic" translation scheme in understanding him—in effect taking him to be speaking our dialect. Then his T and his U—like ours—must differ in content and cannot be empirically equivalent. This is again consistent with (1), since the observational evidence that would lead him to abandon T' in favor of T or U would be evidence for T and not for U. The relevant factor here is conservatism: adopting T would involve less of a change in antecedent view than adopting U would. (And if this sort of difference between theory formulations, involving considerations of conservatism, can have a bearing on the content of the theory formulation, why not also considerations of simplicity etc.?)

Now consider someone who has no theory of electrons and molecules. This person accepts neither T nor U nor any approximation to either. If T and U are nevertheless in his language and have content, they cannot have the same content, since they are logically incompatible. On the other hand, they can hardly have different content. Therefore they must as yet have no content, no actual content anyway. What they have is potential content—each would have content if accepted. Indeed, their potential content is the same. T if accepted would have the same content as U would have if U were accepted. In a derivative sense, then, T and U have the same content, the same potential content.

This suggests that instead of the misguided principle (2), we might try something like the following principle (2'):

(2′) T and U are potentially empirically equivalent, i.e., T in a dialect in which T is accepted is empirically equivalent to U in a dialect in which U is accepted, if and only if T and U are compatible with the same observational evidence.

(2′) is not refuted as (2) is by the 'electron' and 'molecule' example. Nevertheless, we may still wonder whether the following principle (1′) is not more reasonable:

(1′) T and U are potentially empirically equivalent if and only if T if accepted would be supported to the same extent by the same observational evidence as U would be if U were accepted.

(1′) differs from (2′) because T and U might be compatible with the same observational evidence, although T is much simpler than U. In that case T if accepted might be better supported by the evidence than U would be if U were accepted. It might be true, for example, that if one accepted U one ought to change one's view and accept T instead. But it is a moot point whether that would show there is a difference in content between T when accepted and U when accepted. Quine *may* well think that it would not—on the grounds that in this case our preference for the simpler theory formulation T is justified only by considerations of beauty and convenience and should not be taken as indicating that T is more likely to be true than U, so that our preference for T should not be taken as indicating any difference in cognitive content between T and U. But I am not sure what Quine's position really is here.

It might be objected that to accept T is to take T to be true, so that, if there are reasons of beauty and convenience to accept T rather than U, these are reasons to believe that T rather than U is true. But that argument is mistaken. One might suppose that T if accepted and U if accepted would both be true, being equivalent in content, but that T if accepted would be a more useful formulation of this content than U if accepted would be. (Consider the 'electron' and 'molecule' example again. We can have reasons of conservatism for accepting that T rather than that U without having reasons to think that that U, if accepted, would be false. On the contrary, our reasons for accepting that T are also reasons for thinking that U, if accepted, would be true.)

Although it is not clear to me whether (1') or (2') yields a better account of potential empirical equivalence, in what follows I will use the phrase "potentially empirically equivalent" in the sense of (2'), and I will understand Quine's use of "empirically equivalent" to mean potentially empirically equivalent in this sense.

II

Clearly, even if T and U are potentially empirically equivalent according to ($2'$), the evidence might support acceptance of T rather than U, for example, for reasons of conservatism if T or an approximation to T is already accepted, or perhaps for reasons of simplicity if T is much simpler than U. Certain cases of what Quine calls "gratuitous branching" might illustrate the second case:

> Thus suppose we had an adequate theory of nature, and then we were to add to it some gratuitous further sentences that had no effect on its empirical content. By ringing changes on these excresences we might get alternative theories, logically incompatible, yet always empirically equivalent. This gratuitous branching of theories would be of no interest to the thesis of under-determination. [P. 323]

This "gratuitous branching" is of "no interest" to the thesis of under-determination presumably because it does not yield a case in which we must choose between two potentially empirically equivalent theory formulations that are equally supported by the evidence. In a case of gratuitous branching reasons of simplicity would clearly favor our original adequate theory formulation.

I will suppose that the thesis of under-determination is the following thesis: *We are always at least implicitly faced with a choice between two potentially empirically equivalent theory formulations that are equally supported by the evidence.* Quine never states the thesis in exactly this way, but I believe that this way of putting the thesis brings out the main issue. For example, it helps to make clear why gratuitous branching is of no interest to the thesis.

Here is another kind of case. Suppose as before that we had an adequate theory of nature, formulated as T. Let U be the infinite theory formulation equivalent to the conjunction of all and only the observation conditionals implied by T, supposing these to be (infinitely) axiomatized using Craig's method.[11] And let V be a finitely axiomatized theory formulation consisting in the claim that the axioms of U are true in the language of U plus a finite theory of truth for the language of U.[12] Here too is an example that is of no interest to the thesis of under-determination. For in this case again the theory formulations T, U, and V are not equally supported by our evidence; T is clearly preferred, although the reasons for this are perhaps more obscure than in the previous case. T is preferred to U because U is infinite and we cannot explicitly accept each of an infinite number of axioms. And even if U had only a finite number of axioms, there would still be so many of them that T would be preferred on grounds of convenience.

V is finitely axiomatized and not noticeably less convenient *in certain respects* than T, so it may seem that there is not that sort of reason to prefer T to V. But there are other respects in which V is less convenient than T. The problem is that both U and V are parasitical on T. Our discovery and formulation of U and V depend on our discovery and formulation of T. I take it that Quine recognizes the relevance of this sort of factor in the following remark contrasting "loose" formulations like T with "tight" formulations like U (my emphasis):

> We, humanly, are capable of encompassing more true observation conditions in a loose theory formulation than in any tight system *that we might discover and formulate independently of any such loose formulation*. [One version of the thesis of under-determination says] that for each such formulation there will be others, empirically equivalent but logically incompatible with it and incapable of being rendered logically equivalent to it by any reconstrual of predicates. [P. 326]

Here the tight system U is taken to be not relevant to the thesis of under-determination because we do not discover and formulate U independently of our loose formulation T. Presumably then V is also to be disqualified, since it too is parasitical on T. (Maybe a theory derived from T by adding "gratuitous further sentences that had no effect on its empirical content" could also be disqualified on this same ground. In the passage just quoted Quine makes no other provision to rule out cases of gratuitous branching, although perhaps because of his prior discussion of the point he expects us simply to assume some further restriction to rule this out.)

How can the fact that V is parasitical on T make T a more reasonable theory formulation to accept than V, given the evidence? Conservatism might be a factor here, if we already accept T. But the point holds even if T is not yet accepted and is merely being considered. The reason, I suggest, is this: When we accept a theory formulation, that is not the end of the matter. We do not expect the theory formulation to remain as it is. We know we will be modifying it in various ways, improving it in the light of new evidence and new ideas about the subject. In seeking a "convenient" theory formulation, we are not only seeking a formulation that is conveniently short and easy to remember and convenient for purposes of deriving consequences; we are also seeking a formulation that can conveniently be modified and improved, given new evidence and new ideas about the subject. The formulation V, which is parasitical on T, may be convenient in the former respects, for it is short, easy to remember, and efficient to calculate with; but V will not be convenient in this last respect. If we were to accept V, then in order to make theoretical progress we would have to look back at T, consider what changes we would have made in T had we accepted it, given our new evidence and ideas. Seeing that we might have arrived at a modified formulation T′, we could then calculate the corresponding V′. But clearly in this case it would be much more efficient simply to begin by accepting T, making modifications in that as we think appropriate, forgetting entirely about V and V′.

Of course, if through some fluke it turned out that we could operate directly with V, making fruitful theoretical advances directly from that starting point without having to refer back to T and T′, then this objection to V would fall away; in that case the later modifications of V would not be parasitic on modifications in T. But we were envisioning a case where we have every reason to think that the later modifications of V *will* have to be parasitic on modifications in T.

Let me mention an actual example in which one theory formulation was parasitic in this way on another. Some years ago I attempted to construct something like a phrase structure grammar of part of English, containing no syntactical transformation rules, a grammar that would account for all the data accounted for by a transformational grammar that Noam Chomsky had described.[13] I believe I was successful in doing that, although the point is controversial[14]—and I believe that I could now in a similar way construct similar phrase structure grammars without transformations rules that would correspond to various more recent grammars. But this, if true, does not show that linguists were or are faced with a choice between two theory formulations equally supported by the evidence—Chomsky's transformational grammar on the one hand and my nontransformational phrase structure grammar on the other hand. For my nontransformational grammar was completely parasitic on Chomsky's grammar, and theoretical improvements in the nontransformational formulation would have to be parasitic on the improvements that Chomsky and others have made in his formulation, since my formulation apparently did not offer a useful autonomous framework for further theoretical progress. So the possibility of my sort of nontransformational grammar does not show that it was or is reasonable for linguists to construct grammars without transformation rules. (Recent arguments against transformation rules from within Chomsky's theoretical framework—arguments that appeal to "trace theory" and rules of anaphora or binding as they apply to traces—are another matter.)[15]

We are concerned with the thesis that theories are under-determined by even all possible observational evidence. I am supposing that this thesis is to be formulated in the following way: *We are always at least implicitly faced with a choice of two potentially empirically equivalent theory formulations that are equally supported by the evidence.* The idea is this: Suppose T is a theory formulation we currently accept or are considering accepting. Then the thesis is that there is another theory formulation U, normally, I suppose, one we do not accept and have not even thought of, such that U is compatible with exactly the same observational evidence as T and, if we were to be aware of U, we would be faced with the choice between T and U, where either choice is equally supported by the evidence. We have to bring in the condition "if we were to consider U," because it is not clear how our evidence could give us reason to accept U if we have never even considered U. Even if we do consider U, it might seem that T will always have an edge because of the value we attach to conservatism, especially if we already accept T. So perhaps we must suppose not just that U is considered but that U has actually been adopted by a number of people and that we have learned U well enough to be able to operate easily within its terms and discuss with those who accept U issues that arise from the perspective of U. But then it is not clear why we must *choose* between T and U. We might as well accept both theories so that we can talk both with those who accept T and with those who accept U.

Quine puts the point like this: "Where there is forever no basis for choosing, then, we may simply rest with both systems and discourse freely in both . . ." (p. 328). But I would quibble at the phrase "forever no basis for choosing." True, T and U are compatible with the same observational evidence. But surely neither T nor U will be our final theory formulation—nothing will ever be that. Both T and U will be replaced with later formulations T' and U' in the light of new evidence and new ideas. And, if neither is parasitic on the other, each theory will develop in its own characteristic way. The point is that one of T or U may be a more fruitful formulation from this perspective than the other. And that is an additional and more important reason why we might want to accept both—such dual acceptance increases our expectation of theoretical advance. This further reason might be a reason to accept both T and U even when no one else has done so, after we have simply realized that it is a possible formulation, since either of T or U might yield theoretical advances not yielded by the other. Of course, if one formulation proves more fruitful in this way than the other, then it is not true that there is "forever no basis for choosing" between them.

As Quine formulates the under-determination thesis, U must actually contradict T. He is supposing that U and T make different claims using the same vocabulary. Clearly, however, we do not want to accept inconsistent theory formulations. And here conservatism clearly favors T over U. As Quine points out, the solution is easy: modify the theoretical vocabulary of U so that it does not overlap the theoretical vocabulary of T. "This use of distinctive signs leaves us with two irreducible and unconflicting theories" (p. 328). Now we might accept U in addition to T in order to increase our expectation of theoretical advance.

Quine rules out the case in which T or U can be translated into the other formulation by reconstrual of predicates, as in the 'electron' and 'molecule' example and also as in an example due to Poincaré:

> Here we have one formulation of cosmology that represents space as infinite, and another formulation that represents space as finite but depicts all objects as shrinking in proportion as they move away from center. The two formulations, again, are empirically equivalent. But again the example is disappointing as an example of under-determination, because again we can bring the two formulations into coincidence by reconstruing the predicates. [P. 322]

But the cases are not the same. Consider the case where U is exactly like T except that 'electron' and 'molecule' have been reversed and marked in some distinctive way so as not be to confused with their occurrences in T. We might have a reason to accept both T and U if some people already accepted T and others already accepted U and we wanted to be able to talk to both groups. But accepting both formulations would not improve our expectations of theoretical advance, so we would not have that sort of reason to accept both formulations. T and U are so similar that we must expect them to develop in parallel ways in the light of new evidence and theoretical ideas. The same cannot be said for cases in which, although one of T or U can be mapped onto the other by reconstrual of predicates, the mapping is more complex, as in Poincaré's example. For in that case it seems quite possible that T and U might develop in different ways, so that it might be that we would improve our expectation of theoretical advance by accepting both. Actually, in this particular example U is and will almost certainly remain parasitic on T, so we have no reason to accept U. But it is not evident that this must always be so just because T or U can be mapped onto the other by reconstrual of predicates.

NOTES

1. W. V. O. Quine, "Two Dogmas of Empiricism," *From a Logical Point of View* (Cambridge: Harvard University Press, 1953; 2d ed., rev., 1961), pp. 20-46, quoting from p. 42.

2. W. V. O. Quine, "Epistemology Naturalized," *Ontological Relativity and Other Essays* (New York: Columbia University Press: 1969), pp. 80-81.

3. W. V. O. Quine, "On the Reasons for Indeterminacy of Translation," *Journal of Philosophy* 67 (1970): 178-83, quoting from p. 179. As I have observed elsewhere, the argument in this paper for indeterminacy of translation does not seem to work: Gilbert Harman, "Comments on Michael Dummett," *Synthese* 27 (1974): 403.

4. W. V. O. Quine, "On Empirically Equivalent Systems of the World," *Erkenntnis* 9 (1975): 313-28.

5. *Ibid.*, p. 318.

6. Cf. W. V. O. Quine and Joseph Ullian, *The Web of Belief*, 2d ed. (New York: Random House, 1978), p. 105.

7. W. V. O. Quine, "On Simple Theories of a Complex World," *The Ways of Paradox and Other Essays*, rev. and enl. ed. (Cambridge, Mass.: Harvard University Press, 1976), pp. 255-58.

8. *Ibid.*, p. 255.

9. Barbara M. Humphries, "Indeterminacy of Translation and Theory," *Journal of Philosophy* 67 (1970): 167-78, specifically pp. 169-70.

10. Pp. 319-22. Page numbers in the text refer to this article.

11. William Craig, "Replacement of Auxiliary Expressions," *Philosophical Review* 65 (1956): pp. 38-55.

12. Clark Glymour notes the existence of theories like V in "Theoretical Realism and Theoretical Equivalence," *Boston Studies in the Philosophy of Science* 8 (1971): pp. 275-88, at pp. 282, 286, citing W. Craig and R. Vaught, "Finite Axiomatizability Using Additional Predicates," *Journal of Symbolic Logic* 23 (1958): 289-308.

13. Gilbert Harman, "Generative Grammars without Transformation Rules: A Defense of Phrase Structure," *Language* 39 (1963): 597-616.

14. Noam Chomsky, *Aspects of the Theory of Syntax* (Cambridge, Mass.: MIT Press, 1965), pp. 210-11, n. 4; Gilbert Harman, "The Adequacy of Context-Free Phrase-Structure Grammars," *Word* 22 (1966): 276-93, esp. 290-93.

15. E.g., Emmon Bach, "Comments on the Paper by Chomsky," in *Formal Syntax*, ed. Peter W. Cullicover, Thomas Wasow, and Adrian Akmajian (New York: Academic Press, 1977), pp. 133-55, specifically p. 140.

On the Roots of Reference: Quine, Piaget, and Husserl*

J. N. MOHANTY
University of Oklahoma

In the ever-growing literature on Quine, his Paul Carus lectures, "The Roots of Reference," appear to have attracted much less attention than they deserve.[1] And yet in these lectures, apart from continuing some of the main theses (about language and reference) of *Word and Object*, Quine develops some new strategies which are of the utmost philosophical interest and whose significance goes far beyond the behavioristic framework that pervades them. It is not my purpose to add to the already available criticisms of that framework, particularly in connection with the question of language learning. I would rather follow two methodological principles. One, formulated by Quine himself in his reply to Chomsky, is: "The more absurd the doctrine attributed to some one, *cateris paribus*, the less the likelihood that we have well construed his words."[2] I would therefore look beneath the absurdities of a behavioristic framework for elements of philosophical insight, which, to be sure, are never lacking in Quine's writings. This, then, leads to the second methodological principle: Since it is not infrequently the case that philosophical theories, professing radically different, and even opposed, points of view (such as realism, idealism, mentalism, behaviorism), are found to share in common philosophical problems and theses that are "beyond the conflict of standpoints,"[3] it is often necessary to separate a philosopher's "standpoint" from his fundamental, and more enduring, insights. I believe this needs to be done in the case of *The Roots of Reference*. If an autobiographical remark is permitted, I should add that my great admiration for Quine's philosophical writings has never been less because of the radically different "standpoint" from which I philosophize. I would not have written this essay were that not so.

---

* An earlier draft of Sections I–III of this paper was read by Chris Swoyer and John Biro, to both of whom I am indebted for their extensive comments.

I. Quine and the Psychogenesis of Reference

Quine gives us an account of the "psychogenesis of reference." This is an account of the way we learn to refer to objects, or to speak referringly of objects. It is necessary first of all to specify what Quine means by "reference" or "referring to objects" and also by "psychogenesis." To begin with "reference," there is no one sense in which philosophers use it. One may distinguish among at least three different senses, the first two of which are the opaque and the transparent senses. In its opaque sense an expression (or the occurrence of an expression) refers only if the object referred to exists. In the transparent sense, however, this implication does hold. There is no doubt that Quine's use of "reference" is in the second, transparent sense. The principle, "Don't refer to what isn't," appears to be a piece of moralizing advice but, in fact, gives expression to a theoretical commitment: the alleged reference to what is not is not genuine reference at all. Reference is not aboutness, referential opacity is only seemingly referential. Not all transparent senses of "reference" are Quinean, however. It is possible to subscribe to the transparent sense of "reference," while at the same time holding that naming may be a referring act, or that names, *qua* names, refer. One only needs a certain theory of proper names, such as Russell's (or Kripke's), to be able to hold the latter view. Now this surely is not Quine's. For Quine, reference not only is transparent but is achieved only through the logical apparatus of quantification and identity. Use of proper names does not show the existence of their objects. "Pegasus" not only may be used by persons who deny the existence of Pegasus but is in fact used in that very act of denying. The existential import is carried not by the name but by the existential quantifier—which is particularly evident in the case of, "There are unspecifiable real numbers" where the values are not objects with names.[4]

The full force of Quine's views extends even beyond this rather uncontroversial thesis about names. For Quine, to refer to red is not the same as being able to discriminate red or recognize red. Even if the child utters "red" in the presence of red things or, asked to point to red, performs his ostension successfully, this does not guarantee that in so doing he is referring to red. Reference involves more than the simple ability to acknowledge a presence.[5] What does Quine mean by saying that the child, when uttering "red" in the presence of red, or when pointing to red while uttering "red," is not referring at all? The clue to what he may mean is provided by the consideration that, for Quine, the child's case parallels that of an adult foreigner. It does not help, then, to be told, "To say that he [the child] refers to the color would be to impute our ontology to him."[6] For, although it may *appear* odd to ascribe any ontology (including ours) to the child, it may well be the case that the foreign adult's ontology and ours overlap at many points. What is it, then, about the case of a child's or foreign adult's uttering "red" in the presence of red, or pointing to red while uttering "red" that should count against saying that the child or the foreign adult is referring to red? Quine goes on to tell us that the verbal response "red" does not imply that "red" is being used to name a color.[7] It may in fact be naming, instead of a color, a patch, a body, or an episode. We are thus led to Quine's well-known thesis about the "inscrutability of reference": objective reference is "inaccessible to observation," that is, "behaviorally inscrutable." But even if one concedes Quine's last point, one may nevertheless point out that the child or the foreign adult is referring, although we cannot be so sure to *what* he is referring. Quine's stronger thesis that in such cases there is no reference at all would need the support of some other premise in addition to the proposition that objective reference is behaviorally inscrutable. Probably Quine thinks that, in order for us to be able to say that an expression refers, we must *be able to specify* what it refers to, and since we cannot do this, to say that the utterance "red" nevertheless does refer is vacuous and useless. We cannot *in any case* specify reference except in the context of a background language. But this thesis—so closely connected with the thesis of inscrutability—that reference is nonsense, except relative to a background language (and a manual of translation), would apply to the child's or the foreign adult's utterance of "red" in the presence of red as much as to the native speaker's sentences faultlessly using the referential apparatus of existential quantification and identity. These remarks are meant not to diminish the merits of Quine's sense of "reference" but to insist that Quine has not satisfactorily shown why the child's or the foreign adult's utterance of "red" does not refer at all.

This is why I have distinguished Quine's sense of "reference" from the two others, including even the simple transparent sense. In fact, Quine's sense of "reference," on his own admission, is somewhat remote from the ordinary usage of "reference" or allied expressions ("being about . . .," "being of . . .," "refers to . . ."). Quine would be the first to admit that the idea of objective reference is alien to large parts of our ordinary language, even if it has its roots in ordinary language. Quantification and variables are alien to the vernacular (but do have close counterparts there in pronouns and phrases such as "there is").[8] For Quine both science and philosophy (which is continuous with science) reconstruct rather than describe the framework of ordinary language. Part of such reconstruction is the regimentation of science and of philosophy. It is of *this* reference that Quine gives us a psychogenesis.

What does he mean by "psychogenesis"? Obviously, it is to be an account of how the child learns to refer in Quine's sense of "reference," which is then the same as an account of how—by what steps—the child learns quantification and identity. Since on his own admission quantification and all the rest of that logical apparatus do not belong to the vernacular, and since the child learns his mother's tongue, Quine adds that he is concerned not how the child *does* but how he *might* achieve reference.[9] As a matter of fact, this way of putting it is rather misleading. What the child does learn at first is to refer in a sense of "referring" that is not Quinean, a sense that is embedded in perception and ordinary language; if Quine's thesis about psychogenesis is correct, then that is the only way the child can learn quantification and so learn to refer. Quine does not, however, want to assure us that his sketch will hold its own as a factual account. All that matters is that it is correct in its essential features: "My concern is with the essential psychogenesis of reference . . . ." "We approximate to the essentials of real psychogenesis while avoiding inessential complications. . . ."[10] For anyone who is familiar with Quine's conception of philosophy, such an assertion should come as a surprise. Is it the case that philosophy can give only the essential structure of psychogenesis while scientific psychology gives its actual process? Quine, to be sure, does not claim that the actual learning process runs parallel to this essential structure. Or is the essential structure a mere "caricature"?[11]

An analogy comes to the mind. In his *Crisis*, Husserl gives an account of the genesis—not psychological but historical—of Galilean physics.[12] Part of the account consists in showing how the exact concepts of geometry arise out of the vague, inexact concepts of everyday world, for example, how the concept of an exact circle arises out of the everyday concept of more or less circular shapes. Now Husserl—not unlike Quine—does not worry if the actual historical process of the genesis of geometry, and so also of Galilean physics, corresponds to his account. His account is *eidetic*. Whatever the historical process may have been, the eidetic structure of the genesis would have been exemplified. I will return to this ascription of an essentialism to Quine in a later context in this paper.

II. *Quine and Kant: Is "Objective Reference" Parochial?*

Since Quine's idea of objective reference hangs together closely with the regimentation of language and with the structure of formal logical theory of predication and quantification, the psychogenesis of reference amounts to the psychogenesis of that formal logical theory. It should be recalled that there is, in the tradition of Western philosophy, another theory which ties the concept of objective reference to the structure of formal logic—not, to be sure, to the apparatus of quantification, but to the interrelated structure of forms of judgment. But, unlike Quine, Kant, his percursor in this regard, would consider it perverse to speak of the psychogenesis of that innate structure. For Quine, "the whole apparatus, and with it the ontological question itself, is in this sense parochial—it is identifiable in other languages only relative to analytic hypotheses of translation which could as well have taken other lines."[13] It may be useful to pursue this point, and the contrast with Kant, a few steps further.

It is, of course, a matter of empirical investigation whether the truth-functional logic, with quantification, is peculiarly Western—perhaps only contemporary Western—or whether it also characterizes the conceptual frameworks of many other communities, present and past. The question is rather: Given a community whose conceptual scheme contains a different logic in which there is no translation for, "There is a . . . such that . . .," shall we be justified in saying that a member of this community *refers* to objects? Such a question may be stopped, at the very outset, by making use of the Quinean thesis that anything that we say about the referential structure of a radically different language can only be relative to analytical hypotheses of translation to the home language. But this scepticism confuses two different questions: (1) how we ascertain what the logical apparatus of the foreign language under consideration is and (2) *given* that that logical apparatus does *not* contain quantification, whether we should say that the users of the language do not refer at all, that is, do not speak of objects. The second question may be answered in the affirmative, if "objective reference" is definable only in terms of the quantificational apparatus. The latter is, most probably, what Quine maintains. In a certain sense of "objective reference" there can be no doubt that the idea of objective reference is encapsulated in that logical apparatus. But this is a higher order, or at least a distinctive, intellectual achievement, and to say that prior to it there is *no* objective reference in any sense at all would be the height of parochialism.

I want to suggest that the Kantian thesis regarding the *universality* of objectivity and the Quinean thesis that objective reference is parochial are not mutually incompatible. As a matter of fact, I want to go even further and say that both are compatible with Brentano's concept of opaque reference. Brentano's sense concerns "aboutness": every mental act is *about* an object; this object, however, need not exist. There does not appear to be anything parochial about this sense of "reference"; it is not an achievement peculiar to a linguistic framework. If ordinary English conforms to the Brentano thesis, so also would *any* ordinary language in which men would necessarily express their thoughts, talk about their thoughts, beliefs, hopes and fears, and would talk about what they think, believe, hope for or fear. The nature of the objects referred to may differ from community to community; they may be material objects, spirits, gods, demons, things, events, or processes. But the Brentano sense of "reference" does not require any specific types of objects to be the objects of reference; hence its universality.

What I am suggesting is that this, most rudimentary, sense of "objective reference" forms the foundation on which all the others, including the Quinean—despite Quine's explicit rejection of Brentano's mentalism—are *founded*. By this I mean that only beings whose thoughts, beliefs, etc., are *about* objects in the Brentano sense could *eventually* speak of objects in the Kantian or the Quinean senses. The Kantian thesis gives the talk of "objects" a first comprehensive determination in terms of the function of judging with its various logical forms; the object, in this strict sense, must be a sense intuition brought under one or more of the modes of synthesis involved in judging. In effect, as contrasted with the Brentano thesis, one refers to objects only in judging. The object, truly, is the object of judgment; and the forms of judgment and the underlying modes of synthesis (or categories = concepts of object in general)—although they come to their own in the intellectual achievements of Aristotelian logic and Newtonian physics—are not mental in the sense in which feelings and desires are. Further, the object, according to this Kantian determination, does not stand alone, but is constituted by rules that insert it into the total contexture of objective experience, into a coherent framework—a requirement that is stronger than the Brentano assignment of an object for each act taken by itself—characterized by Kant as "the unity of selfconsciousness." Although Newtonian physics was, for Kant, the ideal case of such a framework, it need not be the only one. In fact, *any* framework which provides objective rules of synthesis would specify at least parts of the Kantian requirements for objectivity.

The Quinean requirement for objective reference is to be understood in the context of the development not of physics but of formal logic since Kant. Quantification theory, Quine writes, is less than a century old.

III. *Acquisition of Objective Reference*

One of the most interesting strategies of *The Roots of Reference* is to show, in the context of an account of the child's learning to refer, how referential language along with its logical apparatus develops out of what we can call preobjective experience. This over-all strategy is all the more interesting because a very similar movement of thought is to be found in so non-Skinnerian a theorist of child psychology as Piaget and in philosophers as different from Quine as Husserl and Merleau-Ponty. In the succeeding sections I propose to institute comparisons, in brief outline, of Quine's strategy with those of Piaget and Husserl with a view to isolating those elements in his thought which a cognitivist and a phenomenologist may find worth salvaging from the Skinnerian framework, and also to indicate directions in which Quine's over-all theory needs to be supplemented. Let us begin with Quine.

We leave aside Quine's talk of "sensory receptors" and the physiological processes. We begin with what, independently of physics and physiology, one needs to begin with: "a prior tendency on the child's part to weight qualitative differences unequally"[14] so that some differences *must* count for more than others even at the prelinguistic level, if the child is to learn at all. This similarity is "perceptual similarity," which has, "for all its subjectivity, a degree of objective validity"[15] inasmuch as these similarity standards are intersubjective. (Quine's *explanation* of how this intersubjectivity is achieved is evolutionary—biological; as is reflected by his talk of "receptors" and the like, but we need not concern ourselves with this *explanation*. Our concern is rather with the description.) The other basic concepts (each with a strong descriptive "backing," and each "detachable" from physiology and the like) that Quine introduces are "trace," "salience," and "pleasure." (Each has a behavioral manifestation, and behind each one may *posit* a hypothetical mechanism, which again we pass by.) Traces are what relate a present perceptual datum to past ones: the trace of a perceptual experience preserves information adequate to show perceptual similarity between this experience and later ones.[16] Salience is the correlate of noticing: the perceptual field is "a field of gradations" rather than "just one or several clean-cut stimuli."[17] "Trace" and "salience" are connected inasmuch as present salience is affected by past experience. All this has a perfectly descriptive sense, even if, in Quine's view, "This is all meant to be, in the end, a matter of physiological mechanisms, manifested in behavior."[18] Perceptual experiences are pleasant or unpleasant in varying degrees, and the trace of an experience preserves its pleasure or discomfort. There is a drive in the subject to increase the similarity with past unpleasant ones.

Given these basic concepts of perceptual similarity with a degree of intersubjectivity, trace, salience, and pleasure, Quine can move on to the learning of observation sentences such as "Red" and "Mama." Pointing heightens salience. The mechanisms of assent and dissent ("yes" and "no") are learned with the help of perceptual similarity and the pleasure principle. But learning single-word sentences such as "Red" and "Mama" is not yet learning to *objectify*. We have already mentioned that, for Quine, merely to acknowledge the presence of red is not to refer to red. There are additional reasons for holding this view. For the infant, "Mama," "red," and "water" are of the same type; they are not terms for things, but each stands for "a history of sporadic encounter, a scattered portion of what goes on."[19] Their use is "pre-individuative," they are all mass terms at this point. It is with individuating terms that the process of objectification begins. Learning to objectify, then, is, *at first*, learning to individuate, and to pick up the scheme of enduring and recurrent physical objects. At the purely linguistic level this involves learning to use the plural form and also such forms as "that apple," "an apple," "some apples," "another apple," "those apples," as well as the "is" of identity as in, "This is the same apple as the one seen yesterday." When "Mama" is separated from "apple" and "water," "Mama" becomes the singular term *par excellence*. Mama is spatio-temporally visibly continuous (though interrupted by casual and partial eclipses); her identity is a matter of shape. "Red," "water" and "sugar" stand for discontinuous occurrences. Their shapes are amorphous; Mama is a body.

It is not surprising then that, since objectivity relies so heavily on individuation and the individual term *par excellence* is "Mama," "Bodies are the charter members of our ontology, let the subsequent elections and expulsions proceed as they may."[20] They are the objects *par excellence*. Physical science then replaces this notion of body by "the more inclusive, more recondite, and more precise notion of *physical object*."[21]

Perhaps the most important step in this process of objectification—to the final goal of quantification—is learning the distinction between singular and general terms, between "Mama" and "dog." Learning to use "dog" is learning to recognize a second-order similarity, i.e., similarity of similarities. (Each dog is a body and so exhibits first-order similarity based on continuity of shape, displacement, etc.) Furthermore, learning "dog" is not learning mere presence, it is to learn its individuative force, in other words, what to count as one dog and what as another. Like "red" and "water," there are simultaneous scattered occurrences to which 'dog' applies; like "Mama," each dog is one gestalt, a body. More complex observation terms are attributive compounds, such as "yellow paper," or such compounds as "Mama-in-the-garden," each of which may be construed also as an observation sentence ("Yellow paper is there"; "Mama is in the garden").

The child is now on the road to learning predication: occasion sentences by learning (through query, assent, and dissent) the circumstances in which to assent to or dissent from the sentences; standing and eternal sentences by that and a transfer of conditioning from the nonverbal to the associated verbal stimulus in terms of traces and salience. From specific sentences he learns by generalization the mode of composition. But at this stage the similarity he senses between "The dog is an animal" and "Snow is white" is "a tendency in the sound of the first term to dispose him to assent to the second."[22]

Truth functions are next in line. Negation of occasion sentences is learned through query and dissent; negation of standing sentences, through negative conditioning. Conjunction is learned by learning the circumstances in which it commands assent and the circumstances in which it commands dissent, and similarly for alternation. One of Quine's interesting ideas in this connection is to "found" the truth functions on a more primitive relationship, which he calls the "verdict function."[23] Verdict logic is three-valued; the three verdicts are assent, dissent, and abstention. Verdict functions can be learned by induction from observation of behavior. They are prior to our two-valued logic. Compared to them, truth values are higher-order theoretical achievements.

With this apparatus at his disposal the language learner is not very far from being able to refer in the strictly Quinean sense. He needs to learn the relative clause (by which general terms may be constructed from sentences by substitutional transformation, as in, "I bought Fido from a man that found him" ⟶ "Fido is such that I bought him from a man that found him," in general: $\ulcorner Fa \urcorner \longrightarrow \ulcorner a$ is a thing x such that $Fx \urcorner$), the *such that* construction, and its variable (which is the most primitive form of the variable, a regimentation of the relative pronoun). When the relative clause in conjoined to the categorical ("Everything x such that Fx is G," etc.), our language learner has learned to refer; the variable has become objectual.

I think, that in this account reference matures in three stages: first, with the separation of "Mama" from "red" and "water," i.e., with the appearance of individuative terms; second, with the universal categorical, "A dog is an animal" (Quine calls this the earliest phase of reference worthy of the name), and, finally, in the relative clause inserted into the universal categorical whereby the variable 'such that' turns objectual. Quine concedes that the child, even the lay adult, does not really know about variables, not to speak of the distinction between substitutional and objectual quantification. "Still I am schematizing what I think is the real development."[24]

Several features of this account need to be noted at this stage: First, for Quine, bodies are objects *par excellence*. They are the sorts of objects which are spatio-temporally and visibly continuous and which retain an identity of shape in spite of deformation and displacement. When he speaks of man being "a body-minded animal, among body-minded animals," apparently he is talking about all human beings and not merely those who share "our" object-positing pattern. Second, using an idealistic jargon but a scientistic kind, too, Quine speaks of *positing* objects. Further, to posit one object rather than another (to choose "rabbit" as the referent of "gavagai" rather than something else) is to impose our "provincial" pattern, rather than settling what the fact of the matter is, since ultimately there is no fact here. In this, I sense, as in an earlier context, a missing link in the argument: it may be that where we would posit rabbit, the native would posit rabbithood or whatever else. But this "inscrutability" of reference or "indeterminacy of radical translation" does not imply that the "object-positing" pattern itself is parochial. *Our* object positing, i.e., *what* we posit, may be parochial, and yet, in an important sense, to posit some object or other may be *an* essential feature of man's relationship to his world.

This leads me back *again* to the alleged 'linkage' of fully developed objective reference to the quantifier. Earlier I pointed out what seems to be its difference from the Kantian thesis about objective reference and insisted on its compatibility with both the Brentano and the Kantian positions. I now want to return to that theme in order further to explore the peculiar character of Quine's thesis. One way of doing that is to ask what it is about the quantificational apparatus that captures objective reference at its best, as contrasted with the earlier stages, viz., the individuative term (or single-word sentence) and the universal categorical.

I find in Quine's writings several plausible answers to such a query:

1. The mere word "red," when uttered even in the presence of red, may be fulfilling one of several different functions: it may be naming a color, a patch, a body, or an episode, or it may be an occasion sentence. There is no way of settling what the word refers to.

2. "Red" may be functioning as a general term true of many objects (as in, "This is red"), or it may be a singular term naming a single abstract entity (as in, "Red is a color"). Ostensively, the abstract singular term and the concrete general are indistinguishable.

3. It is meaningless to ask absolutely what the word refers to; one can

only ask this relative to a background language. It is not clear why these difficulties would not arise in the case of "(∃ x) (x is red)." The inscrutability of reference and the indeterminacy of translation vitiate as much the distinction between singular and general as they do the apparatus of quantification. Both are, on Quine's view, parochial, in fact objective reference itself is parochial.

These three then are not satisfying as answers to the question what it is about quantification that captures objective reference at its best as contrasted with individuating terms and universal categoricals.

Another line of answer is suggested by Gilbert Harman.[25] "Mama," "Fido," "Red," according to Harman, as uttered by the child, refer not to objects but to *occasions*. So also with sentences such as, "This is a dog," where "a dog" is a predicate of certain occasions but not yet of objects. The same is true even of identity statements such as, "This is the same dog as this": here, for Harman, "there is no reason to suppose that the 'this' s refer to dogs rather than to presentations or occasions." Harman wants to say that the truth conditions for these sentences can be purely phenomenalistic. With the quantified sentence it is otherwise. I am not convinced that this account of the difference would do. If "occasions" are presentations, then neither "Fido" nor "This is a dog," refer to presentations. Neither the language-learning child nor the lay adult not using the quantificational form refers to presentations. The former may be referring to mama as a discontinuous series of occurrences and using "Mama" as a mass term. But each such occurrence is not a presentation. Besides, we are talking about a stage where "Mama" has been separated from mass terms, where the language learner has learned to use singular terms. Even if the single word sentences admit of phenomenalistic truth conditions, the sentence, "This is a dog," does not. The "this" refers not to a presentation but to what is presented; it serves to *identify* for the auditor what the speaker is talking about. Even if Quine is right that this identificatory function lapses under regimentation, the reference, independently of that regimentation, is already objective, not phenomenalistic.

I will mention one more unhelpful answer before suggesting what appears to me to be the real gain with the introduction of the quantificational construction. According to it, in the transparent sense of "reference" which Quine accepts, reference must be to an existent. Add to this Quine's thesis that the existential quantifier encapsulates the most general meaning of "existence." It is then only natural that the same existential quantifier will encapsulate the function of objective reference. This answer is certainly consistent with what Quine has said but does not help us understand why it is that the prequantificational stages of language learning do not confer on the learner the ability to refer in the strict sense to something that exists. Even if this answer is unhelpful, it nevertheless suggests the direction in which we should look. One may distinguish between referring to an entity (that exists) and referring to an entity *as* an existent. The transparent sense does not attain full maturity, unless reference is made to an entity *qua* existing, in other words, unless the fact that the entity being referred to exists is not merely "presupposed," not merely "implied," but explicitly "shown" in the very form of the referential expression. Perhaps "Red," suitably interpreted, does refer to an existent color. "This is a dog," if true, does refer to a dog. But none of these expressions contains a part which shows that the reference exists. "There is an x, such that" does precisely this. It fully explicates the sense of transparent reference. Reference is here not only to what is but to it *qua* existing. In the jargon of idealistic metaphysics objective reference is here fully self-conscious.

Two other related considerations follow from what has just been said. In the first place, by paraphrasing the name as a predicate and making the variable of quantification the vehicle of reference, the object referred to is *detached* from its name. What is is not a dog or red but something, an x, which is such that it is a dog or red. This is only to be expected: referential or objectual quantification needs nameless objects, or at least that the name and the named be separable. Even if the object has a name, it *could have been* nameless. The use of the variable makes this explicit. Second, the referential function of the quantifier also brings out a connection between Quine's thesis that objective reference best takes place through the apparatus of quantification and his later thesis about the inscrutability of reference. The first made its appearance much earlier than, and independently of, the latter. Now we begin to see that the latter was implicit in the former. If the reference is not to a rabbit but to an x such that it is a rabbit, it also becomes evident that many alternate descriptions may be true of this x. Of this x itself we can say very little, if anything at all. It is not a rabbit, for "rabbit" as a name has been paraphrased into the predicate "is a rabbit." The x admits of different true predications. Add to this the thesis about reference to a background language, and we have got rid of the last vestige of the fact of the matter. Quine's theses cohere well enough.

IV. *Piaget*

In this section I propose to draw attention to only those thoughts of Piaget which bear on the child's construction of "object." The important point is that, for Piaget, acquisition of speech needs an already constituted substructure. If speech were a system of conditioning and conditioned reflexes, an infant could acquire speech as early as the end of the first month, when the first conditioned reflexes already exist. "A long practice of pure action is needed to construct the substructure of later speech."[26] A notable feature, therefore, of Piaget's theory is the important role assigned to what is called the sensory-motor stage, during which the child acquires its most rudimentary sense of "objectivity" but *independently of language*. What is for us the outer world is, to begin with, for the infant, a series of moving pictures that appear and disappear, without substantiality, permanence and location.[27] There is no one objective space but "a series of spaces differing one from another and all centered on the body proper."[28] The visual, tactual, and auditory spaces, all centered on the body, lack coordination. They are called by Piaget "ego-centric spaces," not only not coordinated but also not including the body itself as an element in a container.[29] During the first six to eight months of an infant's life the world provides only sensory pictures, open to perpetual destruction and rematerialization. The only identity objects have for him concerns their practical significance. It is the schema of action that confers a certain permanence. "The aim of sensori-motor intelligence is practical success, not truth."[30]

Central to understanding Piaget at this point is his notion of *schema*. Though to begin with schemata are characterized by the behavior sequences to which they refer, it would be wrong to identify a schema with its associated behavior sequence. Rather, a schema is a cognitive structure, generated by the assimilatory functioning. Objects are assimilated *to* something. That to which an object is assimilated is a schema of action. The nipple is assimilated to the schema of sucking.[31]

For the infant, the nipple and sucking form one single, indivisible experience. The object is not yet separated from the action schema. The identity of the object is the identity of an action schema. There are no objects as such, only undifferentiated action-object structures. Objectification of reality emerges out of this primitive amalgam. The first stage in this process is the sensorimotor period during which one and "the same" object comes to be inserted into a whole network of intercoordinated schemata (e.g., of sight and hearing). Thereby the object gets detached from *any* one schema, and the original unity with the action schema is disrupted. Thus the more the subject is active the more is experience objectified.

It is during the sensorimotor period that the infant begins to learn that objects exist even when outside perceptual field and to coordinate their parts into a whole recognizable from different perspectives.[32] This achievement no doubt comes about in various stages. Without going into the detailed account of these stages,[33] which Piaget supports by skillful observations, I mention only the following facts about this process: The object is, in the first place, a practical object rather than a substantial thing. The progressive dissociation of the object from action is indicated by the child's searching for a vanished object in a new position, for a whole when only a part of the object has been seen; also in the child's attempt to set aside obstacles which prevent perception, in the combination of visual and tactual searchings, and, finally, in search "in a comprehensive spatio-temporal universe."[34] As the object becomes detached from action, the child also—as a correlate of that process—locates his own body and his own bodily movements along with other objects and their movements. True objectification begins with the body's becoming an item among other items within an aggregate system.

The construction of the object is not, for Piaget, either an *a priori* deduction or the result of empirical groping. It is not the former, for gropings are necessary (for example, the child does begin by searching for the object where he has found it the first time). But the sequence of achievements is not haphazard; it rather shows "a progressive comprehension."[35] The process is not a mere unfolding of an innate mechanism. What is innate is at most the function of assimilation. The sequential structures are achievements. Piaget calls this process "constructive deduction."

If Piaget's conclusions are valid, objectification is not *completely* a linguistic achievement. Language, it should nevertheless be admitted, makes possible higher-order objectifying achievements, but the prelinguistic phase already records gains on which language builds. Brown agrees with Piaget that semantic notions such as "nomination," "recurrence," and "nonexistence," abilities for "recognition, anticipation based on signs, the concept of the enduring object, awareness of a single space that contains the self as well as other objects," are developed in the period of sensorimotor intelligence.[36]

Returning now to Quine, I should say at the outset that it would be wrong to accuse Quine of being insensitive to the many other aspects of the situation of language learning than those portrayed by him. It is obvious that he is concerned to emphasize only one important aspect of it. Nevertheless, what should be pointed out is that his theory of language learning presupposes nothing in the infant, but an innate standard of perceptual similarity and the concepts of "trace," "salience," and "pleasure." If Piaget's thesis is valid, then this much of mechanism is too simple for language learning. What is necessary is that the infant be able to detach the object from the action schema to which it initially belongs. The infant thereby already acquires a rudimentary concept of object before it learns to speak. The roots of objective reference go deeper down than where Quine locates them. But, in that case, when the infant begins to utter the first holophrastic sentences, such as "Mama," it is in fact already referring. Quine's thesis that Mama is at first a history of sporadic encounters, a scattered portion of what goes on, would still be valid. During the first six to eight months of an infant's life, the child's world has only sensory pictures, open to perpetual destruction and rematerialization.[37] But soon the child acquires the concepts of unperceived existence and permanence of things. When it utters its first holophrastic speech, "Mama," it already refers to an object. According to McNeill,[38] holophrastic speech has three characteristics: (1) words are linked with action; (2) they are imbued with emotion and so have an expressive aspect; (3) they refer to things. The referential function, however, never appears at this stage alone; moreover, the holophrastic single word is not a mere labeling. Children never use mere labels; there is a predication and an assertion.[39]

V. *Husserl*

Husserl's *Experience and Judgment* contains investigations into the genealogy of logic, and since Husserl shares the view that objectivity in the strong sense is constituted by formal-logical operations, these investigations may be regarded as being about the genesis of objectivity.[40] The genesis which Husserl portrays is less clearly psychological than Quine's; its relation to the child's acquisition of language and construction of reality is difficult to ascertain. It is closer to a "rational reconstruction" of the formal logical concepts. Husserl would characterize the genesis as "transcendental phenomenological," meaning thereby that the entire account presupposes the *epoché* by which all reference to the constituted world of things and persons is suspended, so that the rational reconstruction has to fall back upon the evidences within the meditating ego's own life of consciousness. Whatever the plausibility or validity of such a genetic enquiry, the present encounter with Quine requires from us that we as much "put within brackets" Husserl's transcendental-phenomenological point of view as we already have the behaviorism of Quine.

Husserl begins with the level of receptivity which precedes predicative judgment. At the level of receptivity what is given are not particular objects isolated in themselves but "always a *field* of pregivenness, from which a particular stands out and, so to speak, 'excites' us."[41] It is a field of "prominences and articulated particularities."[42] Similarity and contrast are the most general forms of connection among the contents of the sensuous field.[43] Similarity is a matter of degree, but the like is always contrasted with the unlike. In passing from the like to the like, the new like is presented as repetition; between the new and the old there is a "blending," a partial coincidence. Association by similarity is basic for Husserl—association understood not as a psychophysical natural law but as the "purely immanent connection of "this recalls that.""[44] The resulting "prominences" in a field have their "affective" power. A "prominence" "strikes" us.[45] A sound or a noise or a color strikes us with more or less obtrusiveness. This is what Husserl calls the "stimulus." The stimulus upon the ego is "transformed" with the ego's giving way, the being-attracted, the being-affected, and turning-toward or being-awake of the ego.[46] Turning toward the object (which is not yet an *object* in the strict sense) awakens an *interest* (not in the sense of having to do with a specific act of will), understood as a positive feeling.[47] The object has for the ego either a value or a disvalue. "To affect," then, at the level of pure receptivity, means to stand out from the environment, to attract interest to itself.

The perceptual "interest" may be obstructed, or it may continue to be progressively satisfied. Obstruction may give rise to disappointment, where there arises a *conflict* between the still living intentions ("uniformly red and uniformly spherical") and the content of sense which is presented ("not red, but green," "not spherical, but dented".)[48] This superposition of a new sense on the one already constituted and the displacement of the first by the second give rise to the original phenomenon of negation. This is not yet a negative predicative judgment. Likewise, the obstructions of perceptual interest generate the original phenomena of modalization (prior to the judgmental modalities), when the original certainty turns into "questionable," "probable," and so on.

There are three stages in which the process of objectification develops *within* the domain of receptive, prepredicative experience. First, an element within the sense field needs to be simply "apprehended": this is the lowest level of the unobstructed exercise of perceptual interest. This is followed by an explication of the "internal horizon" of the object, i.e., of all that the object is, its "internal determinations"; this explication is made by following the direction of the expectations which have been awakened. At the next stage the perceptual interest turns to the objects copresent with the already apprehended datum and determines its relations to them; these are the "relative determinations." In the course of this process of development the logical categories of "substrate" and "determination" ("quality" and "relation") are constituted, although in the strict sense logical categories pertain to predicative judgments.

Predicative judgment brings about a new level of objectification, the correlative of which is an active synthesis of the elements (S and *p*) which earlier—at the level of receptive explication—were apprehended in a mode of passive synthesis of coincidence. Whereas *p* originally emerged as an enrichment of sense of S, a new cognitive interest returns to S, identifies it as being "again" there as S, and actively brings about the transition to the new sense *p* accruing to it. As a result of this activity and the cognitive interest motivating it, the object substrate of receptive explication becomes the subject, and the determination *p* becomes its predicate. In receptive explication, the S is clarified, explicated as being *p*, but the "being-determined-as" is not apprehended. In predicative judgment, this being-determined-as is a component of the constituted objectivity. New forms are thematized: the subject form, the predicate form, and their unity in the proposition form. The "copulative" form of unity expressed by "is" is "that to which the objectivating consciousness in its different levels ultimately aspires, and thus objectivation in the pregnant sense attains its goal in this copulative positing of the "is.""[49]

An important stage in the development of predicative activity is marked by the achievement of the sense of identity. The cognitive interest, while making a new predication *r* of S, may "retain" the previous determinations p and q as sedimented into S (though no longer self-given), arrives at the sense "the same S" which was *p* and *q*, is also *r*. If, in the past, *p* and *q* were receptively explicated determinations of S, S*p* and S*q* may have already entered into a passive synthesis of identity, which may then subsequently be given the predicative form "S which is *p* is identical with S which is *q*."[50] The function of judgment of identity, then, is to "gather together the acquisitions of judgment" from different contexts and to hold them together in a new judgment. It is important to recall that, for Husserl, the notion of identity belongs to a developed concept of object. An object is one which is not merely being perceived here and now, but to which one can return again. Identity is constituted by identificatory acts. The identifying act posits the object as the same in different temporal positions. Identity is thus, to begin with, a temporal concept; it is only as applied to abstract entities (which Husserl often calls "irreal objects" or also "objects of understanding") that identity *seems to be* an atemporal concept, whereas in reality it still pertains to time: in the first instance to the lived, immanent time, if not to objective, natural time; they also possess an "*omnitemporality*, which, *nevertheless, is a mode of temporality.*"[51] Whatever is an object must be such that one can return to it again. But this is a constituted achievement, not a passively given datum.

Husserl, then, proceeds to trace the genealogy of more complex forms of predicative judgment: of the "has-judgment" (S has p) which, of course, he regards to be as primitive as the "is-judgment"; of the comparative judgment (a is larger than b); of the attributive form (initially through a subordinate clause "S which is p, is q," and then through an attributive adjective). These lead to the operation of substantivization, which constitutes states of affairs (*sachverhalten*) as categorial objectivities, which however have their origin in the receptively given relational situations (*sachlagen*); to the acts which transform the receptive act of plural contemplation into *one* object, i.e., a set; to the origin of modalities of judgment ("possibly," "actually," and "necessarily"); to the origin of judgments of existence ("A exists," "A does not exist"); and finally to the constitution of empirical universals on the basis of receptively given empirical types, culminating in the constitution of essences, or *eide*, and essential judgments.

In this account several theses stand out with prominence: (1) objectivity, in the developed, critical, and scientific sense, is constituted by formal-logical operations of predicative determination, identity, and modalization through confirmation ("yes, actually so"). (2) Beginning with the concrete, sensuously perceived individual up to the abstract *eidos*, there is an ascending series of constitutive achievements. Of these, the individual object *is*, in the strict sense; the others have a sort of quasiobjectivity. (3) Although predicative thinking constitutes objects in the strictest sense, prepredicative, receptive experience also presents sense contents which "anticipate" such objectivities. (4) The formal-logical operations themselves are "anticipated," "pre-figured" in prepredicative experience, such that in an important sense logic extends far beyond the domain of propositions and predicative thought and into the domain of receptive, passive experience. Thus, writes Husserl:

> ... logical activity is already present at levels in which it was not recognized by the tradition and that, accordingly, the traditional logical problematic begins at a relatively higher level, but that, above all, it is precisely in these lower levels that the concealed presuppositions are to be found, on the basis of which the meaning and legitimacy of the higher-level selfevidences of the logician are first and ultimately intelligible.[52]

VI

1. The similarities, both in the program and in the actual execution

of it, between Quine's "psychogenesis" and Husserl's "genealogy" are striking. They are also instructive. They show that such concepts as "stimulus," "affection," and "pleasure," "habit," "association," and "trace" have a place, independently of the behavioristic and physicalistic framework in which they are usually found. Even within a purely phenomenological psychology they have their legitimate role inasmuch as they "describe" features of prepredicative experience. Should one call for an *explanation* of these features, a physicalistic and biological-evolutionary explanation may be as good as any other. For the phenomenologist, understanding of the structure of prepredicative experience is simply in need of no explanatory-theoretical schemata.

2. Further, all three—Quine, Piaget, and Husserl—agree that there is a genesis of objective reference and also that the most developed *sense* of "object"—that of scientific discourse—is constituted by logical operations. While this much is held in common, there are deep differences in details. As we have noted in connection with Piaget, the most rudimentary concept of objectivity is constituted before acquisition of language and through sensorimotor intelligence. For Husserl, there is no stage of conscious life which is not marked by intentionality, although higher-order objectivities presuppose lower-order ones, and "object" in *the strictest sense* is characterized by identity, predicative determination, judicative confirmation ("yes, actually so"), and ascription of existence. This, however, does not imply that prior to scientific-critical activity there is no objective reference. The Brentano thesis still holds good.

3. Both Quine and Husserl emphasize the concept of identity. An object must be such that it can be identified, which implies also that it can be distinguished from others (of the same kind as well as of different sorts.). For both, identity, in its origin, concerns temporality. Husserl's thesis in this connection has been noted. Let us listen to Quine: The primitive inception of identity is "as a mere temporising locution, helping to sustain a prolonged ostension."[53] "But this role is one that identity later outgrows."[54] However, beyond this point, there are vast differences. For Quine, the connection between the concept of object and the concept of identity demands that, as long as one may be said to be using terms to refer, he remains answerable to the demands of substitutivity of identity. This rules out intentional discourse from referring in the strictly Quinean sense. Not so with Husserl, for whom identity is inseparable from difference, so that the identity of an object maintains itself in and through the different *noemata* referring to the same object. There is no reference pure and simple; reference is always mediated by *Sinn* or *noema*, and identity is always being constituted through the

39

overlapping coincidence of *noemata*. The object *simpliciter,* in itself self-identical, is the cherished goal of ontology but not a phenomenological datum. This is as much true of physical objects as of abstract entities such as numbers. The latter also are presented under some description or other; the identity of each maintains itself in and through these different descriptions. To each such *noema* there corresponds a set of intentional acts. Substitutivity of identity obtains for a domain of entities fully sundered from the process of their constitution, and therefore from all reference to the acts which posit them. Phenomenology, being concerned precisely with these acts and their intentional correlates, is not bothered by the failure of substitutivity under act contexts. Ontology cannot but worry about it.

4. It is also a common desideratum of the two investigations that formal logic is founded upon, or may be traced back, for its "origin," to a more primitive logical structure, a "proto-logic', characterizing prepredicative experience. Husserl argues, in *Experience and Judgment*, that formal-logical concepts like negation, conjunction, and disjunction originate from structures of everyday prepredicative experience, such as disappointment of an anticipation,[55] retaining-in-grasp of one object while apprehending the next,[56] and, vacillating between two apprehensions with inclinations to believe either of the two.[57] Like Quine's verdict logic, this prepredicative logic is not two-valued. While Quine's logic is to be laid bare by phenomenological "attending to" what goes is open to learning by observation of behavior, Husserl's prepredicative within one's conscious life prior to predicative judgments.

5. This brings us to two major differences between the Quinean and Husserlian projects which threaten to make the similarities already indicated look insignificant. For one thing, Quine's psychogenesis is explicitly an account of *language learning*, a chapter of developmental psychology. Husserl's genealogy of logic—in fact all genetic phenomenology—is neither an account of language learning nor one of developmental psychology. Husserl's sense of "genesis" is closer to what may be called rational reconstruction, not in terms of theoretically posited entities (such as sensations) but in terms that are descriptively "verifiable." It is not as though the infant begins with what Husserl calls prepredicative experience from which, as he grows up, he also progresses toward performing predicative acts of growing complexity. It is rather as though prepredicative experience continues to be the basis and the foundation for all higher-order cognitive strivings. Though not explicitly a theory of language learning, the genealogy does provide an essential skeleton for any cognitive growth and so of growth in linguistic skill; just as the Quinean psychogenesis, though explicitly a theory of

language learning, is also—as this paper has emphasized—an account of the gradual, stage-by-stage constitution of scientific objectivity, not in terms of intentional acts but rather in terms of acquisition of logico-linguistic tools considered in abstraction from the intentional acts making them possible.

6. With his explicitly learning-theoretical and behavioristic framework, Quine's psychogenesis would almost seem to be reductionistic, logic almost rendered a fragment of psychology, and, as Quine never ceases to emphasize, philosophy continuous with science. And yet Quine knows very well that formal logic, for example, is not continuous with verdict logic, that regimented language is a reconstruction of ordinary language. Husserl's genealogy, coming at the end of a long chain of philosophical thinking on logic which began with a powerful critique of psychologism, cannot but understand the talk of "genesis" in a somewhat Pickwickian manner. What, in fact, Husserl claims to show is that prepredicative experience exhibits stuctures which foreshadow, anticipate, or are analogues of the structures of the higher, predicative thought. The cognitive interest that characterizes predicative judgment is, however, something new; the talk of "genesis" does not therefore annul the radical discontinuity between prepredicative receptivity and predicative spontaneity.

7. The Husserlian sense of reference is "opaque," the Quinean "transparent." They belong to two different levels of discourse, the former to the phenomenological, the latter to the ontological. From the standpoint of phenomenology, ontology is naïve insofar as it looks upon the constituted objects as though they were not constituted; its naïveté consists in forgetfulness of the acts of positing that first make the domain of objects possible. For a (physicalistic) ontology, phenomenology belongs to the level of prescientific description which needs to be overcome in a scientific-philosophical reconstruction. In all fairness it should be said that Quine's ontology seeks to overcome the naïveté by explicitly recognizing physical objects as well as commonsense bodies as posits. Neither Husserl nor Quine would agree that posits are *ipso facto* unreal.[58] Of the three types of posits he recognizes, Quine ascribes *evidential* priority to sense-data, *conceptual* priority to commonsense bodies, and *natural* priority to physical particles.[59] For Husserl, evidential priority belongs ultimately to the constituting acts with their intentional noetic-noematic structure; among the posits themselves there is a founding-founded relationship: physical objects are founded on sensory data, and the particles of physics on (insofar as they are idealizations of) the commonsense bodies. Physicalism, for phenomenology, is guilty of not recognizing that the objects of physics, the framework of

physics, and most importantly its denial of intentionality, are themselves achievements of intentional acts coperformed by the community of scientists.

8. Finally, a remark about the methodology pursued in this paper. I proposed that we abstract from the behavioristic framework of Quine and the transcendental-phenomenological framework of Husserl and then look for general features of Quine's psychogenesis which would be acceptable to phenomenology. Against this method it may very well be argued that those features that are salvaged are not indifferent to the backgrounds from which they are abstracted, that as in a gestalt situation they are radically transformed when inserted into a different contexture. I agree with this. I would nevertheless insist that, like all identity, of 'theme' is itself a function of the various contexts into which it can enter and the range of alterations it undergoes through those changes in contexture.

NOTES

1. W. V. O. Quine, *The Roots of Reference* (La Salle, Ill.: Open Court Publishing Co., 1973). Henceforth referred to as RR.
2. D. Davidson and J. Hintikka, eds., *Words and Objections: Essays on the Work of W. V. Quine* (Dordrecht: Reidel, 1969), p. 304.
3. I owe this insight to Nicolai Hartmann's "Diesseits vom Idealismas und Realismus," *Kant-Studien* 29 (1924).
4. W. V. O. Quine, *Ontological Relativity and Other Essays* (New York: Columbia University Press, 1969), pp. 92f.
5. RR, p. 83.
6. Ibid., p. 82.
7. Ibid., pp. 83f.
8. Ibid., p. 124.
9. Ibid., p. 101.
10. Ibid., p. 100.
11. Ibid., p. 105.
12. E. Husserl, *The Crisis of European Sciences and Transcendental Phenomenology*, trans. D. Carr (Evanston, Ill.: Northwestern University Press, 1970).
13. Davidson and Hintikka, *Words and Objections*, p. 320.
14. RR, p. 19.
15. Ibid., p. 19.
16. Ibid., p. 25.
17. Ibid., p. 25.
18. Ibid., p. 26.
19. Quine, *Ontological Relativity*, p. 7.
20. RR, p. 85.
21. Ibid., p. 54.
22. Ibid., pp. 66-67.
23. Ibid., pp. 77-78.
24. Ibid., p. 124.

25. G. Harman, Review of *The Roots of Reference*, *Journal of Philosophy* 72 (1975): 388-95.
26. J. Piaget, *The Child and Reality: Problems of Genetic Epistemology*, trans. A. Rosin (New York: Grossman Publishers, 1973).
27. *Ibid.*, p. 14.
28. *Ibid.*, p. 15.
29. *Ibid.*
30. R. Brown, *Psycho-Linguistics: Selected Papers* (New York: Free Press, 1970), p. 223.
31. J. H. Flavele, *The Developmental Psychology of Jean Piaget* (Princeton, N.J.: D. Van Nostrand Co., Inc., 1963), pp. 52-53.
32. Piaget, *The Child and Reality*, p. 12.
33. For a good account of these stages see J. Piaget, *The Construction of Reality in the Child* (New York: Basic Books, 1954) esp. Chap. 1, "The Development of the Object Concept."
34. *Ibid.*, p. 91.
35. *Ibid.*, p. 94.
36. R. Brown, *A First Language: The Early Stages* (Cambridge, Mass.: Harvard University Press, 1973), p. 199.
37. See E. Vurpillot, "Development of Identification of Objects," in V. Hamilton and M. D. Vernon, eds., *The Development of Cognitive Process* (New York: Academic Press, 1976), p. 202.
38. D. McNeill, *The Acquisition of Language: The Study of Developmental Psycholinguistics* (New York: Harper & Row, 1970), pp. 20-21.
39. *Ibid.*, p. 23. See also P. Menyuk, *The Acquisition and Development of Language* (Englewood Cliffs, N.J.: Prentice-Hall, 1971) p. 101.
40. E. Husserl, *Experience and Judgment: Investigations in a Genealogy of Logic*, rev. and ed. L. Landgrebe; trans. J. S. Churchill and K. Ameriks (Evanston, Ill.: Northwestern University Press, 1973). Henceforth referred to as *EJ*.
41. *Ibid.*, p. 72.
42. *Ibid.*
43. *Ibid.*, pp. 74f.
44. *Ibid.*, p. 75.
45. *Ibid.*, p. 76.
46. *Ibid.*, pp. 78-79.
47. *Ibid.*, pp. 85-86.
48. *Ibid.*, p. 88.
49. *Ibid.*, p. 215.
50. *Ibid.*, pp. 235f.
51. *Ibid.*, pp. 260-61.
52. *Ibid.*, p. 13.
53. *RR*, p. 115.
54. *Ibid.*, p. 59.
55. *EJ*, pp. 88-91.
56. *Ibid.*, p. 245.
57. *Ibid.*, p. 91-99.
58. W. V. O. Quine, *The Ways of Paradox and Other Essays* (New York: Random House, 1966), p. 251.
59. *Ibid.*, pp. 251-52.

Quine's View(s) of Logical Truth*

MICHAEL E. LEVIN
City College, City University of New York

I. *Introduction*

The effort to undermine the distinction between necessary and contingent truth is a theme that dominates Quine's work. It has led him to argue at length that the laws of logic have no special epistemic status, but his accounts of the topic show strains and apparent inconsistencies. My aim here is to clarify Quine's view of logical truth. The discussion will be largely confined to propositional logic. Predicate logic raises further problems about ontology and reference (see [17], 60–61), and anyway propositional logic generates the main philosophical issues. Kleene, for example, has traced the oddities of intuitionistic predicate logic and arithmetic to the replacement of the classical propositional law $--p \supset p$ by $-p \supset (p \supset q)$ ([8], 82, 101).

Quine's quarrel with necessity explains his desire to demote logical truth. Such ostensibly nonlogical necessary truths as "Bachelors are unmarried" are such only because they become logical truths when synonyms replace synonyms; such truths inherit what necessity they have from logic. The ostensible necessity of mathematics also arises from logic. Russell's identification of Peano's axioms with valid quantificational formulas has fallen into disfavor, but this disfavor has not extended to the view that a theorem T of a set of axioms A can be re-

---

* This paper had a difficult gestation. Some years ago I wrote a quite bad piece on Aristotle's *Metaphysics* Γ, which contained some scattered remarks on [27] that a student of mine thought interesting. After a number of conversations with Alan Berger, these remarks became a paper I submitted to the *Australasian Journal of Philosophy*. They rejected the paper, but the remarks of two anonymous referees brought many issues into better focus. I owe them a debt that I have been unable to acknowledge until now. Meanwhile, my students Richard Smokovich and James Murphy were constantly after me to explain just what Quine thinks the status of logical truth is. When I was invited to contribute a paper to the present volume, I combined what was salvageable of the paper with what I had learned from my discussions with Berger, Smokovich, and Murphy—and, again, my wife, Margarita.

garded as the consequent of the logically valid conditional $A \supset T$. Since neither A nor T need be true in all models, the necessary mathematical truth involved must be $A \supset T$. The status of mathematical truth thus reduces to that of logical truth. Because modern empiricism recognizes no claimants to the title "necessary" beyond such truths as "Bachelors are unmarried" and "$A \supset T$," logic emerges as the source of all the necessity there is.

Modern empiricism has also supplied a well-known account of the necessity logical laws appear to have: they are true by convention, true in virtue of the meaning of the logical connectives. Thus, for example, "$pv - p$" is said to be true because "$-$" is defined as the sign for reversing truth value, and "v" is so defined that "pvq" is true just in case at least one of $\{p, q\}$ is. Empiricism welcomes the idea that all necessity originates in our own decisions and linguistic activity. This "linguistic" theory of logical truth ([19], [25]) has been Quine's main opponent over the decades and the background against which he has articulated his own views. I will argue here that Quine has never abandoned the main tenets of his initial assault on it in [27] and that his positive account of logical truth bears a rather paradoxical relation to his rejection of conventionalism therein. Quine rejects conventionalism not because the gap between the meaning of the logical constants and the truth of the logical laws is too wide but because it is too narrow. To the extent that he understands "meaning," he finds the meanings of the constants too closely tied to the truth of the laws for one to explain the other.

I would begin to expound this remark at once were Quine's account of logical truth not complicated by another theme: his holistic conception of knowledge. Quine holds that individual sentences cannot be determinately paired with confirming experiences; sets of sentences meet experience as corporate entities, and so no single sentence is immune from revision. Scientific investigation could lead to the rejection of even purported definitional truths (see [26], 74). (Quine's seeing Lakatos as an ally here may account for his otherwise inexplicable praise in [28] of Lakatos' ridiculous *Proofs and Refutations*.) Quine has not shied away from applying this holism to logic:

> Revision even of the logical law of the excluded middle has been proposed as a means of simplifying quantum mechanics; and what difference is there in principle between such a shift, and the shift whereby Kepler superseded Ptolemy . . . ? ([18], 43). Logic is in principle no less open to revision than quantum mechanics or the theory of relativity ([19], 100).

Such statements sometimes make it seem that Quine denies necessity to logical laws because he thinks they could be shown, or reasonably held, to be *false*. I will call this the *empirical view* of logic. And some writers influenced by Quine have suggested that the logical laws are no more than extremely general empirical hypotheses whose shining record of confirmation to date has given them a transempirical aura (see, e.g., [15]). The Intuitionist Brouwer argued, independently of Quine but in this spirit, that $(\exists x)Fx \vee - (\exists x)Fx$ is valid in the realm of the finite but invalid in the infinite—that its record of success has been tarnished now that the infinite has come into clearer view.

One reason to withold the empirical view from Quine is its implausibility. I consider it in greater detail in Section IV; it suffices to remark here that hardly anyone really believes that "$pv - p$" could go the way of geocentrism, or even "$K = \frac{1}{2}mv^2$." The principle of charity counsels that we do not burden Quine with a view so patently at odds with intuition. But a deeper reason for such circumspection is the conflict between the empirical view and Quine's widely discussed "translation argument." Call a translation of the discourse of a speaker S *deviant* if it attributes to S the denial of a logical law. Quine has argued—in [17], [19], [25] and originally in [27]—that a deviant translation is *ipso facto* a mistranslation. It is unreasonable that S will deny the obvious, so attributing to S the denial of something obvious suggests a mistake in the attribution. Since the logical laws are *so* obvious, a deviant translation is unacceptable. The kind of unacceptability at issue will need careful scrutiny, since for Quine the precept "save the obvious" occupies a shadow zone between inductive generalization and methodological convention. This complication aside, the upshot of the translation argument appears to be that the logical laws *cannot* be denied, that we cannot coherently describe the situation the empirical view so equably envisions. A scientist's apparent denial of "$pv - p$" means only that we have mistranslated him. I will call this the *mistranslation view* ("eisegesis view" is tempting, but the term applies literally only to those translations which deviate because mistakenly homophonic). The mistranslation view goes beyond the claim that we could never know that S has denied a logical law (a claim compatible with the empirical view), for *that* would be altogether too mentalistic. A merely epistemic version of the mistranslation view would, for example, allow S to assent to "$\#(p@\#p)$" and yet mean by "#" and "@" what we mean by "$-$" and "v". Quine will not so detach meaning from public use.[1]

Clearly any account of Quine's conception of logical truth should, so far as possible, reconcile the empirical and mistranslation views and, where this is not possible, give pride of place to the one most in harmony with the rest of Quine's commitments. Furthermore, Quine's rejection

47

of conventional truth and its ilk should not leave him *understanding* these notions. That would be a major concession to conventionalism. Quine's view of "truth by virtue of meaning" should be much dimmer; he should see it as far less clear in point of empirical significance than, say, absolute space.

II. *"Truth by Convention"* Revisited

Quine argues in [27] that conventionality fails to distinguish logical truth: when "true by convention" is properly understood, it becomes clear that *any* truth can be construed as conventionally true. [27] repays close inspection because it contains the germ, and some of the difficulties, of the mistranslation view.

Let "p" be schematic for sentences of an object-language O. Let "$\cdot$" and "$-$" be symbols of O whose intended interpretation is conjunction and denial. In these terms the law of noncontradiction is: every instance of "$-(p\cdot-p)$" is true. Quine explicates the thesis that "$-(p\cdot-p)$" and other logical laws are true in virtue of the meaning conventions governing the logical particles as follows: Imagine an infinite array of sentences of O, some containing "$-$" (say), which for the moment we regard as meaningless. We assign a meaning to "$-$" by convention by arbitrarily assigning a truth value to every sentence of O. "To whatever extent we carry this process, we to that extent determine meaning for the initially meaningless marks . . . '$-$' and the rest. Such contexts as we render true are true by convention" ([27], 90). Thus, if each instance of "$-(p\cdot-p)$" is marked T, "$-(p\cdot-p)$" is true by convention. The trouble is that, even if geometry is definitionally irreducible to logic, this same procedure could be used to make selected postulates for geometry true by conventions governing suitable geometrical primitives ([27], 99). Finally, Quine notes, this procedure could even render statements of empirical science true by convention: "Now we can pick [an] empirical primitive, perhaps 'body', . . . and repeat the process . . . rendering conventionally true all known truths . . ." ([27], 101). Conventionality has failed to distinguish the truth of "$-(p\cdot-p)$" from the truth of anything else. And Quine's observation that the outlined procedure has not been run through "deliberately and explicitly" for either logic or science anticipates the suggestion that it "rationally reconstructs" the genesis of logical truth in some useful way. Quine concludes on the strength of this that it is empty to call anything true by convention.[2]

The mistranslation view emerges when Quine responds to the charge that he is missing the special status of the law of noncontradiction—the fact that consistency must be observed even in the initial assignment of truth values to unconstrued sentences. Empirical principles like "$s = \frac{1}{2}gt^2$" need not be preserved in the assignment of truth values to hitherto unconstrued sentences; doesn't this make noncontradiction special? Quine formulates this consistency requirement as the demand that we not mark both "p" and "$-p$" T, and replies as follows:

> If we make a mark in the margin opposite . . . "p" and another opposite "$-p$," we sin only against the established usage of "$-$" as negation sign. Under the latter usage "p" and "$-p$" are not both true; in taking them both by convention as true we merely endow the sign "$-$", roughly speaking, with a meaning other than denial. Indeed, we might . . . allow no sign of [O] to behave analogously to the denial locution . . . ([27], 97).

Quine says "roughly speaking," of course, because his preferred account —that "$-$" has been rendered untranslatable as "not"—skirts reference to meaning altogether (see [17], 59). At any rate, "$-(p\cdot-p)$" has again been demoted to the status of "People grin," another sentence whose imputed denial would impugn the (homophonic) translation. (Quine holds that, in general, no objective mark selects sentences dissent from which involves deviation from the mother tongue. But, as we will see, he does not apply this doctrine to logic.)

Quine is here using a version of the mistranslation view to reply to the charge that adherence to the law of noncontradiction is somehow necessary. But before we turn to the mistranslation view itself, it should be noted that Quine's reply to this charge seems to rest on a confusion about the language for which consistency must be observed. Consistency in the assignment of truth values to unconstrued sentences is *not* the requirement that "$-p$" always take the truth value opposite that assigned "p." Let us grant that Quine is right on this score: assigning T to both "p" and "$-p$" just disqualifies "not" as a translation of "$-$". Rather, consistency is the requirement that no sentence in O be marked both T and F—that no sentence of O is both given and denied T. This is how noncontradiction is built into our meaning-bestowing activity. More precisely, let B be the metalanguage which assigns truth values to sentences of O, "P" schematic for sentences of B, and "¬" and "&" symbols of B whose intended interpretation is negation and conjunction. It is a constraint on B that all instances of "¬$(P \& \neg P)$" be true. The law of noncontradiction reenters as a truth of the metalanguage in which meaning is conventionally assigned.

It is tempting to reply that, just as O needs no proxy for denial, neither does B. By letting both "p is T" and "¬$(p$ is T$)$" be theses of

49

B, we simply disqualify "¬" as a translation of "not." Or, since falsity is truth of the negation ([19], 83), we could say that "T" and "F" (= "¬T") have been disqualified as translations of "true" and false." (As Quine notes—[19], 87—"Once you upset the interrelations of the logical operators, you may be said to have revised any and all." The completeness of classical logic means that unfixing the usual relations of the connectives also unfixes the semantics, and in the present case the interpretation of the "truth values" being assigned. Logical laws are syntactic expressions of semantic inclinations.) But this move is not as straightforward for B as it was for O. If we can assign more than one truth value to a sentence of O, why say that what we are doing is distributing *truth values*? Such assignments surely sin against the established usage of "truth value." And if we are not, we are not bestowing truth-conditional meaning. If "T" and "F" lose their standard meaning, we are *certainly* not bestowing truth-conditional meaning.

I am not denying that a metalanguage B' for O could be nonclassical; it might distribute n truth values ($n>2$) to sentences of O, more than one of which is designated. Moreover, as Rescher has shown, the assignment of truth values to statements of B' can itself be nonclassical: there are "autodescriptive" n-valued systems that can serve as their own n-valued metatheory (see [29], 81–86, 229). Now Quine himself is skeptical about the title of such values to the qualifier "truth": he refers to "the three or more so-called truth values" ([19], 84). In any case, noncontradiction retains its grip in the requirement that, where v_1 and v_2 are distinct truth values of B', the statement "p is v_1 and p is v_2" must not get a designated truth value.[3] Rescher tries to loosen this grip by exhibiting "quasi-truth-functional" systems in which such values as $<v_1, v_2>$ are assigned to sentences ([29], 170). Why these pairs should be called "truth values" is again the question—as Rescher seems to realize, for he interprets the assignment of $<v_1, v_2>$ to p to mean "p may be either v_1 or v_2" ([29], 169). Anyway, his proof ([29], 178) that an n-valued quasi-truth-functional system is always representable in some n^2-valued truth-functional system backfires, for the univalence requirement holds in the expanded system.

These considerations do not prove the impossibility of a language lacking negation—or, equivalently, that some version of noncontradiction must be a thesis of every body of discourse. They just suggest that one cannot *describe* such languages without using a metatheory which assigns two truth values and is governed by the classical laws. This requirement is not a formal one; it is orthogonal to the plane in which the layers of an autodescriptive system are stacked.[4] Its violation would mean only that what we are doing in such systems is best described as "something like assigning truth conditional meaning." To raise this issue of family resemblance is to anticipate; but it is worth remarking that the argument that noncontradiction is presupposed at some higher level is based on the same style of reasoning by which Quine showed that it was unnecessary at the bottom level O.

My main purpose in reviewing [27] has been to highlight the principle by which Quine avoids having to build the logical laws into O: apparent dissent from a logical law just means that the discourse has been mistranslated. Genuine dissent is impossible. This principle can be viewed as a corollary of a more general lemma: "S's discourse contains proxies for the connectives" are just other words for "S assents to the logical laws." Since there is no absolute requirement that a body of discourse have proxies for the connectives, assent to the logical laws is no absolute requirement either. Such is the use to which Quine puts the lemma in [27]. It and its corollary come to stand on their own in such aphorisms as "An illogical culture is a mistranslated one" ([21], [17]), "Deny the doctrine, change the subject" ([19]), and "The propositional connectives are fixed points in radical translation" ([31], [20]). And here, in high relief, is the strain between the empirical and mistranslation views. Quine's way of showing that "$-(p\cdot-p)$" need not be affirmed not only does not show that it can be denied, it entails that it *cannot* be denied. The point holds as well for the more controversial law "$pv-p$." If our conventional assignment of truth values to sentences of O makes "$pv-p$" false, some deviance in usage is thereby established. Quine sidesteps the necessity of logical laws by making them undeniable. This had led some writers to claim—mistakenly, we will see—that the empirical and mistranslation views are actually inconsistent (see e.g. [6], 15).

III. *The Mistranslation View and Obviousness*

A yet more striking feature of the translation argument (noted by Quine himself in [25]) is its suggestion that logical laws are true *in virtue of the meanings of the connectives*. Nor will Quine's rejection of meanings as grounding translational relations quite annul this suggestion. A conventionalist might agree to eschew meanings and explicate "'p' is true in virtue of meaning" as, simply, "Dissent from 'p' entails a change in usage" (see e.g. [14], 80). The significance of the slogan "We wouldn't accept a deviant translation" clearly hinges on *why* we wouldn't accept one. Quine himself has stressed that our intolerance of deviance proves nothing by itself, for there is an explanation of it that offers no aid or comfort to the conventionalist: logical laws are obvious.

Quine rightly notes that explaining the automatic unacceptability of deviant translations via the obviousness of logical laws and the canon that translation should not impute denial of the obvious keeps logical laws on the same footing with other truths preserved under translation ([19], 82, 96–97). The whole weight of Quine's position, then, rests on his appeal to obviousness. In fact, Quine's use of obviousness is unhelpful and ultimately at odds with the mistranslation view itself. (I argue in Section VI that Quine can accept the slogan that logical laws are true in virtue of meaning without embracing what is objectionable about conventionalism.)

The most natural reading of Quine's translation argument is this: it is always more *likely* that a deviant translation is erroneous than that the translated party S has dissented from a logical law. Quine speaks this way when chalking up the unacceptability of deviance to the fact that "there can be no stronger evidence for a change of usage than repudiation of what had been obvious ... one's interlocutor's silliness, beyond a certain point, is less likely than bad translation" ([25], 112–13; [17], 59).[5] This recalls Hume's argument against miracles: because a miracle is by hypothesis extremely unlikely, it is always more probable that testimony supporting a miracle is mistaken than that the miracle really occurred. For Quine, S's denying a logical law would be a miracle. But the catch is that Hume's argument does not show that miracles are impossible: it shows only that it is impossible rationally to believe in miracles. And Quine must make a similar concession. Even if a speaker is always less likely to have denied a logical law than that the translation which attributes the denial to him is faulty, it does not follow that genuine dissent from a logical law is impossible. All that follows is the irrationality of ever believing we have spotted a case of it. Quine's argument seems to permit the hypothesis that S has denied a logical law some nonzero probability. If the grounds for rejecting this hypothesis are that there is always some incompatible hypothesis with a higher probability, Quine has abandoned the claim that S's seeming to deny a logical laws *amounts* to S's having changed usage. No one supposes the platitude "people grin" is true by meaning, yet no one would accept a translation that attributed its denial, precisely because it is so improbable that a speaker has missed every grin. But this concedes that, under suitably strange conditions, someone could use "people" and "grin" as we do *and* deny "People grin." To keep "People grin" and "$pv-p$" under one heading, Quine must allow that someone could mean what we mean by "v" and "—", and yet deny "$pv-p$."

It is tempting to leave the matter here and let the mistranslation view thus dovetail with the empirical view; but Quine clearly does not mean the mistranslation view this way. Consider his depiction of the deviant logician's dilemma: "When he tries to deny the doctrine he only changes the subject" ([19], 81). If the translation argument concerns probabilities, Quine must weaken his aphorism to: when the deviant logician tries to deny the doctrine, he *probably* changes the subject. This admits the doctrine can be denied and lets the deviant logician off the hook. Or consider Quine's remark that preserving the logical laws under radical translation is a convention ([20], 319). It is no convention that no one doubts that people grin. Indeed, if preserving classical logic is a convention, why appeal to its obviousness, or anything else, to justify rejecting deviant translations? And if we say this convention is *motivated* by the obviousness of logical laws, the mistranslation view becomes incompatible with the empirical view where the convention replaces its motivation. This ties in with the final point, Quine's unwillingness to let anything count as genuine dissent from even a single logical law. Since every logical truth is potentially obvious ([19], 82), any deviance is unacceptable. Quine explains this peculiarity of logic in contrast to other theories partly in terms of its completeness ([19], 83); since all logical truths are provable, someone dissenting from a logical truth will have to dissent from some "first" one in some proof—but that first one will follow by an *explicitly* obvious step from a truth already assented to. Another reason one cannot change just one logical law, Quine might add, is that propositional logic admits a simple finite axiomatization. In this it differs from set theory, say, which is not finitely axiomatizable and is usually presented as a group of eight or so independent axioms and axiom schemata. One can, for example, keep careful track of the consequences of the Axiom of Choice, so that denying it does not unfix the meaning of "ε". So Quine would say, of a man who dissented from "$(p \supset (p \supset -p)) \supset -p$" after assenting to millions of valid schemata, "His connectives behave as ours do over a number of cases, but his '—' and '⊃' cannot be mapped to ours *because* that mapping would be deviant." The presumption of translational error can be overridden when it comes to the denial of most obvious truths. Not so here; so something more must be afoot.[6]

Quine rightly remarks that "one's reaction to denials of sentences typically felt as analytic has more in it of the reaction to ungrasped foreign sentences" ([17], 66). But this only perpetuates unclarity about the translation argument, since a foreign speaker's words may elude us in two ways: we may literally have no idea how to translate them, or else we may have a tentative hypothesis, but one which attributes a belief so bizarre as to discredit the hypothesis itself. The speaker just might mean what it looks like he means in the latter case, if only because there *is* something it looks like he means. With the former there is no such possibility, for we have yet to specify anything that it looks like he means. Which kind of bewilderment does Quine think sets in when we interrogate a man who denies "$pv-p$"? Might he mean what it looks like he means, or is it that it doesn't look like he means anything yet?

IV. "Quantum Logic"

Before acquiescing in the empirical view, and fitting the mistranslation view into it as best we can, we should examine one current motivation for a deviant logic: quantum mechanics. I argue in Section V that Intuitionism presents no real challenge to classical logic. Quantum mechanics at least seems to, and does, it has been argued, on empirical grounds. It seems clear to me, however, that quantum mechanics no more refutes classical logic than the behavior of mature rabbits refutes arithmetic. When the dust settles, in fact, this emerges as a by-product of the translation argument. Since the argument underlying the mistranslation view wars with the best case for the empirical view, we will have to try again to reconcile them—this time favoring the mistranslation view.

Readers who encounter the claim in [15] that some empirical phenomenon violates the principle $(p \cdot (qvr)) \equiv ((p \cdot q)v(p \cdot r))$ are rightly puzzled. Even proponents of "quantum logic"—in which the distributive laws fail—do not say directly that one can have both p and q or r true but neither p and q, nor p and r true. Rather, they represent the quantum theoretic descriptions of microphenomena as a topological space R, and then *interpret* the connectives of *formalized* propositional logic in terms of operations and relations defined on R. Under this interpretation the distributive law fails. The interpretation is rather natural, and a parallel topological representation of classical mechanics under a parallel interpretation of the connectives *would* satisfy the distributive laws. But before deciding what to make of this, let us review the facts of the case.

Electrons can occupy only discrete states of energy. Because of the relations between energy, momentum (M), and position (P), this entails that not every mathematically possible ordered pair of values for M and P, or pairs of intervals on those values, can be satisfied by an electron e: in fact, $\triangle M(e) \times \triangle P(e)$ must be greater than some interval I. Now what this suggests is that the underlying entities of the world are *not point masses*. Rather, one can apply to these underlying entities two parameters M_q and P_q analogous to classical momentum M_c and position P_c—we thus split the concepts "M" and "P" much as special relativity splits Newton's unanalyzed "mass" into "rest mass" and "relativistic mass." Since M_q and P_q are not parameters of point masses, not every statement true or well defined for M_c and P_c will be so for M_q and P_q. In particular, in accordance with the inequality $\triangle M_q \times \triangle P_q \geq 1$, not every pair of intervals on values for $M_q(x)$ and $P_q(x)$ is a physically realizable situation. Call such unrealizable pairs $<\triangle M_q, \triangle P_q>$ *inadmissible*. One can now construct a space R whose points are possible states of quantum systems. In classical physics every possible point $<M_c, P_c>$ of the analogous space is occupied, but because of the inequality $\triangle M_q \times \triangle P_q \geq 1$, there will be gaps in R. We can perform certain operations (like vector multiplication X) on subspaces of R and note that certain relations hold between subspaces of R. Next we associate every sentence A of quantum theory with a subspace /A/ of R; in particular, that subspace of states in which A is true.[7] Thus we may take the values /A/, /B/ and /C/ of the statements A = "particle m is located in the interval $\triangle P_q$," B = "m's momentum lies in the interval $\triangle M_q$," and C = "m's momentum lies in the interval $(\triangle M_q)'$." Finally —and here is the physical oddity of the world as quantum mechanics describes it—both $<\triangle P_q, \triangle M_q>$ and $<\triangle P_q, (\triangle M_q)'>$ can be inadmissible, while m's having a position in $\triangle P_q$ and having momentum in the interval $\triangle M_q \cup (\triangle M_q)'$ is admissible, or physically realizable. In that case /A/X(/B/U/C/) will be nonempty, but both /A/X/B/ and /A/ X /C/—and hence their union—will be empty. Technically speaking, $<R, X, U>$ is a nondistributive lattice. So *if* one interprets the expressions "·" and "v" of propositional logic as X and U—so that /AvB/ is /A/ U /B/—the distributive law fails.

For all its complexity, however, this construction shows only that, suitably interpreted, the notation of propositional logic may come out false. This is hardly news: propositional logic is, formally, a kind of Boolean algebra, and Boolean algebras fail under numerous interpretations. Putnam has simply picked such an interpretation for the symbols normally used as the connectives. As with "—" in language O of Section II, "·" has been endowed with a deviant usage: Putnam is using "·" to mean what we usually mean by "X in certain odd spaces." Indeed, thus transposing the translation argument into the language of interpretation is no real shift. For a formalism T to be true in a model $<t, D>$ just means that, where T_D is the theory descriibng domain D, translation t carries the theorems of T to theorems of T_D (see [10], II). In particular, for an obvious truth to come out false under an interpretation is for it to come out false under a translation; and, as before, this only shows that the interpretation deviates from the standard or intended one.

55

Putnam seems to me simply in error when he writes, "The whole difference between classical and quantum logic lies in this: that propositions do not form a distributive lattice according to quantum logic, whereas according to classical logic they do" ([15], 238). The conceptual novelty of quantum mechanics is its displacement of the point-mass picture of the world. It is the space R in which distribution fails, and it fails because of the behavior of the parameters P_q and M_q. The nondistributativity is paradoxical only if one vacillates between a quantum and a classical construal of sentence A above. "$p \cdot (q v r)$" both "ought" to imply "$(p \cdot q) v (p \cdot r)$" and fail to only if one reads the p classically and q and r quantum-theoretically. Some remarks in [15] suggest that Putnam is doing this:

> 'Indeterminacy' comes in not because the laws are indeterministic, but because the states themselves, although logically strongest factual statements [sic], do not contain the answers to all physically meaningful questions. . . . S_3 is incompatible with Tj, for all j! But it does not follow that S_3 is incompatible with $(T_1 v T_2 v \ldots T_r)$. Thus it is still true, even assuming S_3, that 'the particle *has* a momentum'; and if I measure it I shall find it. [228–30]

But the statements referred to as physically meaningful seem to be so only if "position" and "momentum" are understood classically (also see [4], 526).

One might object that while quantum mechanics need not be so interpreted as to refute classical logic, it *can* be; and that is all the error view needs. I blame the failure of distribution on vector multiplication in the gappy space R, but could we not blame it on classical logic? This objection misconstrues what an interpretation is. If the sentences of a theory (like *uninterpreted* propositional logic) come out false under a mapping from its primitives to some domain, the theory is false under that interpretation. Whether the theory is true or false under some interpretation is the only fact of the matter. If you want a formalism true of the troublesome domain, change the formalism or (if possible) the mapping. Take geometry: it may *surprise* us that a given geometry fails under a certain physical interpretation, but from the logical point of view there is no more to be said.[8] Putnam brands "essentialist" the view that the primitives of logic (or geometry) are defined just by their containing axioms ([16]), but the issue is largely verbal. Any uninterpreted system (geometrical or algebraic) determines a class of structures whose identifying trait is satisfaction of that system. These "schematic diagrams" exist, and it is pointless to forbid the familiar algebras and geometries to be such. Anyway, Section V introduces a sense in which the logical constants are independent of the logical laws. Embracing this as the "correct" understanding of the constants will do Putnam no good, however, for under it "quantum logic" is not deviant.

Putnam tries to dismiss the translation argument on the grounds that we do not possess a sufficiently refined notion of "change of meaning" ([15], 233). But if not, "refutations" of the laws of logic come *too* ready to hand. If a function f is not 1—1, it can easily happen that $f(A \cap B) \neq f(A) \cup f(B)$. (Let $A = \{x\}, B = \{y\}, x \neq y$ and $f(x) = f(y)$.) If we interpret $\cup$ as "v", $\cap$ as "·" and f as "—", De Morgan's law fails. If Putnam is right, we have no compelling reason to dismiss this as a play on words. Indeed, if the notion of meaning change is all that unclear, mating rabbits refute $1 + 1 = 2$. Surely *here* we should say that our physical domain does not satisfy, not that it *refutes*, arithmetic. Perhaps we might *stop using* arithmetic if such things happened often enough, but no more follows. Were Putnam right about meaning change, there would be no need to reach into quantum theory for a counterexample to classical logic.

Putnam appeals to an ordinary "operational meaning" in terms of tests that "and" (etc.) are said to have, tests that, conducted at the microlevel, refute the distributive law. But it is surely as appropriate to take the "ordinary operational" sense of "and" which carries temporal connotations as refuting the commutative law. If one refutation is bogus, so is the other.

V. *Two Kinds of Deviance: Two Ways to Translate the Connectives*

The upshot of the translation argument is that no one can *deny* the logical laws. But the translation argument also permits conceptual schemes which have no counterparts at all to the standard constants and in which, consequently, the logical laws are *inexpressible*. You cannot be illogical, but for all that the translation argument shows, you can be alogical. It is just this that reconciles the mistranslation and empirical views. No empirical evidence, indeed nothing, could refute the classical laws; but, roughly speaking, evidence could move us to stop using logic—to shift to a system of concepts which have no match in our present system. These are, *modulo* the translation argument, two descriptions of the same thing. Think of our propositional connectives as building blocks, so interlocked that only one structure can be built with them. Nobody could use these same blocks to build in other ways than ours. But one could use other building blocks. In fact, the distinction I am drawing is no more than that between denying p and simply not affirming p. One may refrain from affirming p without denying it if the elements out of which p is built are not in one's lexicon. Pages 83 to 87 of [19] suggest that this is how Quine sees the "shift" deviant logicians propose:

> whoever denies the law of excluded middle changes the subject. This is not to say that he is wrong in so doing. In repudiating "$pv-p$" he is indeed giving up classical negation, or perhaps alternation, or both; and he may have his reasons. . . . The intuitionist should not be viewed as controverting us as to the true laws of certain fixed logical operations, namely negation and alternation. He should be viewed rather as opposing our negation and alternation as unscientific ideas, and propounding certain other ideas, somewhat analogous, of his own.

Let us call a translation of S's discourse *weakly* deviant if it maps nothing to our connectives, or, equivalently, translates none of the sentences S affirms or denies as a logical law or instance thereof. Finally, let us term *normal* a translation which attributes the classical connectives to S. The mistranslation view permits weakly deviant translations, forbidding only deviant ones. If in [18], 43 and [19], 100 Quine is saying that we might someday speak in a way which admits only weakly deviant translation into our current ways, the view espoused is consistent with the mistranslation view. Quine himself notes ([17], 243 and [19], 89) that a speaker may have no counterpart for the existential quantifier, the question of his "referential intent" being ill-formed. Neither does a speaker *have* to have proxies for the connectives. This, indeed, was the lesson of [27].

Consider a parallel from another area of discourse. Perhaps the law that kinetic energy $K = \frac{1}{2}mv^2$ is conventionally true in the sense that any translation that attributes its denial is *ipso facto* a mistranslation. This would be compatible with the existence of conceptual schemes in which nothing at all quite corresponds to "kinetic energy." One could lack (or drop) the law and the concept, using different conceptual equipment for explaining the motion of bodies. Thus there may be no precise counterpart in modern physics for the old "*vis viva.*" Quine sees the difference between "$K = \frac{1}{2}mv^2$" and "$pv-p$" in that a translation might well attribute the denial of "$K = \frac{1}{2}mv^2$" and yet be acceptable, contrary to the supposition of this paragraph. At least, Quine sees no objective answer to the question "How much must doctrine about energy change before the subject does?": see [17], 16. But logic admits no deviance. Correlatively, Quine sees no objective way to determine the kind of revision physics should be said to have undergone if "$K = \frac{1}{2}mv^2$" were denied—whether the "K" of the new physics should be translated normally, or (as best we can) weakly deviantly. No such ambiguity hedges the revision ostensible denial of a logical law comes to.

The appearance of even weak deviance can be illusory; where homophonic translation is bewildering enough to suggest weak deviance, a heterophonic translation may match components of one scheme to components of another with no real discrepancy in judgment or the "building blocks" used. The Intuitionist, who seems by his denial of "$pv-p$" to have abandoned negation, can be interpreted normally in classical logic supplemented by talk of time. Remember, the Intuitionist believes that mathematical objects are created by human thought (see [7], 2, 17–18). It is natural, then, to take his "p" as our "p is now true" and his "$-p$" as our "p will never be true." So interpreted, his "$(\exists x)Fx \vee - (\exists x)Fx$" is something we ourselves would sometimes deny: "either an F exists now, or there will never be an F." Both disjuncts fail if there are no F's now but will be someday. We need not share the Intuitionist's metaphysics to repudiate two merely contrary alternatives. Such repudiation is no more a retreat from "$pv - p$" than is rejection of "The King of France is either bald or nonbald." If the Intuitionist permits himself temporal locutions, we can explain our "$-p$" to him as "p is false at times." Even if he kicks away the ladder of explanation and just presents us with his axiomatized propositional calculus, we can still translate his system normally, if heterophonically, so that his theorems come out as clear truths. (The temporal interpretation of Intuitionism is not the only possible one. Another is Kleene's notion of "recursive realizability," which ties the Intuitionistic conception of truth to the notions of partial and general recursiveness; see [8], 501–16, and Kleene's brilliant [9].) The notion of weak deviance countenanced by the mistranslation view is stronger than this: there can be schemes that permit no irenic interpretation of their deviant notations.

How can Quine permit speakers who do not follow the classical laws to have a *logic* at all? It is here that he can utilize the notions of partial analogy and family resemblance. Logic can be identified not only by its laws but also by the role it plays: logic can be said to be whatever underlies all inference, under some behavioral criterion for inferring that transcends conformity to classical logic. (James Murphy has pointed out to me some difficulties in developing such a notion of inference, but I cannot pursue that issue here.) Why a weakly deviant body of discourse should be allowed to embody a logic at all involves such more specific questions as why a connective which disobeys some classical law governing negation should be allowed to be negation. The translation argument takes both logic and negation to be *immanent* notions: logic is *our* logic, and negation is whatever satisfies our rules for negation: "Negation and alternation are immanent rather than transcendent" ([19], 87; see 19–22 for a general discussion of immanence and transcendence). But the looser conception of logic just broached, one compatible with the mistranslation view, is transcendental: logic is the foundation of inference, and the logical particles are those syncategorematic expressions used to build assertions and studied by logicians. "Negation" is any particle that behaves sufficiently like our "not"—which obeys, say, 75 per cent of the classical laws. In its immanent sense, a deviant logic is impossible; in its transcendent sense, a weakly deviant (but not deviant) logic is possible. Quine seems to have this thought in mind when he writes "The logics of two cultures will be . . . incomensurable at worst and never in conflict, since conflict would simply discredit our translation" ([19], 96). What especially supports this interpretation is the fact that, in general, Quine holds that we sometimes transcendentally extend properly immanent grammatical notions by "felt family resemblance" ([19], 19).

Discussions of quantum logic often conflate the two senses or simply take the question of "alternative logics" in its transcendental sense. M. Gardiner does the second ([4], 518–22):

> we must first ask what a logic is. In the first sentence of the . . . *Prior Analytics*, Aristotle wrote that "the subject of our inquiry is demonstration." . . . Pierce wrote that "[logic] . . . is the classification of arguments. . . ." Quine has also claimed that "the chief importance of logic" lies in the techniques it provides "for showing, given two statements, that one implies the other. . . ." [T]he crucial question in deciding whether quantum logic is a logic is whether . . . all inferences in quantum theory use standard logic; or whether . . . some inferences require rules based upon quantum-logical implication. . . . What . . . would . . . make us . . . regard $<P,\rightarrow>$ as a logic? Presumably, if it turned out to be a good idea to use it to govern proofs . . . to infer from any . . . proposition [p] any proposition [q such that $p\rightarrow q$].

Birkhoff and von Neumann just present a formal system, satisfiable in R, which agrees with classical logic in some but not all respects ([1]). This transcendent usage is permissible so long as it is recognized that "changing logic" in this sense involves no denial of the standard laws. Putnam's obliviousness to this may explain his conviction that shifting to new connectives amounts to rejecting classical logic as empirically false. He grants that " 'a language which does not have a word V which obeys such-and-such patterns of inference does not contain the concept *or* . . . in its customary meaning,' " and notes correctly that "it does not

... follow that an optimal scientific language *can* contain such a word as V" ([15], 231-32). His conclusion that the evidence suggests that there are no "precise and meaningful operations on propositions which have the properties classically attributed to 'and' and 'or' " is consistent with the error view. But he erroneously suggests that such a rejection of classical logic amounts to taking the evidence to suggest that "it is *more likely that classical logic is wrong.*" Putnam claims that "this bypasses the issue of whether adopting quantum logic is 'changing the meaning' of 'and', 'or', etc.," but it does nothing of the sort. Putnam has accepted Quine's diagnosis that one has shifted to a weakly deviant system of inference simply incommensurable with logic.

The quantum logician must distinguish two questions: "Should the nonstandard interpretation of the symbols in my Boolean algebra count as negation, etc.?" and "Is the Boolean algebra, so interpreted, *a* logic?" The answer to the first is "No," but the answer to the second may well be "Yes." One can reject a certain account of the quantum-logical interpretation of "·" and agree that the nondistributive Boolean laws form a (weakly) deviant logic. This does not require the new constants and formulas to be matched with our old ones. In this sense empirical discoveries could justify abandoning the apparatus of classical logic—laws, constants, and all.[9]

Similar remarks apply to particular connectives. Speaking immanently, any particle "&" violating commutativity is ipso facto untranslatable as "·". But we might relax our scruples if "&" played a role in its home language like the one "·" plays in ours. If "&" was a binary connective, favored by mathematicians and obeying some of the laws "·" obeys, we might call "&" a *conjunction-like* connective bearing a family resemblance to conjunction. We might, on the strength of this, map "&" to "·" and call the system containing "&" a *logic-like* system. Such systems might not be truth-functional but might admit of valuations analogous to the assignment of truth values. Quine can allow deviant logics in this sense: logic-like systems with connective-like particles.

Quine is under no obligation to specify how similar a particle C' must be to a classical connective C for C' to be C-like and translated as C. Judgments of similarity are matters of degree, not so much right or wrong as reflections of our innate sense of similarity (see [21]). There may be no objective point at which such translation becomes intolerable. When "connective" is understood transcendentally, translation of the connectives is indeterminate, the line between weakly deviant logics and what is not logic at all being unclear. Three of Quine's most characteristic ideas meet here: (weakly) deviant logics are permissible precisely when translation of the connectives is indeterminate, i.e., when logic is conceived transcendentally. Indeed, the hypothesis that Quine himself has not sufficiently registered the deviance/weak deviance distinction goes far toward explaining his desultory flirtations with quantum logic (e.g.: "[Consider] the proposal to change logic to help quantum mechanics. The merits of the proposal may be dubious, but what is relevant just now is that such proposals have been made" ([19], 100)). Nor need Quine tell us which of the two conceptions, transcendent or immanent, is the "right" one for radical translation and the assessment of alternative conceptual schemes. As long as what each one will permit is clear, and we have all the facts straight, it does not matter.[10]

VI. *Meaning and Truth*

If the mistranslation view as expounded here is Quine's final account of logical truth, can the conventionalist not reply that it confuses necessity with inevitability? The conventionalist admits that it is at most a fact of anthropology that men use proxies for the logical connectives. All he holds to be necessary is that, *if* one uses words translatable as our connectives, one must subscribe to certain theses. Not only may the conventionalist freely jettison meanings as entities (see Section III), Quine's main argument for repudiating all talk of meaning—the indeterminacy of translation—is offstage here. Quine has often explained that he rejects meanings not because they are abstract entities (he does countenance sets) but because talk of meaning suggests that the "is translatable as" relation ($=$ the "means the same as" relation) induces equivalence classes where none exist (see [19], chapter 1). The indeterminacy thesis illustrates and evidences the claim that no clear line separates change of belief from change of meaning; and this is why, where indeterminacy reigns, nothing can be true in virtue of meaning alone. But Quine cannot thus deflect the conventionalist, for the line between change of meaning and change of belief is sharply objective when it comes to logic. Quine seems to suggest that, in general, the indeterminacy of translation blocks any entailment from "apparent dissent from 'p' signifies misunderstanding" to " 'p' is true in virtue of meaning." This suggestion is out of order when "p" is a logical law.

I think Quine can, and should, concede all this. Let us call each of the conditional claims the conventionalist is so insistent on—e.g., "If you use a term translatable as 'not,' you must accept 'pv-p' "—a *crucial conditional*. Not only does Quine accept each crucial conditional; they form the backbone of the mistranslation view. But Quine does not see them as the conventionalist does, because for Quine each crucial conditional is the *barest tautology*. The test (criterion, standard) for whether one is using a language normally translatable into ours is that the consequent of each and every crucial conditional is true. Suppose, then, that logical law L is the consequent of some crucial conditional. That crucial conditional does not *explain why* the speaker assents to L, or justify his assent to L, or explain why what he says is true. Presumably, the explanation or justification for a phenomenon must go beyond the phenomenon itself; since "S has the concept of negation (etc.)" is *another way of saying* that S assents to all the classical laws, the former cannot explain or justify the latter. Conventionalism is a theory about why necessary truths are true, a theory which takes the antecedent of a crucial conditional to explain its consequent. This is why Quine can accept all the crucial conditionals without being a conventionalist. Corresponding to every logical truth is a crucial conditional, each one a bare tautology. It is because dissent from even a single logical law entails mistranslation that we cannot explain assent or truth in terms of meaning, however modestly construed.

Quine and the conventionalist agree that the "sudden dissenter" of Section III—so like Wittgenstein's student who suddenly puts an odd construction on the rule "add 2"—is empirically possible. Where they disagree is that the conventionalist sees the sudden dissenter's usage before his sudden deviance as *committing* him to meaning something by "⊃" and "—", and as violating this already incurred commitment to assent to "$(p \supset (p \supset -p)) \supset -p$." Even philosophers not normally considered conventionalists, like Dummett and Putnam, have looked favorably on the idea that some proper subset of the valid wffs give the "core meaning" of the connectives. This is what Quine cannot make sense of. As he says in a different but related context, "To seek what is 'logically required' ... under unprecedented circumstances is to suggest that words have some logical force beyond what our past needs have invested them with" ([22], 490). When the sudden dissenter suddenly dissents, only these two things happen: (1) the dissenter's verbal behavior, which for so long has agreed with ours, ceases to do so. (2) Our translation of his words (or our inductive guess about what the best translation should be) changes. To explain these two changes in terms of a third—a change in what the sudden dissenter's words mean—is to project a feature of our own translational activity, our induction of his linguistic behavior, onto its object. There remains the overwhelming feeling, most present when one is working through a mathematical proof, that one *could not* be using words as the author of the proof does if one dissents from his theorem—and that this *"could not"* has some objective grounding. (Dummett and Moore raised this sort of objection to Wittgenstein's very Quinean ideas about mathematics.) Quine grants this point but sees it as trivial, contraposition on the crucial conditional whose consequent is the theorem.

Still, a voice echoes, does not Quine concede that a logical truth could not be false? And to the extent that the indeterminacy of translation allows other areas of discourse their own crucial conditionals ("If you understand 'kinetic energy,' you must agree that '$K = \frac{1}{2}mv^2$'"), are these other "constitutive principles" not also necessary? The issue, I think, is verbal. If one is impressed by the truth of the crucial conditionals, one may feel that conventionalism best expresses the nature of logical truth. But their intended job was to locate the origin of necessity in our linguistic activities. If you see the very necessity of the crucial conditionals as undercutting this goal by collapsing the needed gap between origin and result, you will find them insignificant. You will almost certainly take the latter view if, with Quine, you see meaning as a phenomenon "on the surface of language."

Two recent publications present versions of some theses I discuss which differ considerably from my own versions:

1. Graham Nerlich advocates (in *The Shape of Space* [Cambridge University Press, 1976]) a more "realist" view of space-time than that canvassed in note 8 below. He takes space (and by implication space-time) to be a definite *thing* with definite properties. If geometry is the attempt to describe this object, geometry is indeed as straightforwardly empirical as botany. Even if geometry is so understood, however, its disinterpretation is the formal object sufficiently rich in structure to interest mathematicians. It seems reasonably clear that it is this disinterpreted theory that mathematicians study. Nerlich's realism provides a natural and historically central interpretation for geometry but leaves unaffected the thesis that geometrical statements are true only under interpretations. There are other bodies of discourse, such as "rational mechanics," in this region between the empirically determinate and disinterpreted.

2. In *Elements of Intuitionism* (Oxford: Oxford University Press, 1977), Michael Dummett construes Intuitionism in a way that is at odds in two respects with my rather standard construal. First, Dummett asserts, contrary to my suggestion in paragraph four of Section V, that the Intuitionist's view of mathematical objects as created by thought is a *consequence* of the Intuitionist's general view of meaning (applied to mathematical statements), rather than a premise from which his view of the meaning of mathematical statements follows (382ff.). This is no place to argue the matter; let me just assert that I find Dummett's reading of Intuitionism eccentric, and his general "constructivistic" theory

of meaning confused and unconvincing. Second, Dummett insists (contrary to what I imply in the same paragraph) that the Intuitionist does not understand classical reasoning—that if he could understand classical reasoning his intuitionistic proofs would be at best "curiosities" (see, e.g., 201). But it is perfectly plain to me that, on Dummett's own showing, Intuitionistic reasoning is capable of classical reinterpretation. The celebrated continuity principles (the Fan Theorem, the uniform continuity of all functions everywhere defined on [0, 1]) result when classically understood restrictions are placed upon the classical notion of "function" in Baire space, classically understood. Also, the topological model for intuitionistic propositional calculus is obtained by mapping $p \supset q$ to the interior of the union of the (open) set $/q/$ and the complement of $/p/$. This classical fact is so manifest that even Dummett alludes to it on 178. This comes rather oddly from someone who claims to find classical reasoning unintelligible. Dummett is evidently using "unintelligible" in that special philosopher's sense in which "so-and-so is unintelligible" amounts to "I disagree with so-and-so."

NOTES

1. "There is no residual essence of conjunction and [negation] in addition to the sounds and notations and the laws in conformity with which a man uses [them]" ([19], 81).

2. Lewis, following Grice and Schelling, has argued that a full-blooded convention can be unstudied and inexplicit ([11]). I find it curious that he neglects this perspective when he turns to necessity, preferring instead a possible-worlds approach. The Gricean notion of convention *seems* richer than the one Quine reduces to absurdity in [27], and the Grice-Schiffer mechanism of infinitely nested recognitions of intentions might yield an interesting account of conventional truth. Quine in his turn might reply that all Grice has supplied is the mechanism by which truth values are distributed during language learning (see [23], 65) and translation, and this leaves the strictures of [27] untouched.

3. Rescher's stipulation that $(Vvp \cdot Vup) \supset v=u$ seems to grant this. I cannot tell whether Rescher intends this stipulation to apply to n-valued autodescriptive systems $(n>2)$, but if not, trouble starts. Let Vip and Vjp, $i \neq j$, both have designated truth values, and define a connective ϕ such that $<i\phi i>=i$ and $<j\phi j>=j$. Any choice of k will violate the requirement ([29], 85) that, if $k \neq <i\phi i>$, $Vip \cdot Vjq \cdot Vk(p\phi q)$ cannot have a designated truth value.

4. Rescher speaks of "absolute metalogical principals" governing the construction of even autodescriptive systems; see, e.g., 233.

5. "If sheer logic is not conclusive, what is? What higher tribunal could abrogate the logic of truth functions or of quantification?" ([19], 81).

6. Some philosophers protest Quine's appeal to "confusion through sheer complexity" (e.g., [19], 102) to explain occasional dissent from logical laws, and remark that most undergraduates will balk, initially, at the simplest tautologies. Speaking intuitively, however, I find that whenever I or a student dissent from a tautology, I have failed to "take it in" in a sense independent of the dissent itself.

7. Assigning sentences values in abstract spaces is standard procedure in metatheory; cf. [10], sec. V.

8. Of course, whether an interpreted geometrical statement is true depends on the theory T_D, which will be empirical if D is. One can in a sense keep a geometry true under an interpretation by changing the physics from T_D to $(T_D)'$, but, strictly speaking, one has changed the interpretation by changing the range of the translational mapping. Nor does the situation change if spacetime is an entity independent of the things in it. Whether a given geometry is true under an interpretation whose domain is spacetime is as empirical a question as that of the relation of a geometry to any other physical domain. The situation is complicated by the fact that some writers take the absolute spacetime of general relativity not as a generalization of Newton's absolute space and time, but as the set of possible point events (see [30], 203; [12], 99); the ontological status of an object partly composed of possibilities is unclear.

9. M. Friedman's gloss on [15] glides right over the distinction I am pressing: "Even if classical logic is somehow forced on us by the meanings of the logical connectives, there is no guarantee that using connectives with *those* meanings is the best way to achieve the aims of science. Using connectives with other meanings might be better—and better in virtue of empirical facts about the world" ([3], 552). Richard Smokovich has convinced me that, even when my distinction is maintained, the question "What sort of facts could make us abandon classical logic?" continues to press. Perhaps the unexciting answer is simply: axiomatized classical logic has fewer models than one supposed. It certainly cannot be that classical logic has *no* models—what are introductory logic courses about? One is tempted to oppose to some of Putnam's more extreme statements the reply of the Episcopal minister who was asked if he believed in baptism: "Believe in it? I've seen it done." But this issue deserves a paper of its own. Let the reflection that one cannot legislate *a priori* what experience will turn up leave us with the undogmatic counsel of Quinean empiricism: Wait and see. Anything can happen.

10. A. Morton ([13]) takes conclusions similar to these to be at odds with Quine's rejection of deviance. His distinction between strong and weak deviance is reminiscent of that between deviance and weak deviance. But he thinks a deviant translation of Intuitionism would be acceptable if Intuitionists used Intuitionistic logic in everyday life and science, and such reasoning shared a core of inferences with classical logic. So Morton is thinking of logic transcendentally. His view that the Intuitionistic connectives would be *enough like* ours to warrant homophonic translation differs only verbally from the view that our hypothetical Intuitionists have a logic-like system. Miss Haack fails equally to appreciate that talk of connectives "partly but not wholly different in meaning from classical connectives" ([6], 13; see also [14], 19–20) is transcendental. The point is more than terminological. If C "differs in meaning partially" from C', C is not translatable as C' except by analogy, and this lets "$F(C)$" be compatible with "$-F(C')$." Similarly, the connective she defines on 19 in terms of assent, dissent and puzzlement—quite similar to that defined by Quine's second "verdict table" on 77 of [23]—can be called "or" only in the transcendental sense. Her unclarity on this point may explain why she attributes to Quine the assumption that "classical logic is correct" ([6], 18–19). If indeed the translation argument *assumes* that classical logic is correct, something has gone haywire. But the assumption she has detected is better expressed as the determination to treat logic immanently for the duration of the argument.

11. These remarks should be compared with [5]. Quine seems to back off this extreme position on logical laws in [23], 78-80.

REFERENCES

1. Birkhoff, G., and J. von Neumann. "The Logic of Quantum Mechanics," *Annals of Mathematics*, 2d ser., 37 (1936):20-46.
2. Davidson, D., and J. Hintikka, eds. *Words and Objections*. Reidel, Holland, 1969.
3. Friedman, M. Review of H. Putnam, *Philosophical Papers, Philosophical Review* 86 (1977):545-56.
4. Gardiner, M. "Is Quantum Logic Really Logic?" *Philosophy of Science* 38 (1971):508-29.
5. Harman, G. "Quine on Meaning and Existence, I," *Review of Metaphysics* 20 (1967):124-51.
6. Haack, S. *Deviant Logic*. New York: Cambridge University Press, 1974.
7. Heyting, A. *Intuitionism*. 3d ed. Amsterdam: North-Holland, 1971.
8. Kleene, S. *Introduction to Metamathematics*. New York: Van Nostrand, 1950.
9. ———. "On the Interpretation of Intuitionistic Number Theory," *Journal of Symbolic Logic* 10 (1945): 109-24.
10. Levin, M. E., and M. R. Levin. "The Independence Results of Set Theory," *Synthese* 38 (1978): 1-34.
11. Lewis, D. *Convention*. Cambridge, Mass.: Harvard University Press, 1970.
12. Møller, C. *The Theory of Relativity*. London: Oxford University Press, 1966.
13. Morton, A. "Denying the Doctrine and Changing the Subject," *Journal of Philosophy* 70 (1973):503-10.
14. Nagel, E. *Logic Without Metaphysics*. New York: Free Press, 1956.
15. Putnam, H. "Is Logic Empirical?" In R. Cohen and M. Wartofsky, eds. *Boston Studies in Philosophy of Science*, Vol. 5. Dordrecht, 1969.
16. ———. "The Refutation of Conventionalism," *Nous* 8 (1974): 25-40.
17. Quine, W. V. O. *Word and Object*. Cambridge, Mass.: MIT Press, 1960.
18. ———. *From a Logical Point of View*. Harper, New York: 1961.
19. ———. *Philosophy of Logic*. Englewood Cliffs, N.J.: Prentice-Hall, 1970.
20. ———. "Reply to Stroud," in [2].
21. ———. "Natural Kinds," in *Ontological Relativity*. New York: Columbia University Press, 1969.
22. ———. Review of M. Munitz, ed., *Identity and Individuation*, in *Journal of Philosophy* 68 (1971):488-90.
23. ———. *The Roots of Reference*. LaSalle, Ill.: Open Court, 1974.
24. ———. *The Ways of Paradox*. 2d ed. Cambridge, Mass.: Harvard University Press, 1976.
25. ———. "Carnap and Logical Truth," in [24].
26. ———. "Necessary Truth," in [24].
27. ———. "Truth by Convention," in [24].
28. ———. Review of I. Lakatos, *Proofs and Refutations*, *British Journal for the Philosophy of Science* 28 (1977):81-82.
29. Rescher, N. *Many-valued Logic*. New York: McGraw-Hill, 1969.
30. Sklar, L. *Space, Time, and Spacetime*. Berkeley: University of California Press, 1974.
31. Stroud, B. "Conventionalism and the Indeterminacy of Translation," in [2].

Ontology and Reduction*

RICHARD E. GRANDY
University of North Carolina at Chapel Hill

> We are completely puzzled, then, and you must clear up the question for us, what you intend to designate when you use the word "being." Obviously you must be familiar with what you mean, whereas we, who formerly imagined we knew, are now at a loss.
>
> Plato, *The Sophist*

The concept of ontological reduction is apparently a fundamental one for Quine's philosophy. Facts about ontological reducibility loom large in the argument for the inscrutability of reference, and the latter is used to provide one of the two arguments for the indeterminacy of translation. It is of fundamental importance, therefore, to clarify the concept of ontological reduction and the reasons for defining the term in the way Quine does. I shall argue that the notion is not philosophically useful because it obscures important issues by conflating cases which are quite diverse.

Let us begin by resolving to use the term "theory" exclusively for a recursively enumerable set of sentences closed under deduction, "language" for a set of sentences closed under the usual formation rules (in both cases without interpretation), and "model" for an assignment of a domain and of suitable sets of n-tuples to the predicates of a language.[1] The first question to ask is what types of entities an ontological reduction relates. The most concise statement of ontological reduction is given in the following passage:

> The standard of reduction of a theory Θ to a theory Θ' can now be put as follows. We specify a function, not necessarily in the notation of Θ or Θ', which admits as arguments all objects in the universe of Θ and takes values in the universe of Θ'. This is the proxy function. Then to each n-place primitive predicate of Θ, for each n, we effec-

---

* Michael D. Resnik and Michael P. Smith made several comments on an earlier draft that have led to greater clarity and accuracy.

tively associate an open sentence of Θ' in n free variables in such a way that the predicate is fulfilled by an n-tuple of arguments of the proxy function always and only when the open sentence is fulfilled by the corresponding n-tuple of values. ["Ontological Reduction to a World of Number," p. 218 of the reprinting in *Ways of Paradox*, 2d ed.]

The definition makes apparent that the relation is one that holds between interpreted languages. We will consider an interpreted language to be a triple $<D, I, L>$, where D is a nonempty set, L a language, and I an interpretation of L in domain D of the usual kind. Making Quine's definition more explicit, $<D, I, L>$ *is reducible* to $<D^*, I^*, L^*>$ iff there is a proxy function f such that for every n-place primitive predicate R of L there is an open sentence A of L^* with n free variables such that a sequence σ satisfies $Rx_1 \ldots x_n$ in I iff σ^* satisfies $Ax_1, \ldots x_n$ in I^*, where σ^* is the sequence obtained by taking the images of the elements of σ under f. (That is if $\sigma = <d_1, \ldots d_i, \ldots>$, then $\sigma^* = <f(d_1), \ldots, f(d_i), \ldots>$.)[2] Thus the first point to note is that the reduction relation holds between interpreted languages and not between theories in the sense in which we are using the term, and thus Quine interprets Frege as having shown something about the relation between the pair consisting of the numbers and number theoretic language and the pair consisting of sets and set theoretic language.

In order to bring out the motivation for Quine's definition, it will be instructive to look at a concept which bears some similarity to the notion of ontological reduction and which might pretheoretically be thought to be a candidate for the definition. I have in mind the syntactic notion of one theory being relatively interpretable in a second. T_1 is relatively interpretable in T_2 iff there is a mapping of predicates R_n of T_1 into open formulas A_n with n free variables and a one-place open formula Dx of T_2 such that for any sentence ϕ $(R^1, \ldots R^k)$ of T_1, $T_1 \vdash \phi (R^1, \ldots R^k)$ iff $T_2 \vdash \phi_D(A^1, \ldots, A^k)$, where $\phi_D(A^1, \ldots A^k)$ is the sentence of T_2 obtained from $\phi(R^1, \ldots R^k)'$ by relativizing all of the quantifiers to D and replacing each R^i by A^i.

This notion taken as a criterion of ontological reduction would appear to have a serious defect, but before exploring this, I should mention that the notion does count Frege's, von Neumann's, and Zermelo's exploits as ontological reductions, as well as the usual reductions of fractions to integers and reals to sets of natural numbers. The apparent defect is that there is a form of the Lowenheim-Skolem theorem proved by Bernays[3] which shows that any theory T is relatively interpretable in number theory with the addition of an axiom asserting the consistency of T. Thus on this definition any theory would be ontologically reducible to an extension of number theory.

Having seen what Quine's criterion is and the apparent defect of an alternative, let us consider the question what we want the criterion for. There are four types of cases which Quine includes under the heading "Ontological Reduction":

I. Reduction of a model
II. Finite models, decidable theories, and substitutional quantification
III. Isomorphic models and models of the same cardinality
IV. Legitimate reduction and trivialization

I. *Reduction of a Model*

Under the first heading Quine originally included such examples as the deflation of a universe which had objects that were indistinguishable in the language from one another to a universe consisting of one object from each equivalence class of indistinguishables. He later accepted the suggestion to broaden the class by including some deflations which did not involve proxy functions but in which one simply restricted the universe to a definable subdomain.[4] The reduction of number theory with a nonstandard model to a theory with a standard model was an example.

The general idea is that when we are giving an interpretation of a language it is otiose to have objects in the model which are unnecessary. Thus, for example, a model with indistinguishable objects or one in which a certain subset of the domain could be dropped should not be seriously contemplated as interpretations of the language. That is not to say that they are not perfectly good mathematical objects or that they should be ruled out in studying model theory, but simply that, if we are considering the interpretation as an interpretation of a language which is used by speakers, then the extra objects are excess baggage since the truth value of no sentence would be changed by dropping them.

We might try to give a precise definition then of a *preferred model* of a language; a model M would be preferred iff for any set S definable in the metalanguage in which M is being given, either the restriction of M to S is not a model of exactly the same sentences or else the restriction is isomorphic to the original model M. Thus if there is a definable submodel which makes the same closed sentences true but which is not isomorphic, then the model is not preferred. We need the condition that the restriction be definable to avoid trivialization by application of the strong Lowenheim-Skolem theorem. We need to add the clause about the submodel not being isomorphic in order to permit the natural numbers with the less-than relation to be a preferred model of number theory; without the isomorphism condition this model would not be preferred because we could drop zero and satisfy the same closed sentences, and we could then drop one from that model, and so on.

The motivation for this definition was given in terms of not being able to make sense of speakers of a language talking about objects which are not specifiable in their language, but the more Quinean formulation would be that we are imposing conditions on what the ontological commitments of the language might be. Thus we could paraphrase the criterion just offered by saying that a model is not an acceptable assessment of someone's ontological commitments if that model contains objects which could be deleted without any change of truth values of the sentences of the language.

A slight modification in the definition is required, however. If we consider a model for a theory in which there are indistinguishable objects, then we can construct a model that is intuitively more economical either by using equivalence classes of indistinguishable elements or by choosing a submodel containing one element from each class. Such changes of model do not in general fit our previous definition. In the case of equivalence classes we do not have a submodel, and when we use representatives of the equivalence classes, the set of representatives may not be definable.[5] Thus we are led to the following modified definition: M is a *preferred model* iff for any set S definable in the metalanguage in which M is being specified either the restriction of M to S is not a model of exactly the same sentences or else the restriction is isomorphic to the original model M, and for any equivalence relation R the model defined by forming equivalence classes with respect to R is isomorphic to M or is not a model of the same sentences.

The process of ontological reduction in this case consists of replacing one model by another where the second is smaller either in the sense of being a proper part of the original or else in the sense of being formed from the original by taking equivalence classes. In either case the application of the term "ontological reduction" seems justified.

II. *Finite Models, Decidable Theories, and Substitutional Quantification*

The second class of cases is rather peculiar; to begin with finite ontologies, one would think that a model which contained seven unicorns would represent a different ontological commitment from one which contained seventeen. We are being a bit hasty, of course, in that Quine only asserts that the case of a finite universe of *named* objects a theory has no ontological commitment, but once we are given an upper bound on the number of objects in the universe, we could eliminate our ontological commitments by adding names. The argument to support this claim is unclear. The explanation given by Quine (OR, p. 62) is that "here there is no occasion for quantification, except as an inessential abbreviation . . . . Variables thus disappear, and with them the question of a universe of values of variables." One might think that this claim is supported by the argument given in "On What There Is"[6] that we can eliminate names in favor of variables and predicates, and thus we can reduce all ontological questions to questions about quantification. But it would be a non sequitur to argue that because we can eliminate names and make all ontological commitments depend on variables we can avoid ontological commitment by eliminating variables and quantifiers in favor of names.

I do not think that Quine is using the above argument, but rather that he is invoking a slightly different standard of ontological commitment. The original version was that "we are convicted of a particular ontological presupposition if, and only if, the alleged *presuppositum* has to be reckoned among the entities over which the variables must range in order to render one of our affirmations true" ("On What There Is," p. 13). The second criterion is invoked, for example, in the discussion of the ontology of decidable theories in "Ontological Relativity": "Where we can always settle truth values mechanically, there is no evident internal reason for interest in the theory of quantifiers nor, therefore, in values of variables" (p. 63). The criterion thus seems to be that the ontological commitment of a theory consists of those objects which must be mentioned by a metalinguistic theory which gives truth conditions of the language in question.

If a theory has names for all objects in the model and the set of names (and thus the model) is finite, then we know that a finite list of atomic sentences will totally characterize the model. If we were given a list of all the true atomic sentences then the truth or falsity of any quantified sentence could be effectively determined from the list of atomic truths. Furthermore, since the list of atomic truths is finite we know that there is an effective listing of these.

Thus it follows that there exists a characterization of the truths of the theory that does not mention the objects in the model. It does not follow, of course, that we know how to find such a characterization. There is an ontology-free truth theory for the theory in question, but this does not mean that we have such a theory. Thus, although we know that the ontology of the theory is potentially reducible (to nothing) in the sense that there is a characterization that would do the job if we could find it, the ontology is not reducible in the sense that we can now produce such an ontology-free characterization. Our original intuition that theories that postulate different finite numbers of objects (or different objects) is justified; if a theory postulates three rabbits, then we could in principle eliminate the reference to rabbits in defining truth for the theory, but it can be done in fact only after we know enough about the rabbits to know which decision procedure is the appropriate one.

The issue of the ontology of a theory with substitutional quantification is closely related. We are told that substitutional quantification's "... nonreferential orientation is seen in the fact that it makes no essential use of namehood" (OR, p. 63). I am not certain what the exact criterion for essential use of namehood is in general, but it makes false that substitutional quantificational theories never make such use. This sort of quantification makes no mention of objects when giving the truth conditions of the quantified formulas, but one must still give the truth conditions of the atomic sentences. It is true that in some cases such as arithmetic the atomic truth conditions can be given without appealing to denotation. But in the general case where there is no decision procedure for the truth of atomic sentences, either there will be an infinite number of unstructured constants or else there will be a complex singular terms involving functional expressions. If the truth conditions for *Rab* are given in the usual way in terms of the denotations of "*a*" and "*b*," then the truth theory has not avoided mention of objects. Biconditionals could be given explicitly, e.g., "*Rab* is true iff *Sde*," if only finitely many constants and predicates occur in the language. But I see no way of avoiding either an infinite set of truth axioms or a denotation function if the set of terms is infinite.

III. *Isomorphic Models and Models of the Same Cardinality*

Let us consider now the third class of cases. The first point to be noted is that there are two different perspectives which are used in discussing ontological commitment. In some papers, such as "On What There Is," Quine is discussing what objects must be included in the domain of the quantifiers in order for certain sentences to come out true *given a fixed interpretation of the predicates*. In other papers, such as "Ontological Reduction and the World of Numbers" (in OR), he is discussing the possibilities of varying both domain and interpretation of predicates. When we are discussing ontological commitments from the second point of view, there is no difference between isomorphic models of a language. That is, if we are given such models, there is nothing to choose between them on the grounds of the truth values of the sentences which would indicate that one rather than the other represents the ontological commitments of a speaker of the language. Consequently, from this point of view it seems that the ontological commitments of a speaker must be taken to be to a class of structures—each model must contain not simply objects but objects that stand in appropriate relations to each other. Thus the specification of a model consists not simply in choosing a domain but also in characterizing the interpretation. The ontology of a theory should properly be located in the domain plus interpretation and not in the domain alone.[7]

This point is worth belaboring, for it appears that there are times when Quine himself forgets that the ontology of a model language pair consists in the entire model and not simply in the domain. Thus, for example, he says:

> One ontology is *always* reducible to another when we are given a proxy function f that is one to one. The essential reasoning is as follows. Where P is any predicate of the old system, its work can be done in the new system by a new predicate which we interpret as true of just the correlates $f(x)$ of the old objects x that P was true of. [OR, p. 57]

Apparently what Quine had in mind was the theorem that, given an interpreted language $<D, I, L>$ and a set D^* of the same cardinality as D, we can define an isomorphic interpretation $<D^*, I^*, L>$. But does this theorem justify the claim that we can achieve an ontological reduction? I think not, for the theorem gives us no guarantee that we can characterize the new interpretation I^* without making reference to D and I. The method used in the proof of the theorem to define the new interpretation is as follows: We choose an arbitrary one-to-one mapping f from D to D^*, and for each n-place predicate of L we let $I^*(R) =$

$$\{<f(d_1), \ldots f(d_n)> \; : \; <d_1, \ldots d_n> \varepsilon \, I\,(R)\}$$

But it is difficult to see what ontological savings we have achieved, for in characterizing the new model we have made essential reference to the old. It is only if we concentrate all attention on the bare objects of the domain and disregard the fact that a model is a structure that we can overlook the contribution of the old predicates $R(x,y)$ in describing the new structure. Of course there will sometimes be other coextensive descriptions of the new structure that do not make essential use of the old theory, but our proof gives us no way of finding these.[8]

To reduce the ontology of one theory to another should mean more than finding an interpretation of the language with a different domain. In the case under consideration an arbitrary domain of the right cardinality will suffice, but in the definition of the interpretation all of the old ontology remains. This is a case of ontological disguise, not reduction. Thus when perusing claims about such other philosophical matters as inscrutability of reference, we should examine these with great care to determine whether or not they rest on genuine reductions.

IV. *Legitimate Reductions and Trivialization*

The most commonly cited example of an ontological reduction is the logicist reduction of number theory to set theory. This case is unlike those discussed in Section I, in which we simply reduced the size of a given model, and the fundamental question is whether we can characterize the legitimate reductions in a way that excludes trivialization. One of the things that we learned from the second and third sections is that in assessing claims of ontological reducibility we must carefully scrutinize the way in which the reducing theory is described. Some reducibility claims were seen to be false because the alleged proof does not enable us to describe the new model independently of the first. With these facts in mind let us reconsider the possibility of defining ontological reduction in terms of relative interpretability by looking more closely at the details of Bernays' lemma.

In effect, Bernays analyzed the proof of the Skolem-Löwenheim theorem and showed that the predicates that interpret an arbitrary axiomatized theory T can be explicitly defined within number theory. In the proof of the Skolem-Löwenheim theorem applied to a given theory T, we first construct a maximal consistent set of sentences including T; then a model in the natural numbers is defined using the maximal consistent set. For example, for each two-place relation R in T we define the new relation:

$$R^* = \{<m, n>: Ra_m a_n \varepsilon \, \Gamma T\}$$

where ΓT is the maximal consistent set including T. Thus Bernays' insight was that the characterization of the set ΓT and of the new relations can be carried out in standard number theory with the addition of a sentence asserting the consistency of T.

The important point about the proof of the theorem is that the definition of the new relation R^* *makes essential reference to the theory* T. Compare, for example, the definition of the successor relation in the typical reductions of number theory to set theory—the relation that is mapped onto successor is:

$$\{<x,y>:y=\{x\}\} \text{ or } \{<x,y>:y=x \cup \{x\}\}.$$

In both cases, as in the original Frege definition, no mention of the theory to be reduced is required. The Bernays lemma gives us a way of mapping discourse about an arbitrary domain into discourse about numbers, but what is said about the numbers is still dependent on reference to the original theory. The situation is exactly comparable to that discussed earlier in which equicardinality arguments were seen to not provide significant reductions because the definition of the new model made use of the characterization of the old model.

Thus we can formulate the restriction on relative interpretability that will include the intuitively plausible reductions while blocking trivialization, and we can do this in a well-motivated way. Theory T_1 is ontologically reducible to T_2 if T_1 is relatively interpretable in T_2 and the definitions of the interpreting formulas in T_2 do not make essential mention of T_1. This definition should be taken in disjunction with the definition given in Section 1 that characterizes acceptable reductions in size within a model.

The definition is open to two lines of criticism. First, someone could show it to be inadequate by producing a plausible reduction that is excluded or by producing an implausible reduction that is allowed by the definition. The second criticism would be that the definition is too vague for it depends crucially on the phrase "does not make essential mention." Certainly this is a vague term and one whose clarification would undoubtedly lead us quickly into matters of ontological relativity. However, as long as application of the criterion gives clear and correct answers for the cases in which we have strong pretheoretical views, a range of vagueness may be acceptable. We should not assume *a priori* that the difference between legitimate ontological reductions and unacceptable ones is itself a matter of the greatest clarity.

NOTES

1. This terminology is not always that followed by Quine. In keeping with Quine's assumptions I confine my attention throughout this paper to standard first-order quantificational languages.

2. There is one technical point which is irrelevant to the main discussion but which is worth mentioning. Quine should have included a requirement that the range of the proxy function should be definable in $<D^*, I^*, L^*>$. If the proxy function's range is not definable, then in general there will not be sentences of L^* which correspond to the sentences of L because there will be no way to suitably relativize the quantifiers. For example, on the criterion quoted, number theory is reducible to the theory of real numbers, but the latter is decidable and thus by Quine's lights has no ontological commitment.

3. For a proof see S. C. Kleene, *Introduction to Metamathematics* (Groningen: Wolters—Noordhoff, 1971), p. 398.

4. See the note added to the reprinting of "Ontological Relativity" in *Ontological Relativity* (New York: Columbia University Press, 1969), p. 68.

5. In general the set will not be definable without the axiom of choice.

6. In *From a Logical Point of View* (New York: Harper & Row, 1963), pp. 20–47.

7. Quine seems to take this point of view at one stage in "Ontological Relativity": "It is thus meaningless within the theory to say which of the various possible models of our theory form is our real or intended model. Yet even here we can make sense still of there being many models" (p. 54).

8. There are various ways in which to hide the reference to the old ontology. For example, if the metalanguage is strong enough to define a well ordering of all sets, then we can define the model to be the first one in the ordering with domain D^* that is isomorphic to $<D, I, L>$.

No Entity Without Identity*

DALE GOTTLIEB
The Johns Hopkins University

Semantics, epistemology, ontology: any problem with roots in all three of these studies will be philosophically central and very difficult. Hence the tremendous interest in giving an account of reference. Reference has become the foundation of truth and thus crucial for semantics. Reference is our medium for speaking about the world, and therefore for formulating theories in which we express knowledge of the world. And since many ontological questions are settled (or at least debated) by appeal to the needs of semantics and epistemology, reference is a determinant of ontology as well. An account of reference will therefore have consequences for a broad variety of philosophical issues and will be partly constrained by positions on those issues. Less obviously, the close relation of reference to those disciplines encourages us to use their resources in understanding reference. In particular, epistemological accounts of reference are perennially popular. *To refer to a thing is (or presupposes) that we have (or can get) knowledge about it.* I shall argue that this approach is correct (at least for certain questions concerning reference), though it has been incorrectly formulated by its proponents.

I

Singular terms, predicates, and quantifiers are three types of expression that refer (at least sometimes). Of the three, singular terms are the least fundamental, for three reasons: (1) In context we often use expressions that are grammatically indistinguishable from genuine singular terms and yet intend them nonreferringly. The real referrers are identified via quantification. (2) Singular terms are eliminable from "ideal" scientific language. (3) Singular-term reference presupposes the

---

* An ancestor of this paper appeared as "Some Epistemic Determinants of Reference: The Need of Identity Conditions," in *Views on Language*, ed. Reza Ordoubadian and Walburga Von-Raffler Engel.

possession of a predicate satisfied by the object referred to, which predicate gives the object's "identity criterion."

So far, predicates and quantifiers are on a par. However, predicates seem to be learned first and seem to have a simpler linguistic basis, and hence are taken as the starting point of reference. A common principle concerning predicate reference is this: *An expression is a genuine predicate—that is, "divided reference" or satisfaction conditions are its correct semantic interpretation—only if it possesses an associated criterion of identity.* This is the unmetaphorical content of the slogan "No entity without identity." I shall defend this principle, thought I shall subject it to an epistemic gloss.

In a nutshell, my thesis is this: Predicates require identity conditions because they are the medium of expression for theories that give us objective knowledge. Objective knowledge requires intersubjective checking of information about objects, and that requires identity. It is the business of a criterion of identity to make knowledge of identities possible, but that in a very special sense of 'possible' which is quite different from that advocated by the traditional supporters of epistemological accounts of reference.

One thing about this thesis troubles me: I do not know to what extent it deviates from the account of reference given by the man who, more than anyone else, has structured the conceptual framework in which this problem is currently discussed—W. V. O. Quine. I would like to think of it as a commentary, or perhaps partial extension of his position. Although he has never cast his account of identity in explicitly epistemological terms, I have the hope that his holistic identification of truth conditions and verification conditions leaves room for a project like mine within his framework. For such an identification encourages the idea that there are epistemological prerequisites for the proper functioning of language, and, in particular, reference. Furthermore, in at least one case Quine's stress on identity conditions does take an epistemological turn. His argument against propositions can be summarized thus:

No entity without identity.
Propositions are identical iff the sentences expressing them are synonymous, and this is our only hope for a criterion of identity for propositions.
There is not sufficient "behavioral" evidence for synonymy.
"Behavioral" evidence is all the evidence there is for synonymy.
Therefore, there is no criterion of identity for propositions.
Therefore, there are no propositions.

Thus the failure of identity conditions for propositions is at bottom a failure of evidence. This is the starting point for my account.

II

There is widespread agreement that reference requires clear identity conditions, or a criterion of identity. However, the rationale for the requirement and its precise content are not easily made out in the writings of its proponents. For example, Peter Geach tells us:

> For every proper name there is a corresponding use of a common noun preceded by "the same" to express what requirements as to identity the proper name conveys.... The use of a name involves a criterion of identity, whereby we can make sure of naming the same thing on different occasions.[1]

Why is this the case? Because, in general, "When the same name is used in two acts of naming, *we can always ask* whether the same thing is named." Talking of proper names, Geach says:

> ... we certainly do not give a man the meaning of a proper name by presenting him with the object named. In using a proper name *we claim the ability* (or at least acquaintance, direct or indirect, with somebody else who had the ability) to *identify an object*; and by giving somebody an object we do not tell him how to identify it.[2]

Accordingly, Geach describes a criterion of identity as follows:

> I maintain that it makes no sense to judge whether x and y are 'the same', or whether x remains 'the same', unless we add or understand some general term—"the same F." That in accordance with which *we thus judge* as to the identity, I call a *criterion* of identity.[3]

Thus *what* we need for the use of a name 'N' to be legitimate is a general term 'F' such that via 'is the same F as' we can identify an object and make sure we are referring to the same object when we use 'N' on different occasions. *The reason we need it* is that when 'N' is used repeatedly we can always ask whether the same object is named, and when we use a proper name we claim the ability to identify its bearer.

This account is eminently unsatisfactory. Aside from pervasive vagueness (what could possibly be meant by "via 'is the same F as' we can identify an object" and "we claim the ability"?), it is open to some obvious objections. If we are to make sure—that is, to know—that we are referring to the same object in different uses of 'N' via 'is the same F as', it appears that we must be able to know, for any two things, whether they are the same *F*. Vagueness appears again in the phrase "be able to know," but even so, this requirement is clearly much too strong. For one thing, it would disqualify every proposed criterion of identity hitherto proposed. Spatio-temporal coincidence is supposed to be an adequate criterion of identity for such objects as stones and electrons, yet no one supposes that for any stones (for example, the first stone stepped on by a dinosaur and the first stone stepped on by a mammal) or any electrons we are able to discover their identity or diversity. In addition, there is an unbridgeable gap between the requirement and its rationale. "We can always ask whether different uses of 'N' name the same object"— we can ask, but the *appropriateness* of the question does not presuppose our ability to nail down an answer. Likewise for the claim to the ability to identify the bearer of a proper name: even if we were normally understood to be making such a claim, it would have to be shown that this is a feature of the *semantics* of being a name. (Think of Moore's paradox "P, but I don't believe it.") But it is not even true that we are so understood: 'the first dinosaur' is a fine name for the first dinosaur, even though no one can identify its bearer. And if it is protested that we certainly could identify it if we were properly situated, consider the case of 'the shortest true sentence of arithmetic which will never be known.' (My apologies to the intuitionists among you.)

Peter Strawson offers a far more elaborate account of reference and predication.[4] There are two points at which identity conditions enter. First, in order to make an identifying reference to a particular, a speaker must *know* a sentence of the form "There is one and only one *F*" where that particular to which he refers is the *F*. And of course 'one and only one' requires identity conditions for *F*'s. Second, to use a predicate that introduces a sortal universal, one must be able to recognize the feature that underlies that universal, and one must possess the criterion of distinctness (and, where applicable, the criterion of reidentification) for the particulars that are instances of the sortal universal introduced.[5] (For example, to use 'cat' as a predicate, one must possess a criterion of distinctness for cats and a criterion for their reidentification over time.) Now the second claim is only as clear as the notion of a criterion, and by comparison mud is transparent. From the criticism of Geach we know one thing that cannot be meant: a way of coming to know the facts of identity and diversity in all cases. And the first claim seems likewise too strong: Suppose I say, "The first woman to step on the moon will be an American." Next year, to everyone's surprise, the Russians put a woman on the moon; have I not been refuted? So I must have succeeded in referring to her. And yet I surely did not *know any* of her unique descriptions. As conditions on the understanding of one's language—and this is what Strawson takes them to be—they are both hopelessly vague and also clearly too strong.

Quine's tack is to link identity first to predication, or, in his own phrase, divided reference. His starting point is a detailed reconstruction of the psychogenesis of the linguistic mastery of predication. Successive levels of sophistication are achieved until one is reached where the only interpretation the linguistic behavior will bear is predication. The operant methodological principle is explanation by the minimal satisfactory theory, i.e., the theory according the least linguistic competence. As long as the child merely "announces" the arrival of objects in his vicinity, his behavior is to be regarded as wholly nonlinguistic; he is merely responding selectively to various stimuli. Learning plural constructions awards him mastery of mass terms, but no more. Only when the apparatus of identity enters his linguistic repertoire are we forced to accord him mastery of predication, and therewith, reference. Quine concludes that "the dividing of reference *consists in* settling conditions of identity."[6] As for singular terms, Quine will accord them referential status only after a genuine predicate appears that we can use to pick out an object for the singular term to name. Now how do these observations, if we assume their truth, support the conclusion that the fixing of identity conditions *is* the dividing of reference? Well, if you are a behaviorist at heart, you may think of referring as a particular complex of behavior, on a par with playing chess, say. You then ask: What kinds of behavior *must* a person display to be counted among the referrers? And the answer *will be* the referring, just as moving chess pieces in accordance with the rules of chess (and with at least a minimal regard for prudent strategy) *is* playing chess. Now if referring to apples requires mastery of 'same apple,' it is natural to assume that referring to propositions and people require mastery of 'same proposition' and 'same person.' Hence the need for a criterion of identity as a prerequisite of divided reference.

I think we must grant the plausability of Quine's sketch of learning to refer, and hesitation over behaviorism as an over-all constraint on linguistic theory cannot be debated here. Thus I will accept Quine's argument as *forging* a link between reference and identity. Nevertheless, two aspects of the argument call for further refinement. First, it is still not clear exactly *what* is required when it is said that conditions of identity must be "settled," or that 'same F' must be "mastered." The appeal to language learning suggests the answer: One must learn to use expressions of identity the way knowledgeable, competent language users do. But this must be rejected, since it is empty: since we have all mastered— in this sense—the use of 'same proposition' and 'same person'—with all the vagueness and uncertainty those expressions engender—we would all qualify as capable of referring to propositions and persons. What do we lack for them and have for apples? A criterion in terms of linguistic behavior (citing "smoothness of dialogue" and the like) does not seem to be forthcoming. On the other hand, we cannot require knowledge, actual or (in some sense) potential, of the truth value of all sentences of the form 'a is the same F as b'; we have seen twice already that that is much too strong. Thus *what* Quine is requiring is unclear.

Second, we may ask for an explanation of the significance of the requirement. Even if we accept the identification of reference with a certain complex linguistic competence, and with it the corollary that if a portion of the complex—viz. the "mastery of identity"—is missing there is no reference, we may wonder about the import of this fact for the wider concerns that reference serves. Reference is the backbone of theory construction and ontology, and thus of all systematic knowledge. Thus knowledge is seen to be dependent upon identity: we cannot have knowledge of F's unless identity conditions for F's are "settled." That in itself is not obvious. True, if we do not have clear identity conditions for F's, there is a lot about them we do not know. But there is a lot we do not know about quasars, quarks, tachyons and the Loch Ness monster. We know so little about them that they could easily be confused with other things, yet reference to them is taken for granted. Why does the lack of identity conditions for F's impugn our ability to refer to F's and hence utterly bar knowledge of F's when other informational lacks and unclarities do not?

The two questions must be answered together: What we understand as a criterion of identity indispensible for reference must also be seen as a necessary condition of knowledge. This suggests that a way to proceed is to answer the second question first: We must find some necessary condition for knowledge of objects that will depend upon identity. This is my approach in the next section. For knowledge of F's to be possible, knowledge of their identity and diversity must also be possible—albeit both in a sense of 'possible' that avoids the excesses of Geach and Strawson—and the latter possibility may be taken as the criterion of identity for F's. The result is an epistemological interpretation of Quine's behavioral link between identity and reference.

III

My account is summarized in the following five definitions:

(D1) A predicate 'Fxy' provides an identity criterion for a predicate 'Ax' $=_{df} (x)(y)(Ax \& Ay . \supset (x=y \equiv Fxy))$, and '$Fab$' is epistemically determinate where '*a*' and '*b*' are terms which are epistemically grounded for '*Ax*'.

(D2) The evidential core (of the language of a given theory) = df the set of sentences which can be known without appeal to support from other known or justifiedly believed sentences (of that language).

(D3) S is epistemically determinate with respect to a set M of sentences = df the relations of rational support between S and the members of M are definite.

(D4) A set M of sentences is epistemically determinate = df for every S ε M, S is epistemically determinate with respect to M−{S}.

(D5) A sentence S is epistemically determinate = df there is a set M of sentences such that S ε M; M is epistemically determinate; and M contains the evidential core (of the language in question).

The dependence of reference upon identity is expressed thus:

(R) In order for '*Ax*' to refer to A's, '*Ax*' must have an identity criterion. In order for '*a*' to refer to an object, that object must satisfy a predicate which has an identity criterion.

First I will explain the definitions, and then the rationale for (R).

I will be taking for granted the following mild version of foundationalism. Knowledge requires justified belief. Some sentences can be justifiedly believed without appeal to support from other justifiedly believed sentences; those sentences form the evidential core of a language. Core sentences *may* receive support from other sentences, and belief of a core sentence *may* be prohibited by overwhelming support for its contradictory; it is not claimed that core sentences are evidentially isolated from the rest of the sentences of the language. Rather, the point is that they are also capable of being believed with sufficient justification to count as knowledge even in the absence of external support. The core certainly contains some observation sentences, and perhaps some sentences of logic, mathematics, and "linguistic" truths as well. Noncore sentences require support from other sentences in order to be justifiedly believed. Such support will ultimately be traced back to the core.

Now imagine a sentence S which is not in the core and whose relations of rational support to almost all other sentences are indeterminate. That is, it is not determinate whether or not other sentences confirm, provide evidence for, explain, etc., S and vice versa. Then S is a sentence which possesses no possible justification, and cannot function as part of the justification for any other sentence. With respect to the epistemic use of language, S is a fifth wheel. If we were to identify a sentence's truth conditions with its evidence condition, S would be strictly meaningless. And even if we reject the identification, we can still agree that, for the purpose of formulating theories which express our knowledge of the world, S is irrelevant.

What is wanted is a principled way of excluding S. But S was characterized as having unclear support relations to "almost all sentences," and this vagueness is hard to clean up. We cannot say 'all sentences', nor even 'all deductively unrelated sentences', since the indeterminary of the epistemic relations between S and T may be T's fault and not S's. And to require determinate evidence relations to all sentences whose own evidence relations are determinate would be flatly circular. We must start somewhere; hence the appeal in (D_2) to the sentences which can be known without benefit of previous knowledge or justified belief. (D_3) and (D_4) enable us to extend the evidential core while maintaining determinate epistemic relations among all the members of the growing set. Now it is most appealing to assume that this process of extension provides a unique result no matter what the order of addition of new noncore sentences, but I have no proof of this. Hence the more cautious formulation in (D_5): Any way of adding sentences to the evidential core which preserves the epistemic determinateness of the resulting sets of sentences is acceptable. A sentence is epistemically determinate just in case it can be incorporated at some stage of such a construction. Notice further that, in assessing relations of rational support, we must invoke a requirement of total relevant information: the sense of 'support' intended in (D_3) requires us to assess T's ability to support S in and of itself. If, as we often say, T supports S relative to the background information I, this will be recorded by (D_3) as support for S rendered by the conjunction of T and I and not by T alone.

As the least precise of the group (D_3) deserves special comment. Included in relations of rational support are relations of deduction, induction, confirmation, explanation, etc.: any relation which entitles certain sentences to be cited in giving a reason for thinking that what one believes is true. By requiring only that these relations be definite, we are allowed ignorance of them. And this is necessary, for we are often in the dark even about deductive relations, let alone the rest. Yet, without knowing S's relations to the members of $M - \{S\}$, we may often know that S does have such relations. For example, S may be a complicated concoction of unobjectionable primitive predicates and first-order syntax whose deductive and other relations to the rest of M we know are perfectly definite, even though we do not know in detail which of them S implies, supports, and so on. Furthermore, indeterminacy must be carefully distinguished from irrelevance. The latter is a determinate epistemic relation: unequivocal nonsupport. The former applies only when it is not determinate *whether or not there is support*. The intention of (D3) is to exclude sentences such as, 'This lectern is necessarily wooden', and, 'There will be a resurrection of the dead'—*if* we despair of a clear delineation of their evidence conditions.

To some the suggestion that epistemic relations among sentences may be indeterminate has a paradoxical ring. "Either S supports T or it does not," they say, "although we may not know which. To deny this is to think that S might fail to support T and also fail to not support T—a patent contradiction." But the situation is not so simple. Some epistemic relations exist unknown; this is guaranteed by the undecidability of first-order logic. But there are sentences whose epistemic relations are unclear to us, and we suspect that the unclarity is not due to our fuzzy perception of a clear reality. Perhaps an apt analogy here is vagueness: Is that mound a hill or a mountain? Must there be a determinate answer? Of course not. Similarly, our troubles over personal identity may reflect real epistemic indeterminacy, rather than mere ignorance of epistemic connections. If, after describing cases in the minutest detail, we feel that even though all the relevant facts have been mentioned we cannot decide whether we have one person or two (or more), the reason may be that the sentences expressing those facts do not have a determinate epistemic relation to the sentences which fix the number of persons. Likewise, imagine a possible world in which the craftsman who made this lectern starts to assemble the same wooden planks but, as he starts to work, an evil magician turns them into warm, brown, roughish-feeling ice. Is he making our lectern or another? If we do not expect to find an answer to this question through further analysis and/or description of that possible world, we may diagnose the trouble as a case of epistemic indeterminacy. Or, to take more specific examples, suppose a person's body is unraveled into its component atoms, and then an atom-for-atom isomorphic body is constructed. Let S be 'They are the same person' and S' be 'The second body is constructed out of the same atoms as the first'. Does S' support S? Bodily continuity seems to have some impact on personal identity, but identity of material is usually irrelevant. In this case, however, it is not clearly irrelevant since we do not have spatio-temporal continuity. Yet it is not clearly relevant either. Now it is conceivable, I suppose, that by further analysis of the concept of a person we could arrive at a nonarbitrary determination of the epistemic relation of S' to S. But it is also conceivable that we shall not and that this is due to an inherent vagueness in the concept of a person. Finally, consider the use of enumerative induction in number theory. Fermat's "theorem" holds in the first 10^{100} cases: does that support the theorem? On the one hand, what is 10^{100} out of infinity? On the other hand, we all check cases in deciding what it is worthwhile to try to prove. I suspect that the concept of support is just not precise enough to give determinate answers to these questions. What needs to be appreciated is the possibility of formulating sentences which elude both the criteria for epistemic support and the criteria for epistemic irrelevance so that neither classification is in place.

Though convinced of the possibility of epistemic determinacy, one might quibble with some of my examples. The trouble with persons and lecterns, it seems, is not that what counts for and against the troublesome sentences is indeterminate; we can see, for example, that the unraveling itself counts for a multiplicity of persons while physical and mental continuity and isomorphism support unity. Rather, the indeterminacy here is a matter of degree: there is no way to *settle* the number of persons even on the basis of a complete roster of the relevant facts. This diagnosis, if correct, requires strengthening (D3) to exclude this indeterminacy as well. I acquiesce to this qualification with pleasure. For, a sentence suffering from this sort of indeterminacy is as surely cut off from our knowledge as one whose epistemic relations are indeterminate—and cut off for the same kind of reason. Thus (D3) is to be replaced with

(D3′)   S is epistemically determinate with respect to a set M of sentences = df the relations of rational support between S and the members of M are definite and there is a (conjunction of) member(s) of M which, if known, would justify belief in S over S's negation.

The case of the lectern is now analyzed as follows. S is the sentence, 'This lectern could not have been made of ice in the manner described in the last paragraph'. Let M be the set of all sentences describing (if true) the physical history of the earth. If knowledge of the entire physical history of the earth would not suffice to justify belief in S or its negation, then S cannot be added to M in the process of constructing a maximal epistemically determinate set. Of course, it might be added at a later stage after other sentences satisfying (D3′) have appeared, if the latter would suffice to justify belief in S or its negation. But if we think the existence of such sentences unlikely, we will reject S as epistemically indeterminate.

Finally, (D1) formulates epistemic determinacy for identity. Two problems must be overcome in order to apply the notion of epistemic determinacy to identity. First, that notion is intralinguistic, concerning relations of epistemic support between sentences. Identity is a predicate, satisfied or not by pairs of objects. Strictly speaking, the two pass one another by; we must demand epistemic determinacy of closed sentences in which the identity criterion figures. Second, we must be careful in choosing the terms with which we will close those sentences. We want the epistemic determinacy of sentences of the form 'Fab' to reflect the determinacy of identity for As; therefore we must ensure that indeterminacy is not introduced by a poor choice of terms. For example, spatio-temporal coincidence may be an adequate identity criterion for hats. But if we are required to vouch for the determinacy of 'George's newest hat spatio-temporally coincides with his oldest', we may fail because of our confusions over the identity of persons, not hats.[7] The solution is to isolate a minimum class of terms which are necessary for the existence of knowledge of the objects in question and to use them to create closed sentences for the identity criterion. These are the terms I call 'epistemically grounded' for the objects in question. In order to have knowledge of a particular object, we must have a way of referring uniquely to that object. We may then coordinate this power to refer with predicates and other expressions to form whole sentences which then can be known. But it is not sufficient to have just any means of referring: the means must be commensurate with the kind of knowledge we expect to have of those objects. For example, we can acquire knowledge of physical objects through perception. Thus there must be ways of referring to physical objects which can figure in closed sentences known through perception. In this case we have at first demonstratives coupled with ostension and then proper names (definite descriptions require predicates and identity, and hence are introduced later). Again, knowledge of numbers is acquired through proof. Thus there must be ways of designating numbers which can figure in sentences which are very obviously true (so that they can be used as axioms). In this case we have the various recursive notations for the numbers. In general, each kind of object is associated with certain characteristic modes of epistemic access, and they will help determine what terms are needed for knowledge of the objects of that kind. These terms can then be used to form closed sentences based on the predicate which is to serve as the criterion of identity, and those closed sentences can be tested for epistemic determinacy.

Now let us turn to (R). One might think it trivial: either '$x = y$' with respect to A's is epistemically determinate, or it is not. On the first alternative (R) is satisfied by '$x = y$', and on the second, nothing can satisfy it since identity for A's *simply is* epistemically indeterminate. The situation is not that simple. Sometimes we know that '$x = y$' is determinate with respect to A's and want to formulate a clear criterion of identity which will capture the identity conditions of A's in a useful fashion. Such are the attempts to analyze identity for physical objects in terms of spatio-temporal coincidence. For these cases $(D1)$ formulates the condition of success. Then, there are cases in which we are uncertain whether '$x = y$' is determinate and then discover that it is by satisfying (R). Finally, there are cases in which either '$x = y$' is not determinate, or we are unclear whether or not it is determinate, and we wish to *make* it so by *adopting* a criterion of identity. For example, imagine proposing spatio-temporal coincidence *at a place-time* as an identity criterion for persons. It is pointed out that personal fission is possible, and the result is two persons whose histories develop in a continuous fashion out of what was the history of a single person. Suppose we then revise the criterion to require spatio-temporal coincidence at all place-times, which allows us to say that after fission we have two persons who share a common past (rather than requiring one person who occupies two bodies postfission, or three persons one of whom was annihilated by the fission). Suppose further that we rest content with this identity criterion for persons. Now before we proposed the latter criterion, 'is the same person as', and hence '$x = y$' for persons, was epistemically indeterminate: the needed evidential connections were missing. On the other hand, 'spatio-temporally coincides with at all place-times' was, we may assume, epistemically determinate even before the revision. Thus the result of the revision is not a *discovery* of an identity criterion for persons but a *proposal* to the effect that 'x is a person' be understood so as to be subject to this criterion. That predicate now *becomes* referential through acquiring an identity criterion.

Finally, the rationale for (R). We start with the observation that language is the medium in which theories are expressed and that theories are instruments with which we acquire knowledge. Thus an adequate semantics for a language must at least be compatible with an account of the epistemic efficacy of its theories, if not itself an integral part of such an account. And so the question which lies at the heart of the matter is this: What is the nature of referential epistemology? What epistemological commitments do we incur by adopting a referential semantics? The answer is: We are committed to characterizing our knowledge as *knowledge of objects*. This requires us, at the very least, to acknowledge the possibility of gathering knowledge about the same object from a variety of points of view and at different times. Objective existence—existence as an object—belongs only to that which can be approached from an unlimited number of perspectives, each of which is capable of yielding knowledge of that selfsame thing. It is for this reason that each object can be uniquely described in numberless ways. And it is to coordinate this description-relative knowledge that we must have an epistemically determinate criterion of identity.

To ask for the consequences of portraying knowledge as *of objects* due to referential semantics suggests there is an alternative—nonobjective knowledge. Is such a thing possible? One might think so from Quine's description of the first stage in language learning: occasion sentences. Until the more sophisticated behavior involved in reference is mastered, these are understood as mere signals "announcing arrivals" but seemingly without commitment to, or connection with, any particular objects. An announced "Red!" is just "Red here now" and no tacit qualification "Spatio-temporal object red here now" is implied. Yet it seems that knowledge of such sentences is possible: Doesn't the child know "Red here now" when he utters it after taking a look? Thus there appears to be at least one model for nonobjective knowledge. But this may be an illusion. What of the 'here now' in the occasion sentence? Don't these indicators pick out a spatio-temporal region of which 'red' is being said? If the child says 'Red!' because the previously displayed block was red, even though the present one is blue, he hasn't got the hang even of the occasion sentence; nor has he got it when his "Red!" is prompted by the block on the floor. Occasion sentences require attention to a particular place-time (which varies greatly from occasion to occasion) whose character determines the appropriateness of uttering the sentence. Thus even here we may not have knowledge without objects. Perhaps all knowledge is of objects. If so, then the epistemological commitments of referential semantics are essential to knowledge per se, and the case for (R) will be even stronger.

To establish (R), those reflections must be true, and they must show (R)'s necessity.

As to their truth, I can offer no knock-down argument. But there are surely no current counterexamples: any thing which has ever been contemplated as a candidate for our ontology fits the picture drawn above. Physical objects, numbers, attributes, events, possible worlds, and so on —each is capable of being the object of description-relative knowledge, where the description expresses a characteristic of the object which the knower knows singles it out; and each is *thought of* as capable of having such knowledge coordinated and transferred via coextensive descriptions. Even so-called private objects like sensations fit insofar as the same knower may need to refer to the same sensation in a variety of ways. It follows that knowledge of objects requires making sense of checking the correctness of what one thinks, at least by comparing one's thoughts over time, if not by full-blown intersubjective comparison. Not by accident, then, does our language provide a vast multiplicity of ways of describing the same object. This versatility is crucial to the epistemic character of objects.

But the comparison of one's thoughts over time with each other and with those of others demands, if they are couched in different descriptions, the coordination of those descriptions. This is the role of identity: to enable us to express the coincidence of what is picked out this way and that, so that what we know relative to each way of picking it out may be combined. Now imagine using 'Ax' to "refer to" A's when (R) is not met, that is, when there is no epistemically determinate relation of identity for the A's. How will the gathering of knowledge of the A's proceed? Using other predicates we will concoct unique descriptions for A's: 'the tallest A', 'the A with the smallest square root'—whatever is appropriate. Sentences of the form, "This A is F," "That A is G," will claim their rights at the bar of knowledge. We will ask for intersubjective checking, but when we do, we will find that we seldom come across the same description identifying the A whose claim to F-ness is being investigated. To use your belief that that A is F to corroborate my belief that this A is F, we must somehow discover that that A *is* this A. But we are imagining that there are no predicates coextensive with 'is the same A as' that are epistemically determinate. The result is that there is no way in general of ascertaining identity for A's; thus is lost the sine qua non of objective knowledge: the interplay of beliefs which variously describe the same object. We thus see why (R) is necessary if the adoption of a referential semantics is to contribute to a reasonable account of knowledge.

I will close this section by considering two objections to this rationale for (R). It might be objected that if object-knowledge requires our *ability* to know when two descriptions are coextensive (R) is too weak. Not epistemic determinacy—not definite relations of rational support—is at issue, but the availability of knowledge. This objection is partly mitigated by moving from $(D3)$ to $(D3')$. However, (R) still allows cases in which we know with perfect definiteness that there can be no evidence for the (contingent) identity claims for A's: it will be said that this should be ruled out as well if the rationale is accurate. But I think not. For, while the ability to know when descriptions are coextensive is of great importance in increasing knowledge, lack of this ability does not always signal a failure to incorporate the entities referred to into our conceptual scheme (i.e., a failure of reference): it depends upon the reason the ability is lacking. For example, if the bar to such knowledge is physical—e.g., we are referring to things so remote in time that not enough information survives the increase of entropy to determine identity and diversity—this is not regarded as defeating reference. And it is easy to see that this is not inconsistent with the rationale for (R), since we can easily imagine circumstances in which such knowledge would be available (say, if observers were properly situated in space-time). If we view language as an epistemic instrument whose usefulness is by design independent of spatio-temporal location of its users, we will not regard this case as one in which language's cognitive function fails, and hence the rationale for epistemic conditions of reference must not rule it out (as (R) does not rule it out). This contrasts sharply with cases in which (D3′) is violated: in those cases the language itself does not provide for evidence for the relevant identities, and hence putative reference with its attendant knowledge is *linguistically* defeated.

A second objection may arise over my free use of the word 'identity'. How, it will be asked, does my account fit with the form identity takes in a first-order theory, namely as a principle of inter-substitutivity? After all, identity can be defined in such a theory; how then can it be indispensable? Well, the reason identity can be defined in a first-order theory is that there is a (nonprimitive) predicate in such a theory which is formally indistinguishable from identity. Thus if I claim indispensability for identity on the grounds of its contributions to formally valid inferences, I must be claiming the same for its definiens. That definiens simply states, straight out, that x and y share the same fate with respect to all the primitive predicates of the theory and all objects in the universe. We can then prove that the same holds for any open sentence definable in the theory. Now it is precisely this kind of transfer of information which objective knowledge requires: we want to know when two descriptions can be substituted for one another in the sentences we believe so as to obtain corroboration.

IV

With an account of the function of identity criteria in hand, we can evaluate various proposals for providing them. Let's start with Leibniz' Law:"

$$(L)\ x = y \text{ iff } (F)\ (Fx \equiv Fy)$$

If (L) is correct, it seems that it provides a criterion of identity for any sort of entity; why do we seek anything else? In order to answer this question, we must bear in mind the different purposes for which a criterion of identity may be sought. In particular, there is a world of difference between (*a*) providing epistemically determinate identity conditions where there were none before, thereby *deciding* how identity shall be understood for certain entities, and (*b*) *defining* identity conditions where they are already epistemically determinate, thereby providing an *analysis* of those conditions. I shall call (*a*) the *legislative*, and (*b*) the *analytic*, uses of identity criteria. We may now check (*L*) with respect to each use.

First, (*L*) must be so restricted that it is consistent (e.g., 'heterological' must not be a permissible substituend for 'F'). Second, if (*L*) is to be used legislatively, it must be so restricted as to avoid overt circularity: no substituend for 'F' may presuppose that reference to the entities in question is already established or that their identity conditions are already determinate. This means that if (*L*) were used to provide identity conditions for A's, no predicates purporting to refer to A's may substitute for 'F'. It follows immediately that quantifiers purporting to include the A's in their range are likewise barred, since the open sentences to which they attach would have to be understood as predicates referring to A's. Now, with all these restrictions, what reason do we have to expect that (*L*) will provide acceptable identity conditions? The right side is so weak, we may expect that different A's may still share all the properties which remain in the range of 'F'. For example, imagine using (*L*) for physical objects legislatively (even though this is unnecessary). If no physical objects or relations among physical objects are allowed in the range of 'F', it seems quite likely that (*L*) will be false. Thus (*L*) cannot be used legislatively, at least not across the board.

This objection does not apply to the analytic use of (*L*) since such use is not subject to the restriction against covert circularity. Indeed, I see no reason to think that (*L*) will be incorrect, used analytically. However, I think it will be very unexciting: providing as it does a criterion of the same form for all sorts of entities, it will reveal nothing significant about any. We seek an analysis of the identity conditions of a sort of entity in order to learn something essential to their nature, and this is precisely what (*L*) will not give us. Contrast (*L*) as applied to physical objects to the standard analysis in terms of spatio-temporal coincidence. The former is almost totally uninformative; the latter has deep implications (e.g., the possibility of two numerically distinct but "qualitatively identical" physical objects). Thus (*L*) is of no use in the search for criteria of identity.

I will close with an application of these reflections to Donald Davidson's criterion of identity for events, viz.:

(E) $x = y$ iff $(z)((z \text{ causes } x \equiv z \text{ causes } y) \& (x \text{ causes } z \equiv y \text{ causes } z))$.[8] Davidson admits that the 'z' on the right which purports to include events in its range gives (*E*) "an air of circularity," but since the very predicate '$x = y$' does not appear on the right, he maintains that

(E) is literally noncircular. Some are certain that (E) is circular, though they do not show how to answer Davidson's literalist claim.[9] Furthermore, if 'z' renders (E) pejoratively circular, what does it do to the standard criterion of identity for sets, viz.:

$$(C)\ x = y \text{ iff } (z)\ (z\,\varepsilon\, x \equiv z\,\varepsilon\, y)?$$

Obviously (E) and (C) are equally circular. Nevertheless, only (E) is illegitimate. The reason is that (E) is meant to be used legislatively and hence is subject to the restriction against covert circularity while (C) is meant to be used analytically and hence is not subject to that restriction. There is no question about what does or does not support the identity of sets, and hence there is no difficulty (on this score) in understanding quantification over sets. Thus it is perfectly legitimate to use a set quantifier in giving the criterion of identity for sets, just as it is legitimate to use a quantifier over physical objects, say, in giving a criterion of identity for them. By contrast, the state of event identity is chaotic. There are vast differences of opinion in very simple cases (does Socrates' death = Xantippe's becoming a widow? does my flipping the switch = my alerting the prowler?), and it is clear that no mere development of the details of the cases will settle the issue. Rather, we have a genuine unclarity in the notion of identity for events. This unclarity calls for a proposal to understand events in some particular way which will render their identity conditions determinate. The proposal must provide a criterion of identity in antecedently understood terms; in particular, reference to events must not be presupposed. The fact that (E) uses 'causes' on the right—a predicate understood as satisfied by (pairs of) events—shows that (E) does not meet this condition and hence cannot be used to provide a legislative identity criterion for events.[10]

NOTES

1. *Reference and Generality* (Ithaca, N.Y.: Cornell University Press, 1962), pp. 43, 148.
2. *Ibid.*, pp. 38, 43.
3. *Ibid.*, p. 39.
4. *Individuals* (New York: Doubleday and Co., 1963), Chap. 6.
5. *Ibid.*, p. 209.
6. *Word and Object* (Cambridge, Mass.: MIT Press, 1960), p. 115; *The Roots of Reference* (LaSalle, Ill.: Open Court, 1973), pp. 86–89.
7. Imagine George's body taken apart molecule by molecule and reassembled. Before the transformation George had only one hat. Now the person who owns the reassembled body buys a new hat. The quoted sentence will be true iff the latter person is not George.
8. "The Individuation of Events," in N. Rescher ed., *Essays in Honor of Carl G. Hempel* (Dordrecht: Reidel, 1969), pp. 216–34, esp. p. 231.

9. Cf. Neil Wilson, "Facts, Events and Their Identity Conditions," *Philosophical Studies* 25(1974): 303–21.

10. Quine has pointed out that this presumes we can individuate the *members* of the sets.

Quine on Properties and Meanings

STEPHEN LEEDS
University of Colorado

In this brief survey I want to discuss the bearing of some of Quine's work on the question whether predicates stand for, or express, properties. One point I shall be making is a historical one: that one effect of Quine's writings has been to make it easier to separate two notions that have often been conflated—the notions *property* and *meaning*. I'll begin by tracing some of the sources of this conflation; but before that, it will help to have a rough characterization of the two notions.

Here is Carnap on properties:

> ... the properties of things are not meant as something mental, say images or sense-data, but as something physical that things have, a side or aspect or component or character of the things.... By the property red ... we mean that physical character of the thing which the physicist explains as a certain disposition to selective reflection.[1]

To this I would want to add (as Carnap might have) that there seems to be a connection between properties and the modalities. *Red* is that, the having of which by the rose causes us to see it as we do; it is that which this table would have had, if this table had been red; it is that which, necessarily, all red things have. There are several ways in which we might try to spell out the connection between properties and causal, counterfactual, and alethic modalities—one is to say that predicates express properties in all contexts, but that what distinguishes modal contexts is that here it is the property expressed, and not merely the extension, which is relevant to truth conditions. I should also mention that Carnap's characterization is meant to apply, not only to 1-place relations-in-intension, but to n-place relations-in-intension, for any n. I shall continue to use the word 'property' for all of these.

It is not easy to characterize the notion of meaning in a way that does not already prejudge philosophic issues. I believe, however, that most of the things that have traditionally been said about meaning make most sense if we take as central the connection between meaning and understanding. If we think of meanings as abstract entities which are in some way "grasped," then we will think of this act of grasping a meaning as that which constitutes understanding an expression. If we do not think that meanings are in any but a metaphorical sense grasped, but we continue to say that two expressions may have the same meaning, we will explain this by saying that whatever constitutes understanding the expressions is in some sense the same. And, finally, if we abandon the notion of synonymy altogether, we are still likely to say that a theory of meaning for a language is an account of what it is to understand that language. I do not claim that these three ways of connecting meaning and understanding have always been explicit in classical writings on meaning (least of all the last, which is a quite modern formulation), but I think some such connection has usually been in the background; for example, you will not think that a sentence which is true by meanings alone must be known *a priori* to be true unless you think that to understand the sentence is to have access to the relevant meanings.

Conflation of the two rather different notions I've been discussing is a very old tradition in philosophy. An interesting place to begin looking at reasons for this conflation is in the writings of Frege. Frege's senses are of course meanings. It is not so easy to locate properties in Frege's system. Church, in a review article in 1943 which reawakened interest in Frege, identified the *Sinn* of a predicate-word with a property.[2] Other authors (including Quine at one time[3]) saw Frege's *Begriffe* as properties. This second view has at any rate Frege's explicit endorsement (in *Concept and Object*); on the other hand, the current view has it (on, I think, not entirely decisive evidence) that Frege's *Begriffe* are individuated by their extensions.

What is to be said about Church's suggestion? There is this technical difficulty: we are inclined to think that for each object x there exist such properties as *being in the gravitational field of* x, *being in motion with respect to* x. Frege could not identify such properties with senses on pain of producing a mixture—illegitimate by his standards—of the realm of reference with the realm of sense. One could perhaps relax Frege's system to allow such mixtures (an idea that is anyway attractive if one wants a Fregean account of *de re* belief), but Frege has, I believe, a strong reason for disallowing such mixtures. For Frege senses are representations; they are thoughts, or the elements of which thoughts are composed: it is not at all clear what sort of entity could be constituted by the representation "is in motion with respect to" in combination with, say, the Moon.

There is no indication that Frege thought of senses as what objects had in common, or as playing a role in explaining counterfactuals or causation. Instead, senses are essentially tied up with human thought and speech; they are "modes of presentation"—a vague phrase which, as I read it, did not preclude the possibility of giving a physicalist or behavioral analysis of what it is to grasp a sense. I think the best reading of Frege will find no place in his system for properties. And in the claim which Frege implicitly makes, that senses are the only intensional entities there are, we should see a very bold reductive proposal: that any sentence which has a truth value can either be given an extensionalist analysis or else must be analyzed in terms of senses—i.e., must be seen as being about the ways in which we represent the world. That such a reduction of all intensions to senses was possible became (often in a modified form) an unspoken assumption of much philosophy after Frege—it is implicit, for example, in the idea that to attribute a property necessarily is really to say that a certain sentence is true by virtue of meanings alone, i.e., is analytic. What we should notice about this reductive thesis is that it can—and did—get read as the thesis that properties are meanings: talk of properties, so far as it cannot be extensionally paraphrased, is really (disguised) talk about meanings. Church calls his reading a minor departure from Frege's account; that we no longer see it as a minor departure today reflects the weakened grip on us of the reductive thesis.

The second source I want to mention for the idea that meanings are properties is Russell (here, as with the reductive thesis, one can find earlier exponents of the position). Russell—I mean the Russell of the "On Denoting" through the Logical Atomism period—takes properties to be the denotations of predicates; sometimes when Russell identifies meanings with properties, all that is at work is his habit of using 'meaning' to mean 'denotation'. But for the most part Russell seems to see the relevant distinctions in the way we do today: he uses the word 'property' (and also 'quality') as Carnap does, and his use of 'meaning' is not always unlike ours: he translates Frege's 'Sinn' by 'meaning'. What is involved in Russell's identification of the meaning of (at least some) predicates with the property they denote is not confused usage but rather a quite clear philosophical thesis: that to understand the meaning of (at least some) predicates it is necessary and sufficient to be acquainted with the property they denote (and, presumably, to know that they denote it). From this standpoint the property *red* is not only the denotation of 'red'; it also performs exactly the role a meaning ought to perform—that of being what we grasp in understanding an expression. Like the reductive thesis above, this theory leads to an equating of properties with meanings, but from a completely different point of view;

99

here, meanings do not do the work of properties, rather the other way around: what makes our thinking represent the world is that the properties and objects which constitute the world also are—in a way which is reminiscent of certain medieval realist positions—constituents of our thinking.

The notion of acquaintance is most plausible when applied to the predicates 'red' and 'similar'; it is not plausible to suppose that we are acquainted with the property *electron*. Here I suppose—although I have not been able to find a text which unambiguously makes this move—that Russell would have treated such predicates as he treated most names: he would have said that to know the meaning of 'electron' was to know a definition. A well-worn path leads from here to the idea that the meaning of 'electron' is the property *electron*: a correct definition must be not merely extensionally correct (an electron is one of those things that just made a track in the cloud chamber) but intensionally correct—i.e., it must give necessary and sufficient conditions for something to be an electron, or (what amounts to the same thing) it must be an analysis of the property *electron*. Hence to understand 'electron' is to grasp *electron*—in the sense of knowing its analysis; *electron* may fairly be held, then, to be the meaning of electron. This is of course a very shaky line of reasoning, even if one grants the premise that the meaning of 'electron' is given by a definition—notice for example the covert shift from 'D is a correct definition' to 'D is analytic' to 'D gives an analysis.' It can be made to seem less shaky by making it depend on a modal fallacy which even today is a little hard to see through: "If 'electron' meant 'what I just saw in the cloud chamber', then the property of being an electron would be the property of being what I just saw in the cloud chamber, which it is not. Only intensionally correct definitions will avoid a similar refutation." Shaky or not, some such argument seems to be one source of what became the received view in the 1930s and 1940s—that the meaning of a predicate could be identified with the property it expressed.

It would be generally acknowledged, I believe, that Quine's writings have made the account I just gave look quite unacceptable. I am not sure, however, that we would find such wide agreement on how they have done this; it will be useful to spell out some of the details.

One of Quine's great contributions to the theory of meaning was to see it as a theory—that is, to see the notion of meaning as one that was invented in order to explain, or unify our account of, certain phenomena, and therefore to see it as a notion that might turn out inadequate. I think that it is in Quine's writings that the fundamental question of the theory of meaning fairly explicitly becomes, not "What is the correct analysis of the word 'meaning'," or "How do we recognize synonymy?" but something wider: What is it for a single speaker to be able to speak and understand a language, or, How would you program a computer to speak and understand English? Not that Quine sees no other questions as being important in the philosophy of language. There is a large group of questions having to do with (what one tradition calls) semantics—what makes sentences true, what things are denoted by different sorts of expressions (the question whether predicates stand for properties fits in here). All of these are treated by Quine under "Theory of Reference"; the notion of meaning stands or falls not with the work it might be called on to do here but with the work it does in the account of understanding.

I will briefly summarize Quine's account of what it is to understand a language—an account which is generally felt to be deplorably vague, but which we might more justly think of as schematic. The fundamental notion is that of assenting to, or holding true, a sentence. This is the relation people bear to sentences which we typically test by asking, "Do you believe this?" (and then uttering the sentence). Quine believes this notion to be behavioristically acceptable, despite the obvious defects of our means of testing it; I am more confident that there is such a relation than I am that it conforms, or ought to conform, to any behavioristic standards. A less clear, and even less clearly behavioristic, notion in at least some of Quine's writings is that of a network of beliefs. I know no way to make this idea precise without going beyond anything Quine has explicitly said—here is one way (among many) in which one might try to explicate it: To each sentence (except occasion sentences) S and to each set X of sentences, there is associated a probability of assent to S conditional on assent to all members of X; to each occasion sentence S is assigned probabilities of assent conditional on various sorts of stimulation. When stimulation occurs, assent (and dissent $=$ assent to the negation) propagates through the network in accordance with the conditional probabilities. All of this perhaps explains why I assent today to a sentence which yesterday I would have denied. It does not say enough—even in general terms—about the connection between assent and behavior other than that of saying yes and no to queried sentences: My assent to "It's raining outside" has an important connection to my putting on a raincoat. Quine would perhaps be willing to speak of another relation, that of desiring-true, which people bear to sentences, and perhaps also of a network of desires. The account begins then to look in some respects like a Bayesian picture—I do not know exactly how far Quine would be willing to move in that direction.

Sketchy as it is, the account just given contains enough detail to support Quine's major negative theses about meaning. Consider first the thesis that first appears in Quine's writings as the claim that there are no meanings. So stated, this thesis needed from the start to be taken with a grain of salt: it was not (at that time) Quine's intention to deny that, for example, the synonymy class of a word (one plausible candidate for a meaning) could exist. Rather, the point seems always to have been to repudiate what Quine later called the "myth of the museum"— the idea that we can understand a predicate by in any sense grasping or being acquainted with or perceiving a property or concept. Against this position Quine advances what are really two claims: First, that the perception of, say, a property cannot be all there is to understanding a predicate: perception alone will not set up the network of conditional assent to sentences. Second, that an account of understanding needs to postulate no kind of acquaintance or perception other than ordinary outer perception: although one cannot characterize my understanding of the word 'red' without mentioning that my eyes are sensitive to red light, one can characterize that part of the network which constitutes my understanding of the word 'number' without postulating anything like Russell's acquaintance with the concept 'number'. I choose the example 'number' by way of reminding the reader that the claim I am attributing to Quine has been denied: it is sometimes held that a certain sort of inner perception of the numbers or the concept 'number' must be assumed, if we are to explain the way our dispositions to assent to sentences containing 'number' evolve over time.

If Quine is right as against Gödel and Church, one avenue by which properties have been thought to play a role in the theory of meaning has been blocked: we do not understand the meaning of most predicates by any sort of inner perception of a property. Nothing so far has been said against the idea that a large part of understanding the predicate 'red' is being able to recognize the property red when one sees it—and I think that nothing Quine says should be taken as denying this. One may therefore say that in a certain limited sense *red* is the meaning of 'red': *red* plays a distinctive role in any account of what is involved in understanding 'red.' Does the property *electron* play any distinctive role in an account of how we understand 'electron'? The answer would be yes, if the familiar account discussed earlier were correct: if to understand 'electron' were in effect to have an analysis of *electron*. It is here that Quine's (and also Hempel's and Putnam's) arguments seem decisive. 'Electron' is understood by coming to assent to not one definition but a cluster of statements involving the word 'electron'. These statements are only contingently coextensive, by anyone's reading of 'contingent';

they cannot then all be analyses of the property *electron*. There is no reason to suppose that any of them must give an analysis of *electron*, but even if one of them did, this fact would play no role in an account of what it is to understand 'electron': for no statement in the cluster occupies a privileged position—the statements, if any, that give a correct analysis of electron are as much linked to other statements in the network, as prone to being denied, given the appropriate stimulation, as any others.

The upshot of all this is the following: properties, whatever virtues they may otherwise have, have no role to play in the theory of meaning. There is no sense in which to state what property a predicate expresses is to explain how the predicate is understood, nor is it the case that, given the network of beliefs in which our understanding of a predicate consists, one can "read off" the property which the predicate expresses. It is important, however, to recognize the limitations of this argument. It shows that, if you take meanings as playing a certain role in an account of understanding, then properties are not meanings. Although many philosophers have understood meanings in this way, not all have —not every philosopher who speaks of the connotation or intension of a predicate is refuted by Quine's argument. An Intensionalist may accept everything that has been said so far and also say that predicates express properties—he may propose that there is an analogy between the way predicates express properties and the way in which names have denotation. That a name has the denotation it has (if any) is in part a result of the meaning of the name—that is, the network of beliefs that constitutes our understanding of that name. But one cannot characterize the meaning of a name by giving its denotation; two names can have different meanings but the same denotation; a name can be meaningful but have no denotation at all. If we are willing to think of properties as Russell did—as entities that exist independently of our means of describing them—we may think of predicates as aimed at properties in the way that names are aimed at objects: there will in both cases be more than one way to hit the target; in both cases our arrow may not be aimed at precisely one target; whether our arrow hits a target may depend not only on how well the arrow is named (how precisely we have described Cicero or *electron*) but also on whether there is a target there (whether Cicero or *electron* exists).

There are thus two very different ways in which Quine's work can affect one's attitude toward properties. If we subscribe to Frege's reductive thesis, then we will be inclined to abandon the notion of property altogether: there seems to be no way to reduce talk about properties to the network theory of meaning. For example, we cannot understand '*red* entails *colored*' as material mode for " 'All red things are colored' is unrevisable, or constitutes the meaning of 'red'." If, on the other hand, we had seen properties in the Realistic way that Russell and the Carnap of our earlier quotation did, then we will respond by disentangling properties from the theory of meaning. The result will be a certain "freeing up" of our notion of property. We will no longer expect that synonymy of predicates is a necessary condition for identity of the properties expressed (though if any notion of synonymy survives, it will presumably be a sufficient condition); we will be able to notice—what had not been noticed before, or had to be dismissed as an anomaly—that it is reasonable to say that the property temperature is the property mean kinetic energy.

Of the two paths just sketched, the second has lately become familiar—it has been taken by Kripke and Putnam, among others. Quine's sympathies seem to lie with Frege's reduction. Not that Quine has been unaware that the equation of properties and meanings is a substantive philosophical thesis: the two notions are presented as distinct in *Methods of Logic* and *Word and Object,* and their identification is mentioned only as an "interesting suggestion" of Church's in "On Reification of Universals." But the suggestion is treated with respect even when McX makes it, and is apparently taken for granted in *Philosophy of Logic*[4]—indeed, Quine's use of the term 'attribute' as neutral between the Realist's properties and the Conceptualist's concepts seems designed to encourage the identification. And when the identification is made, it is attributes-as-meanings that seem the more fundamental notion: synonymy, not necessary coextensiveness, is the criterion for identity of attributes.

I think it would be profitless to speculate on the depth of Quine's commitment to Frege's reduction. Quine has at least one good reason—the obscurity of identity conditions—for thinking there are no attributes, and quite excellent reasons for disbelieving in meanings; no doubt he thinks the relations between these two categories of nonexistents of less than crucial importance. But for those of us who are not persuaded of the nonexistence of properties, it is interesting to notice some places in Quine's writings where the reductive thesis seems to be assumed. One obvious place is in the equating of necessity with analyticity. Troubles with analyticity will not be thought to cast discredit on necessity (as Quine thought in "Two Dogmas" and also in the later "Necessary Truth") unless necessity is construed not as a property of (o-place) properties but as a property of sentences, e.g., unrevisability.

Another place in which we may see Frege behind the scenes is in

Quine's treatment of *de re* modality. One need not accept the reductive thesis to sympathize with Quine's rejection of many *de re* claims as essentialistic—one may think that properties exist and yet deny that many of them are had necessarily. But it is not difficult to detect in Quine a reluctance to admit even such theses as $(\forall x)(N(x=x))$, or even the schema $(\forall x) \sim N (Px)$—and here, in rejecting quantification across operators as being even meaningful, Quine stands with Frege, and for reasons similar to Frege's: 'necessary' is a predicate of sentences (for Frege—of thoughts), and one cannot speak with respect to each x of *the unique* sentence (thought) that attributes 'is P' to x.

Lastly, the reductive thesis seems to be at work in Quine's treatment of 0-place intensions. Quine's name for these is 'propositions'; propositions are always characterized as the meanings of sentences; two sentences express the same proposition if and only if they are synonymous. Those of us who see a distinction between the meaning of a predicate and the property it expresses will see a parallel distinction in the 0-place case as well. In Quine's writings things tend to go the other way: because propositions are thought of as the meanings of (closed) sentences, it becomes natural to think of attributes as the meanings of open sentences.

Some of Quine's work in logic can be used to give an attractive account of 0-place intensions (not considered as meanings) and the way in which sentences express them. Consider how Quine eliminates variables by the use of predicate functors: predicate letters are taken to stand for their extensions, and the logical symbols are taken as functors which map extensions (or pairs of extensions) to extensions. Thus, "There are people who love each other" can be written (in a notation less general than Quine's) *EEKLConvL*: here *Conv* is an operation which takes the converse of an extension, *K* takes two extensions into their intersection, and *E* is an existential projection. The same notation may be read intensionally: take *L* as expressing the relation-in-intension *loves*; then *ConvL* is the intension *is loved by*, and *KLConvL* is *loves each other*. *E* takes any $n+1$-place intension to an n-place intension: *ER* is the attribute which holds of $(a_1 \ldots a_i \ldots)$ iff *R* holds of $(b, a_1 \ldots a_i \ldots)$ for some b. Here 0-place intensions appear in a natural way as the result of applying *E* to a 1-place intension; we also are able to give an iterative definition of 'Sentence *S* expresses intension *I*' without, for example, making use of possible-world semantics. It is natural to identify two 0-place intensions just in case their biconditional is necessary. Alternatively, one can take this as a definition of necessity: A 0-place intension (let us say, 'proposition') is necessary iff it is the proposition '0 = 0.' As for *de re* necessity: *P* holds necessarily of x if the proposition $P(x)$ is necessary, i.e., $=$ '0 = 0.' (Notice that the locution 'the proposition $P(x)$' is acceptable in this context, in the same way that the locution 'the property of being in the gravitational field of x' is acceptable.) In general, I think it is useful to pursue accounts of intensions like this one, in which the apparatus of possible worlds and possible objects seems to play no role—though closer investigation would be needed to see if that apparatus was lurking in the background. The reason for trying to avoid possible worlds is that a full-blown use of that apparatus—e.g., to give a definition of truth for modal sentences—seems inevitably to quantify over possibilia; nothing persuasive has ever been said against Quine's remark that unless you are prepared to say that something exists you have no business letting it into the range of your variables.

I want now to say something about the bearing of Indeterminacy of Translation on the issues I have been discussing. An argument I have heard advanced which purports to show that sentences do not express (0-place) properties is the following: If sentences expressed properties, we could make sense of synonymy: two sentences would be synonymous just in case they expressed the same property. But synonymy makes no sense, etc. This argument of course fails, given the distinction between properties and meanings. However, relatives of this argument, based on Indeterminacy of Translation, seem to have a better chance of succeeding: if we adopt the constraint on translations that they must preserve the property expressed, then translation will surely be much more determinate than Quine argues that it is.

This is not the connection between 0-place intensions and translation which Quine draws in *Word and Object*; rather the converse: if translation were determinate, then we could posit propositions as what is preserved in translation—since translation is not determinate, this way of defending propositions fails (though others may succeed). I think that Quine was wise to draw the connection in this way, rather than that of a paragraph back, because of an analogy that might be drawn between expressing properties and the various relations of the theory of reference. As the Intensionalist wants to say that sentences express propositions, so Quine—like any of us—wants to say that predicates have extensions, that names denote, that sentences have truth values. But if the first thesis contradicts Indeterminancy of Translation, so must the second: translation by pairing names and predicates that have the same denotation or extension would be much more determinate than Quine thinks translation actually is.

We are now in the area of the problems that Quine discusses in *Ontological Relativity*. It is not my purpose here to try to resolve the questions that arise when we try to reconcile Indeterminacy of Translation (and Inscrutability of Reference) with our inclination to say that 'rabbit' by definition has as its extension the set of rabbits; what I do want to point out is that, however these are reconciled, a similar reconciliation will be available to any Intensionalist who wants to maintain that sentences express propositions and also wants to agree with Quine about Indeterminacy. For example, we may find it acceptable to say that all of our discourse about numbers is in a certain harmless way ontologically inscrutable—in that there is no sense in which our behavior, dispositions, or history singles out one abstract entity rather than another to be the referent of the numeral '3'; we may then go on to say that semantical discourse about arithmetic—e.g., "Peano arithmetic has many non-isomorphic numerical models"—is no more infected by Inscrutability, no less acceptable than nonsemantical discourse within arithmetic—'2+2 = 4.' Similarly, the Intensionalist may admit that in a certain sense no single correct map exists from predicates and sentences onto intensions, but he may go on to say that this ought not prevent us either from talking of properties or from positing semantical relations that hold between our words and properties—in both cases, what we say may, we hope, be true under at least one interpretation.

I have not dealt with what I take to be Quine's central objection to properties—that their identity conditions are obscure. Some forms of this objection seem to me to demand too much of the Intensionalist. The Intensionalist should not be asked to supply a general criterion for when two predicates express the same property, any more than he should be expected to give a criterion for when two singular terms denote the same object. Nor does it seem appropriate to ask for a clear-cut criterion of identity: although we have such a criterion for sets, it is not obvious that we do for physical objects—"physical objects are identical iff they occupy the same space-time points" seems likely to turn out circular, once we start looking for a criterion of identity for space-time points. What does seem to me an appropriate demand is that Intensionalists give us more general and systematic reasons for identity statements about properties than they have so far given. So long as properties were required to bear the weight of a theory of meaning, there was an obstacle in the way of meeting this demand; now that the obstacle has been removed, we may hope that Quine's scepticism will soon be overcome.

NOTES

1. *Meaning and Necessity* (Chicago: University of Chicago Press, 1960), p. 27. Carnap also identifies properties with Frege's senses; this is, I shall argue, a mistake.

2. *Philosophical Review* (1943): 301.
3. In "On Frege's Way Out," *Mind* 64 (1955): 145–59.
4. *Philosophy of Logic* (Englewood Cliffs, N.J.: Prentice-Hall, 1970), p. 67.

Can Epistemology Be Naturalized?

M. J. CRESSWELL
Victoria University of Wellington

Quine believes that epistemology is best studied as a branch of empirical psychology:

> It studies a natural phenomenon, viz., a physical human subject. This human subject is accorded a certain experimentally controlled input —certain patterns of irradiation in assorted frequencies, for instance— and in the fullness of time the subject delivers as output a description of the three-dimensional external world and its history. The relation between the meager input and the torrential output is a relation that we are prompted to study for somewhat the same reasons that always prompted epistemology; namely, in order to see how evidence relates to theory, and in what ways one's theory of nature transcends any available evidence.[1]

The view is appealing. As Quine goes on to observe, most of the traditional problems of epistemology can, on this view, be tackled making free use of psychology. Why then the nagging feeling that we are getting something for nothing; the feeling that the traditional philosophical problems are not really solved? Quine seems to have the feeling too because in several places he tries to make clear exactly what he is and what he is not claiming. On page 75 he mentions the objection of "earlier times" that the naturalizing of epistemology is circular. His reply is that the objection applies only if one's aim is the validation of the grounds of empirical science. Quine claims that the objection has little point against one who is simply trying to understand the link between observation and science.

Despite the title, it is not the point of this paper to quarrel with what Quine has done in EN. Indeed, it seems to me that treating it as part of natural science may well be the only legitimate way of studying the relation between observation and theory. My aim is to discuss a different problem, a problem which is perhaps best described as a problem of metaphysics rather than epistemology. I am discussing it in the context of *EN* because, although it is not Quine's problem, it seems to me one which could mistakenly be confused with Quine's problem.

I. *The Problem of Naturalized Epistemology*

Quine's view of epistemology is as a branch of psychology, and psychology for him seems to be the study of certain aspects of a physical human subject in relation to its physical environment. I take it to be important for Quine that the whole of physical science is an integrated and unified system, ultimately reducible to physics[2] and, presumably, described and codified by a theory stated in a first-order language. The details of the theory are not important; probably it will need to incorporate set theory (Quine in *EN*[3] clearly regards set theory as a rather shakier foundation than we should be entirely happy with, though perhaps it is a necessary one), and, from the work of Gödel, it will not be axiomatizable. What is important is that it be a complete theory about the physical world.

In case this seems an implausible requirement, let us indicate how it might be met. Let us suppose that $\mathscr{L}$ is a first-order language with a number of predicates and, possibly, individual constants. This language is supposed to be adequate for the description of all physical regularities. Among the interpretations of $\mathscr{L}$ there will be those whose domains are the intended domain D of the theories stated in the language $\mathscr{L}$ under its intended interpretations. We let $\mathscr{L}+$ be the language obtained from $\mathscr{L}$ by adding the members of D as individual constants. ($\mathscr{L}+$ will then be a 'language' in a rather abstract sense only because D will almost certainly be nondenumerable.) Clearly the expressive capacity of $\mathscr{L}+$ will be such that any two physically distinct situations can be distinguished by sentences of $\mathscr{L}+$.

Let us now suppose that we have two physical theories T_1 and T_2 in the language of $\mathscr{L}+$. Let us suppose that T_1 is the correct physical theory (I am taking it that Quine assumes that there is at least one correct physical theory); in particular suppose it to be a fact that a certain object O, say a copy of *Word and Object*, has (at a certain time) printing on its cover and that a percipient, P, is in such a state that we can say that P knows that O has printing on its cover. Since T_1 is the correct physical theory, then the sentences of T_1 will between them say that P does know that O has printing on its cover. T_2 is an incorrect physical theory; according to T_2, O has (at that same time) no printing on its cover and (according to T_2) P knows that it has no printing. It is important that T_1 and T_2 are whole theories because Quine has stressed that it is only theories as a whole which can be said to have empirical consequences.[4] It may not be possible, short of having T_1 and T_2 as whole theories, to say that the one describes the case in which P knows that O has printing on it, and the other the case in which P knows that O has no printing on it.

Our position so far then is this. Relative to T_1, P knows that O has printing on it; relative to T_2, P knows that O has no printing. But we said at the outset that T_1 is the true theory and T_2 a false theory. This means that *in reality* P knows that O has printing and that T_2 is false in claiming that he knows that it has no printing (he cannot know both because what is known must be true).

The metaphysical question then is this: What is it that makes T_1 true but T_2 false? This question has often been posed as an epistemological question, viz.: How can we know that T_1 is the correct theory and T_2 the false theory? Quine has suggested that we naturalize our epistemology. This means that we rephrase the question about what we can know so that it turns into the question about whether a certain relation holds between a physical observer and the objects of his knowledge. Now this relation holds in one theory between an observer and a book which does have printing on its cover and in another theory between an observer and the same book without printing on its cover. And the problem is that although according to the true theory T_1, P knows some facts which ensure that T_2 is false, yet, according to the false theory T_2, P knows some facts which ensure that T_1 is false. What the naturalized epistemology *does* tell us is that, *provided we are working with the true theory*, it is simply a matter of empirical psychology (together I suppose with a certain amount of semantics) to decide what sorts of things human beings can know and what is the relation between sensory stimulation and the production of descriptions of the world. What it *does not* tell us is what counts as being the true theory in the first place, or how, in any absolute sense, we may come to know which theory is the true one.

II. *The Indexical Solution*

One reply is to deny outright that truth and knowledge can ever be absolute and to say that they must always be relative to a theory. We can think of a theory as a description of a possible world. T_1 is a world in which P perceives that O has printing on it, while T_2 is a world in which P (or, if you like, a counterpart) perceives that O has no printing on it. Such an approach is taken and defended by David Lewis, except for the identification of the worlds with the theories (6, p. 85f). According to Lewis truth and falsity are always relative to a world, though of course some statements are true in all worlds or false in all worlds; but that is not what is usually meant by absolute truth or falsity. Lewis uses a temporal analogy. When we speak of something being true or false *now*, we mean true or false relative to the moment of speech. At t_1 a sentence '*a* now' is true iff *a* is true at t_1; at t_2 the same sentence is true iff *a* is true at t_2.[5] Although we may dignify some particular moment as the present and try to invest it with some kind of reality above that possessed by the past and the future, this extra reality is spurious and the fact remains that for scientific purposes we make do with a relative concept of temporal statements. The temporal illustration is important in examining Quine because he has made it clear that he does accept this sort of relativity in the case of temporal statements.[6] However, he has made it equally clear that he does not accept this sort of relativity in the case of modality (except for acknowledging the use of something like possible worlds in the analysis of some manifestly nonlinguistic propositional attitudes such as the beliefs of animals]10, pp. 139–60]).

III. *The Atomist Solution*

A quite different type of solution is one which says that T_1 is the true theory because that is the way things are, in other words, that in some sense the nature of reality makes T_1 true and T_2 false, and further that the nature of reality is such that we can know that T_1 is true and T_2 false.

One form this answer might take is that of logical atomism, viz., that each atomic sentence of T_1 corresponds to a fact, a fact being thought of as a number of objects standing in a certain relation [14, p. 60f]. In a solution of this kind we must remember that it is not merely in their being a model of T_1 that their being facts consists, for T_2 (assuming, as we are doing, that it is a consistent theory) also has models, but none of *its* models contain only facts. But even if an atomistic solution could be made to work, it would not help Quine, because he rejects the idea that the separate sentences of the theory correspond to separate bits of reality (e.g., in [8, pp. 42–46]). Of course, one could still embrace a kind of atomism which said that reality was a complex of atomic facts but that there was not a direct correspondence with sentences of the theory and the atomic facts which make the theory as a whole true. To me this seems like a confession of the logical inadequacy of atomism. The appeal of the classical atomist solution is that it explains precisely why T_1 is true but not T_2. It is because at least one of the models of T_1

contains *facts* for all the atomic sentences while none of the models of T_2 has this property.

In any case an atomism even of this kind still seems incompatible with the kind of holism Quine wants. He certainly has no sympathy with any theory which would make the atomic facts simple facts about our experience, each logically independent of all others. That is precisely the doctrine he is arguing against in the latter part of [8] and the early part of *EN*, and his objection there is to the existence of facts of this kind, not merely to their being paired with atomic sentences.

IV. *The Holistic Solution*

If the reality which makes the true theory true and the others false cannot be split up into logically separate parts, then we must treat it as a single undifferentiated whole. And once we give up the requirement that there be a one-to-one correspondence between atomic facts and atomic sentences, there is no reason to suppose that a single theory only is the correct one. So we do not need to assume, as we have been doing, that T_1 is the only true theory but merely that reality does not rule out as false any of its sentences but does rule out as false some of the sentences of T_2. This perhaps explains why the phenomenon which Quine describes as "ontological relativity" in an essay of the same name [10, pp. 26–68] (henceforth *OR*) is unworrying. In *OR* he makes the point that we can only make statements about the ontology of a given theory, or statements which compare the ontologies of two given theories, if we move to a background theory in which we can talk about both. On the holistic solution to the problem this need not matter, since reality may not be sufficiently constraining to force a decision between rival ontologies. Such indeterminacy would suit Quine.

The idea of reality as an undifferentiated something is very reminiscent of the metaphysical views of F. H. Bradley, whose Absolute had just those properties.[7] The entities involved in T_1 would form part of what Bradley called appearance and a question immediately arises of their status vis à vis reality. Bradley in fact says in several places that he is unable to answer the question of why and how it is that reality appears to us in the form that it does. Presumably what this means is that there is an unanalyzed (and perhaps unanalyzable) property which T_1 has but which T_2 lacks which makes the former true but the latter false. And even to speak of a property is misleading, since properties and relations are things which have their place within T_1 or T_2.

We may note in passing that a holistic view of reality of this kind requires that the notion of a self be part of appearance and not part of reality. For Quine the self is a physical organism and so would take its place within T_1 and be part of appearance rather than reality. And while Bradley is no materialist, the self is for him, too, unreal. Bradley is also unlike Quine in that he adopts something like a possible-worlds theory of appearance,[8] but this is simply a question of the most convenient way to codify experience; and as noted above there need be no unique theory which does this job. It is perhaps worth pointing out that even a solution of the kind outlined in Section II cannot entirely escape the postulation of a reality distinct from appearance unless it actually identifies the possible worlds with the theory, which Lewis at least seems loath to do.[9]

If this solution solves the metaphysical question of which theory is the (or a) true theory, then what is the status of epistemology? Perhaps all we need to say is that, since epistemology has been naturalized, the problem of knowledge is automatically solved by being a relation which holds between a human physical subject and an object in the true theory. I think that this is right provided that we accept that the metaphysics is not itself based on epistemology. And at least some views of reality seem to have made it a defining condition that it square with appearance. Quine himself speaks of the "tribunal of experience" [8, p. 41] as the final arbiter of the correctness of a theory; and Bradley in fact takes this to its conclusion and simply identifies reality with experience. It is of course a holistic experience of a rather funny kind since, as we saw, even selves are part of appearance and not part of reality. Bradley calls it the Absolute, and, although we can perhaps see how he might be driven to postulate it, it is still rather difficult to grasp its nature. Even more difficult is to see how it might be related to appearance. And at precisely the same point Quine's metaphors about the tribunal of experience never quite get the elaboration we feel they need. There need be no shame in this; Bradley certainly acknowledges that this problem is the hard one and the one which he does not solve. But he points out that a failure to explain *how* appearance and reality are linked is not an argument against the fact that they are somehow linked, and he considers that he has proved that they are linked by proving that they can be and that they must be.

To claim that Quine is a latter-day Bradley may sound a little ridiculous, yet it seems to me that, of the solutions I have described to the problem of naturalized epistemology, it is this one which gives him the most of what he wants. For any detailed examination of issues in the theory of knowledge must be studied as part of appearance. There is, for a Bradleyan, very little that can be said about the Absolute except that it is what makes theories true, to the extent that they can be true. Quine of course has a much more sympathetic attitude toward theories: He would no doubt see Bradley's preoccupations with the Absolute as unhealthy, morbid, and useless; yet in the end is he not asking us to accept a theory as true because it measures up as a whole to our nontheoretical experience? A sentence quoted by J. J. C. Smart in [3, p. 7] from p. 2 of [9] is almost pure Bradley: "immediate experience simply will not, of itself, cohere as an autonomous domain." Postulation of theoretical entities is the only way by which our total experience of the world can be explained, and for Quine the best of these theories is the physical one.[10]

V. *Some Pseudo-Solutions*

In the last three sections I have tried to describe some solutions to the problem of naturalized epistemology which was posed in Section I. In the present section I want to show that some other purported solutions to the problem are in fact not genuine solutions, or that insofar as they are solutions they reduce to one of the types already discussed.

The first of these is to make use of the previously mentioned notion of ontological relativity (OR, pp. 26–68). Broadly speaking, we say that the statement that T_1 is the correct theory and T_2 the incorrect theory is a statement in a metatheory M about T_1 and T_2. The first point to notice is that M is not being used here in the way Quine seems to have in mind in OR. In that essay the kind of case he seems particularly interested in is where M makes a statement about which of the models of a theory T is the intended one. The point is that by definition no two structures which verify exactly the same sentences of a language can be distinguished by sentences of that language. The present issue is rather different. It is not a problem about how to say that T_1 is correct and T_2 is not. It is a problem about what constitutes T_1's being correct and T_2's being incorrect.

Since the expressive power of T_1 and T_2 is the same and since they are supposed to be capable of giving a complete physical description of the world, there can be nothing which M can say which they cannot already say. If there are some facts about the world which are expressed in M but not already expressed in T_1 then this shows that T_1 is not already the complete and correct theory of the way the world is. To be sure, if these facts about T_1 can be expressed within T_1 then there are all sorts of problems involving self-reference. I would be the last to pretend that these problems are easy, but I would point out that they cannot help but arise in any case in any theory which attempts to describe the phenomenon of knowledge within a system in which the knower is part of what can be known. T_1 can, and does, assert its own truth. From the point of view of T_1 its own sentences proclaim their truth and therefore, by implication, proclaim T_2's falsity. But of course the sentences of T_2 proclaim T_1's falsity.

A second pseudo-solution is one which, in the case of single sentences at least, Quine seems to give some support to. It is "what Wilfred Sellars has called the disappearance theory of truth" [11, p. 10]. This is the view that for the sentence "snow is white" to be true is just for snow to be white.[11] This view is of course true, but what that seems to show is merely that we can pose the problem without using the notion of truth and ask what it is for snow to be white. Our problem does not disappear, and it was various possible answers to that problem which were explored in the last two sections.

A more radical solution is to claim that we have not been set a problem, that it does not make sense to ask whether T_1 or T_2 is right, still less to give reasons for which one it is. It seems to me that if this reply is viable then it reduces to one of the two we have considered. Consider the person who says that it makes no sense to suppose that T_1 or T_2 is either true or false. Now what is clear is that relative to T_1 certain sentences are true and others false, and similarly relative to T_2. So this reply reduces to the view that truth is relative to a theory and that it makes no sense to speak of the truth of the theory as a whole. Such a reply is roughly the one we attributed to David Lewis in Section II.

It is interesting to note that this shows why the coherence theory of truth in an extreme version is wrong. For if coherence is the *only* test of truth, then there is nothing to favour T_1 over T_2; both are consistent and complete. Of course, those who have adopted a coherence theory of truth have not taken it in a version as extreme as this. Bradley requires that truth give a coherent account *of experience*.

Consider though the person who says that although T_1 is the true theory and T_2 the false theory it makes no sense to ask for reasons why this is so. For reasons, he says, can only be given relative to a theory, and we are now asking for reasons to be given outside the theory. It seems to me that this reply reduces either to the metalinguistic reply discussed at the beginning of the section or to the solution described in Section IV but without the identification of reality with experience. For it seems to say that the truth or falsity of a whole theory is an unanalyzable property of the theory and cannot be taken to be explained within the theory.

VI. Conclusions

What is the moral of this? Is it that Quine has gone wrong? I think not, for as observed in Section IV the Bradleyan solution to the problem puts the detailed questions of epistemology fairly within the province of the theory which correctly explains our experience. And indeed in the latter part of EN [10, pp. 83–90] Quine shows, in an illuminating way, how it is that many of the traditional questions of epistemology do seem able to be better studied as psychology. How close the new forms of the problems are to their traditional forms is not for me to say, but a protest against the tendency for epistemologists to be armchair psychologists would certainly not go amiss. In fact, the only point that I want to insist on is that naturalized epistemology, however indespensable its methods may be, and however superior to traditional procedures in the theory of knowledge, is dependent upon, and not a substitute for, a metaphysical justification.

NOTES

1. This quotation is taken from p. 82 of the essay "Epistemology Naturalized," which I shall refer to as EN, in [10, pp. 69–90]. For a general picture of the foundations of Quine's philosophy I have relied on Reeves [12].

2. Quine's naturalism is stressed in [10, p. 26], and a clear statement of the primacy of physics occurs on p. 303 of [3].

3. E.g. [10, pp. 69 and 73].

4. E.g. [8, p. 41] and [10, p. 79].

5. The detailed semantics of 'now' is slightly more complicated than described here but in ways which are presently irrelevant (*vide* Kamp [4]).

6. E.g. [9, pp. 170–76]. Both Lewis [5] and Prior [7] take seriously the parallel between worlds and times, the former to argue that all worlds and times are equally real, the latter to argue that even the past and future of our own world are unreal. Lewis comments on the parallel at p. 185n. of [5].

7. I have attempted an exposition of Bradley's metaphysics in [2]. Detailed references to Bradley's works may be found in that article.

8. *Vide* section 6 of [2].

9. Not only Lewis but also my own work in [1, p. 38] is subject to the same comment. The problem of selecting the true model of the theory is discussed in Sec. 4 of Routley [13], where points like those made in the text are used as a general criticism of model-theoretic semantics. As Routley puts it a little later in his paper, "Every theory is correct according to its own lights."

10. As mentioned earlier Bradley was not a materialist, but I argue in Sec. 4 of [2] that his metaphysics is not incompatible with materialism when materialism is taken as a theory of our experience.

11. Another passage in which Quine seems to endorse this view is in [10, p. 24]. I am grateful to David Lewis for drawing these passages to my attention.

REFERENCES

1. Cresswell, M. J. *Logics and Languages*. London: Methuen, 1973.
2. ———. "Reality as Experience: A Study in the Philosophy of F. H. Bradley. *Australasian Journal of Philosophy* 55 (1977): 169–88.
3. Davidson, D., and K. J. J. Hintikka. *Words and Objections: Essays on the Work of W. V. Quine*. Dordrecht: Reidel, 1969.

4. Kamp, J. A. W. "Formal Properties of 'Now'," *Theoria* 37 (1971): 227-73.
5. Lewis, D. K. "Anselm and Actuality," *Nous* 4 (1970): 175-88.
6. ———. *Counterfactuals.* Oxford: Blackwell, 1973.
7. Prior, A. N. "Modal Logic and the Logic of Applicability," *Theoria* 34 (1968): 183-202.
8. Quine, W. V. O. "Two Dogmas of Empiricism," *From a Logical Point of View.* Cambridge, Mass.: Harvard University Press, 1953. 2d rev. ed., New York: Harper and Row, 1961, pp. 20-46.
9. ———. *Word and Object.* Cambridge, Mass.: MIT Press, 1960.
10. ———. *Ontological Relativity and Other Essays,* New York: Columbia University Press, 1969.
11. ———. *Philosophy of Logic.* Englewood Cliffs, N.J.: Prentice-Hall, 1970.
12. Reeves, A. L. "The Foundations of Quine's Philosophy," *Philosophical Studies* 30 (1976): 75-93.
13. Routley, F. R. "Meaning as Semantical Superstructure: A Universal Theory of Meaning, Truth, and Denotation."
14. Urmson, J. O. *Philosophical Analysis.* Oxford: Clarendon Press, 1956.

Warrant and Meaning in Quine's Clothing

MARK PASTIN
Indiana University

Of course, the title should be "Warrant and Meaning in Quine's Clothing—After Alterations to Suit the Tailor." It is the fate—happy in my own view—of great philosophers to be plundered by invaders pursuing their own purposes. I plunder. Quine can teach those who take the notions of warrant, meaning, and reference seriously a great deal about how to live reflectively with these notions. I have two Quinean themes in mind. The first is the corporate view of language:

> The dogma of reductionism survives in the supposition that each statement, taken in isolation from its fellows, can admit of confirmation or infirmation at all. My countersuggestion ... is that our statements about the external world face the tribunal of sense experience not individually but only as a corporate body.[1]

The second is the inscrutability of reference:

> I have urged that we could know the necessary and sufficient stimulatory conditions of every possible act of utterance, in a foreign language, and still not know how to determine what objects the speakers of that language believe in.... If we then go on to assign the sentence some import in point of existence of objects, by arbitrary projection in the case of the heathen language or as a matter of course in the case of our own, thereupon what has already been counting as empirical evidence for or against the truth of the sentence comes to count as empirical evidence for or against the existence of objects.[2]

These two themes have a plausibility outside the general Quinean framework. Now that philosophers of language, led by Dummett, are again allowing that a theory of language must comport with a theory of evidence, points related to these themes must be made. I place these points in an epistemological framework to show how they must be accounted for in epistemology and how recognition of these points is happily consistent with a trenchant, reformed empiricism.

I believe that an adequate theory of language must directly employ epistemic notions. This is not because I accept some axiom requiring that a theory of language explain what it is to know or understand units of the language. I am concerned rather with requirements to be placed on a theory of language if it is to meet adequately the needs of epistemology. To explain what I have in mind, it is necessary to introduce some background.

I speak of warrant conditions and relations of sentences. Sentences are linguistic entities of a language which are used to make statements. It is familiar that people sometimes use different sentences to make the same statement. I reflect this in my jargon by saying that the sentences uttered by each speaker express the same proposition. Talk of propositions is useful in describing such cases even if we ultimately wish to do without propositions. Propositions also have the role of objects of belief: If I believe your statement, I believe the proposition expressed by the sentence you utter. Finally, some sentences may, without modification to the language in which they are formulated, express different propositions, and thus be used to make different statements on different occasions. There is much that should be said about all of this, but not here.

It is tempting to say that the warrant conditions of a sentence are the conditions under which one could be warranted in believing the proposition(s) expressed by the sentence. This is not right. There are circumstances in which the proposition expressed by a sentence is warranted for a person, in the sense that he has good evidence for it, although he is not warranted in believing the proposition expressed by the sentence. What is required is not just that the person believe the proposition but also that the belief be "based on" the evidence in a way that somehow corresponds to a pattern of warranted inference from the evidence to the proposition. So the primary notion is that of a sentence (more exactly, the proposition expressed by a sentence) *being warranted for* a person *at* a time. An advantage to taking this notion as primary, rather than that of a person being warranted *in believing* a sentence (the proposition it expresses) at a time, is that it does not directly require that we examine belief in explaining the warrant conditions of a sentence, although psychological notions may still be required for the explanation.[3] I address warrant relations of sentences later.

What should an account of the language in which a sentence is formulated say about the warrant conditions and relations of the sentence? It is not easy to answer this question since the answer depends on our view of what a theory of evidence should say about the warrant conditions and relations of a sentence. I think it is clear that a theory of language, conjoined with a theory of evidence, should fully determine the warrant conditions and relations of sentences of the language. This goal of epistemic completeness can be given fairly precise formulation. Three factors can be distinguished as contributing to determination of the warrant conditions and relations of a sentence: (1) basic facts concerning the use of the sentence (that information about the sentence or its constituents which might plausibly be included in a language theory for the sentence), (2) contingent facts stated in nonepistemic terms about circumstances of use of the sentence, and (3) general warranting principles—principles belonging to a theory of evidence. We can say that a theory of language is epistemically complete for a sentence of a language if the theory provides information of type (1) which, when combined with information of types (2) and (3), determines the warrant conditions and relations of the sentence.

This notion of epistemic completeness requires tightening up and explanation. Since a particular sentence may bear warranting relations to many other sentences, we must be clear about just which relations are at issue in assessing epistemic completeness. Thus I speak of a theory of language L being epistemically complete with respect to sentences $p_1, \ldots, p_n$ of language L. Ideally $p_1, \ldots, p_n$ will be a broad set of sentences closed under the relevant warranting relations, although we shall often have to settle for less. Note that room is left for theories of language that do not assign a parcel of meaning to each sentence of the language. I use 'S' as a person variable and 't' as a time variable. $D(l, S, t)$ is a true description of S's condition t, and is formulated in nonepistemic terms in a metalanguage for l compatible with L. $WP(l)$ is a set of true *general* warranting principles formulated in a metalanguage for l compatible with L and $D(l, S, t)$. A theory of language is to determine the warrant conditions and relations of $p_1, \ldots, p_n$. This means that L is concerned with sentences of the forms 'α warrants β for S at t' (abbreviated 'W $(\alpha, \beta/S, t)$' and 'α is warranted for S at t' (abbreviated 'W $(\alpha/S, t)$'), where α and β are either one of $p_1, \ldots, p_n$ or logical compounds of $p_1, \ldots, p_n$. These are the warrant sentences involving $p_1, \ldots, p_n$.

We can now state a criterion for language theory L being epistemically complete for sentences $p_1, \ldots, p_n$ of language l:

> L *is epistemically complete for* $p_1, \ldots, p_n$ *of* l iff, for all S and t, if W is a warrant sentence of l true of S at t involving only $p_1, \ldots, p_n$, then there are $D(l, S, t)$ and $WP(l)$ such that $D(l, S, t)$ and $WP(l)$ and L logically entail W.

In slightly plainer English: L is epistemically complete for $p_1, \ldots, p_n$ of l iff every true warrant sentence formulated in terms of $p_1, \ldots, p_n$ and true of S at t is logically entailed by L along with a description of S at t in nonepistemic terms and general warrant principles. There is much about this criterion of epistemic completeness that requires elaboration. I focus on two prominent problems, general warrant principles and logical entailment.

A few comments about warrant and warranting will help in explaining general warrant principles. I shall not propose an analysis of 'p is warranted for S at t' here, although elsewhere I argue that this expression is to be analyzed in terms of what S would believe at t were S's beliefs ideal in specified respects at t.[4] There are several senses in which one proposition can be said to warrant another for a person at a time.[5] Here we consider a notion of prima facie warranting: p prima facie warrants q for S at t iff p is warranted for S at t, and q would be warranted for S at t if only propositions necessary to p's being warranted were warranted for S at t. In other words, p prima facie warrants q for S at t iff p is warranted for S at t, and, *ceteris paribus*, this suffices for q to be warranted for S at t.

General warrant principles concern these warrant conditions and prima facie warrant relations. General warrant principles, or, more exactly, warrant principles general with respect to $p_1, \ldots, p_n$, can be formulated without employing nonlogical constituents of $p_1, \ldots, p_n$. I adopt the simplifying view that names are a type of uniquely satisfiable predicate function. Thus warrant principles general with respect to $p_1, \ldots, p_n$ can be formulated without employing the predicate functions that occur in $p_1, \ldots, p_n$ and without restriction to a class of predicate functions including those that occur in $p_1, \ldots, p_n$. Examples of general warrant principles are: (1) $W(p/S,t) \to W(p, p/S, t)$, (2) $W(p, q/S, t) \to W(q, p/S, t)$ (p is the "total evidence" for q), (3) $W(p, q/S, t)$ & $W(q,r/S, t) \to W(p, r/S, t)$, and (4) $\forall S \forall t$ $(W(p/S,t)$ & (q is probable to degree n on p for S at $t) \to W(q/S, t)$. I do not state these as *the* sound general warrant principles. They are examples of the sorts of principles which, if true, would qualify as general principles. The principle 'If S at t takes himself to see that x has proper or common-sensible ϕ, then that x has ϕ is warranted for S at t' would not qualify as a general principle with respect to sentences containing predicates for proper or common sensibles. The idea behind this categorization of general warrant principles is simple: If a principle can be stated without restrictions on predicate functions, it seems to be a principle *of warrant* rather than a principle for specific predicate functions. On the other hand, if a principle is restricted in application to certain predicate functions, that principle seems to be a principle *of those predicate functions*. We shall see that little depends on this sorting of principles.

The criterion of epistemic completeness requires that a theory of language L for $P_1, \ldots, p_n$ together with certain factual information and general warranting principles *logically entail* warrant sentences involving $p_1, \ldots, p_n$. The idea is that given L, together with factual information and general warranting principles formulated in a metalanguage compatible with L, warrant sentences involving $p_1, \ldots, p_n$ should be deducible via inferences authorized in the metalanguage. It is not clear what inferences are to be authorized in the metalanguage, but it is clear that inferences will be authorized by deductive principles which do not require formulation in epistemic terms. How liberally we interpret 'deductive principles' is not essential to anything at issue provided that usual propositional, quantificational, and set-theoretical resources are allowed.

This sketch of a criterion of epistemic completeness does not, by itself, move us closer to an answer to our original question: What should an account of the language in which a sentence is formulated say about the warrant conditions and relations of the sentence? To answer this question we must answer two subquestions: Should a theory of language aspire to epistemic completeness? And, anticipating a positive response, what epistemological information should a theory of language aspiring to epistemic completeness include? Consider the first question. One can apparently fully understand a sentence without knowing all of its warrant conditions and relations, and we often seem to find new ways to determine whether a sentence, which we fully understand, is warranted. These are plausible considerations, but they are not incompatible with the goal of epistemic completeness. The apparent incompatibility rests on the idea that epistemic completeness requires that all warranting conditions and relations of a sentence be stated in a language theory. What is actually required is that the theory of language (or, if one thinks of theories as deductively closed, the axiomatic part of the theory of language), in light of what it says about a given sentence *and* about related sentences, when combined with certain factual information and general warrant principles, determine the warrant conditions and relations of the sentence. Tolerating epistemic incompleteness is less attractive than seeking epistemic completeness. Suppose we have a theory of language which encompasses 'duck' and 'water'. Consider whether the sentence 'That the duck is in the water is now warranted for John' is true. If we suffer epistemic incompleteness, it may be that, given the theory of language, relevant information about constituents of the sentence not encompassed by the theory, full information about John's situation formulated in nonepistemic terms, and general warrant principles, the truth of the sentence is not fixed. Assignment of either truth or falsity to this sentence is consistent with this body of information—a result that I find counterintuitive.

The goal of epistemic completeness is also compatible with the novelty of some warrant conditions and relations. On my preferred reading of '$W(p/S, t)$' this expression means that S would believe p at t if S's beliefs were formed in ways that are ideal in specified respects.[6] This makes questions of warrant conditions and relations matters of contingent fact, subject to novel discovery in whatever ways any contingent facts are. While I claim that this reading plausibly reconstructs our use of epistemic expressions, and thus is, in one sense, a matter of meaning, this claim is consistent with the sort of empirical epistemology envisioned by Quine.[7] This is one step in showing that the gap between Quinean and traditional epistemologies is not as wide as some would make out. Both perspectives have been fairly silent about what is being said when epistemic expressions are used. I believe that when this question is raised the supposed radical difference between naturalized and traditional epistemologies may be greatly reduced. I point out, however, that one who takes basic epistemic principles to be conceptual, necessary, or analytic truths can also argue that their discovery may be surprising.

This brings us to the question of what a language theory aspiring to epistemic completeness should say about warrant conditions and relations. I argue two claims: first, that a theory of language must trouble itself with epistemological information, and, second, that, even if a theory of language does so, that will not suffice for it to do much that is often asked of a theory of language. I know of two ways to press the first claim. If one recognizes a distinction in content between a class of sentences which is epistemologically basic and a class which is epistemologically derivative, one confronts the problem of explaining the nature of warranting relations between sentences of these classes. Elsewhere I argue that there are no good candidates for nonepistemic relations to explain epistemic relations between such sentences, that part of the task of explaining these epistemic relations belongs to a theory of language for the related sentences, and thus that an adequate theory of language must state basic warranting relations.[8] But, since such a distinction between basic and nonbasic sentences is not entirely welcome within a Quinean framework, I press the first claim in a different way. Most epistemologists allow some principles of inductive inference from sample to population, usually along with much richer inductive principles, in an adequate account of knowledge. But the problem of projectibility shows that inductive principles which are not predicate-specific fail to distinguish proper from improper inferences of this kind. In our jargon the point is stated as follows: Inductive principles which are not predicate-specific fail to explain why, given a body of evidence that examined emeralds are green, claims about other emeralds formulated in terms of 'green' are warranted while claims formulated in terms of 'grue' are not.[9] One can take the heroic line that there is no distinction between warranted and nonwarranted claims of these sorts. This is to embrace not only epistemic incompleteness but also a strong skepticism. There is another moral which may be drawn, and which must be assessed before opting for the heroic line: One must specify not only principles but also predicates to which the principles apply. Principles which apply to a restricted set of predicates are just the sort of thing which belong to a theory of language, according to the curriculum I have adopted. How are the relevant predicates to be specified? There is no difference in the truth conditions or nonepistemically characterized inferential relations of, say, 'green' versus 'grue' which explains why inductive inferences on 'green' but not 'grue' yield warranted claims. Thus, *whatever features* of projectible predicates one favors as their qualifying features, that projectible predicates have these features, and that these features qualify the predicates for inductive warrant extensions, must be stated in a theory of language for the predicates that aspires to epistemic completeness. To summarize: Even if the ability of projectible predicates to support inductive warrant extensions "supervenes on" nonepistemic features of these predicates, e.g., their supposed "entrenchment," principles stating that such and such predicates have these features *and thereby* are a basis for inductive warrant extensions must be included in an epistemically complete language theory for the predicates. (I note that my own theory of warrant in terms of what we would ideally believe offers the following sorting of projectible vs. nonprojectible predicates: Projectible predicates are those in accordance with which one would, were one to function ideally, choose to inductively extend one's beliefs.)

Suppose then, if only for the sake of argument, that theories of language include epistemic information, information expressed in terms of the expressions 'W($\_\_/\_\_,\_\_$)' and 'W($\_\_,\_\_/\_\_,\_\_$)'. There are different ways of thinking about inclusion of such information in language theories. We may think of the theories as consisting mainly of specifications of truth conditions and inferential relations (deductive and, perhaps, inductive), and as including epistemic information only where the main part of the theory, together with factual information and general warranting principles, fails to determine warrant conditions and relations. Or we may think of the theories as consisting mainly of warrant conditions and relations for sentence components along with ways of generating warrant conditions and relations of sentences from those of their components. I prefer the former view. Part of an adequate explanation of the warrant conditions or relations of a sentence is to indicate features of its truth conditions or nonepistemic inferential relations which, together with a general account of warrant and warranting, suffice for it to have these epistemic roles. If it were uniformly possible to find such features, there would be minimal need—only specification of ways in which epistemic features "supervene on" nonepistemic features—for epistemic information in a language theory. But the language theories, e.g., phenomenalistic theories, which go furthest in supporting such a supervenience are inherently problematic.

Granting that there is some epistemic information in a language theory, we now consider the relation of epistemic information to other information in the theory. Certain Quinean themes apply here. To draw issues as sharply as possible, I ask what control epistemic information exerts over the other information in a language theory that includes epistemic information from which *all* the warrant conditions and relations of a set of relevant *sentences* follow. I focus on *results* of a language theory in terms of warrant conditions and relations for *whole sentences*, rather than on the statements in the theory (the axioms of the theory) concerning warrant conditions and relations for sentence components from which these results for sentences follow, to avoid begging questions to be raised. I contend, first, that these results may be viewed in accordance with a holistic conception of language such as Quine's, and, second, that, however viewed, these results leave basic issues of reference undecided.

In "Meaning and Perception" I try to support the claim that, even within a strict empiricist framework (all empirical knowledge is based by deduction or by [roughly enumerative] induction on sentences describing a person's present or recalled sensory experience), a language theory can be epistemically complete.[10] Rather than repeat the tedious details of making this claim stick, I shall just explain the strategy. The key problem on this approach is to explain how the warrant conditions and relations of physical sentences, contingent sentences which do not report anyone's present or recalled sensory experiences, can be explained by inductive and deductive warrant-preserving inferences from sentences about sensory experiences. If we allow that certain epistemic information belongs to a theory of language for sentences, in this case, physical sentences, the solution is fairly simple. An adequate theory of language for physical sentences yields results which state (1) that physical sentences warrant sensory sentences, (2) that sensory sentences warrant physical sentences, (3) that counterfactuals having subjunctive counterparts of sensory sentences as antecedents and consequents (if such and such experiences should occur, such and such further experiences would occur), conditional sensory sentences, warrant physical sentences, and (4) that physical sentences warrant conditional sensory sentences. Given a *rich supply* of results of these kinds, warranting relations between physical and sensory sentences are results either of the language theory or of inductive generalizations in terms of sensory experiences plus results of the language theory. Accounting for warranting relations between physical sentences (or complex sentences involving both physical and sensory sentences) is more complicated. If physical sentence p warrants physical sentence q, this must be explained in terms of sensory sentences warranted by p, warranting relations among these sensory sentences, and sensory sentences warranting q. These resources are available in an empiricist framework supplemented by results of language theories for p and q. The general strategy is to explain warranting relations between physical sentences in terms of results of a language theory establishing sensory sentences as intermediaries between physical sentences.

These considerations presuppose that the results of a language theory will specify warranting relations of individual, logically simple physical sentences to sensory sentences. This presupposition is a form of the view that "each statement, taken in isolation from its fellows, can admit of confirmation or infirmation."[11] But the important thing to note is that nothing about the strategy for establishing epistemic completeness depends on taking individual, logically simple physical sentences, rather than sentences expressing all or part of a theory or cognitive system, as that which is at the center of warrant relations to sensory sentences. Thus, even within traditional empiricism, there is nothing to preclude "holizing" the results of a language theory. Depending on how we "holize" results, and continuing to assume that a language theory has a rich supply of epistemic results, epistemic completeness can still be established. If we take the results of a language theory to specify warranting relations only for whole theories or systems, the epistemic completeness of the theory for sentences expressing the theory or system can be argued exactly as it was for individual, logically simple physical sentences. Reference to warrant conditions or relations of a sentence which is part of the theory must then be viewed as elliptical reference to the warrant conditions or relations of the theory to which the sentence belongs. There is a less pure but, I think, more plausible way to "holize."

On this view, results of a theory of language state warrant conditions and relations both for individual, logically simple sentences and for whole theories, but epistemic completeness for an individual sentence can be established only by considering the warrant conditions and relations of a theory to which it belongs. This view recognizes that individual sentences seem to have some warranting conditions and relations ('This is red' seems to be warranted by 'This looks red to me') independent of an encompassing theory.

These approaches to "holizing" assign a special role to sensory sentences. But nothing essential turns on identifying the sentences in terms of which physical discourse is tied by language theory to evidence as *sensory* sentences. It is essential to recognize a point at which perceptual input is cognized and as such becomes the evidence, together with recalled past cognized perceptual input, against which beliefs about the physical world are epistemically evaluated. But no assumption about the form of this cognition is necessary to the above picture.

There is also nothing to preclude results of a language theory which relate physical sentences, or whatever sort of sentences are taken *not* to formulate perceptual cognitions, to one another. The core required is that sentences formulating perceptual cognitions be the only contingent sentences having warrant conditions and that appeal to these sentences be necessary in determining the warrant conditions of all contingent sentences.

This completes what I shall say to support the claim that language theories which include epistemic information and aspire to epistemic completeness can treat language holistically. I turn to the claim that a language theory which includes enough epistemic information to sustain results of the forms considered, and to be epistemically complete via these results, leaves open basic questions concerning reference of sentence components. This claim is the counterpart in a framework that includes notions of warrant and warranting of Quine's claim that the sorts of things talked about by a sentence are not determined by the sentence's stimulation conditions. To support my claim, I underscore a restriction observed to this point. The results of a language theory appealed to in arguing its epistemic completeness for physical sentences (be they individual sentences, theory fragments, or whole theories) are warranting relations of physical sentences to evidence sentences (sentences having warrant conditions as well as warrant relations—sensory sentences in the empiricist view) and inductive generalizations from evidence sentences. I call this limited set of results of a language theory the *empirical component* of the theory.

A first approximation to my point is made by observing that sentences which are contraries, and which clearly differ in referential import, may be indistinguishable with respect to the epistemic results that constitute the empirical component of a language theory for the sentences. Thus the contraries 'Lo, there is a dagger before me' and 'Lo, there is no dagger before me, but there is a perfect dagger hallucination', where a perfect dagger hallucination is a hallucination that neither I nor anyone else can detect through all actual and possible perceptions, have the same linguistic empirical components—although the results would be generated differently given the different structures of the sentences. One may suspect the notion of a perfect dagger hallucnation, arguing that it is parasitical on the notion of a dagger so that a claim of a perfect dagger hallucination could be warranted only for someone for whom dagger claims, or claims about objects sufficiently resembling daggers, are warranted. To meet this problem, we might try imagining people who had conceptual schemes that allowed that reality is occasionally undetectably "gappy." That is, in the conceptual scheme of the imagined people, the world usually is as it seems to be, populated with tables, chairs, pi-mesons, etc., or we could, at least in principle, find out that things are not as they seem to be. But in rare cases it seems that there is an object of a certain kind, when there is not and when there is, in principle, no way to find out that there is not. We might imagine further that these people have words for tables, chairs, and pi-mesons, as well as words to be applied when there seem to be such objects but the objects are undetectably absent. Thus there might be "bookgaps," "chairgaps," and "pi-mesongaps." 'This is a pi-meson' and 'This is a pi-mesongap' would have the same linguistic empirical components, while they obviously are contraries and differ in referential import, the former requiring the existence of a pi-meson while the latter requires that there be none. This sort of case seems not to rest on the sort of parasitism alleged in the preceding example, but it does require a good stretch of imagining.

Another way to support the claim that linguistic empirical components do not determine referential import is to note that various reductionist programs to translate physical and theoretical sentences into an evidentially more basic jargon would yield translations of physical and theoretical sentences having the same linguistic empirical components as the physical and theoretical sentences, but different referential import. Thus on one reading C. I. Lewis wished to translate (preserving identity of proposition expressed by the sentences) physical sentences into conjunctions of sentences of the form 'If one should have such and such sensory experiences, one would, in all probability, have such and so sensory experiences.' On a successful translation of this kind the physical sentence and its translation have the same linguistic empirical components, since the point is to translate the physical sentence into the empirical evidence relevant to it, but different referential import—physical objects in one case, sensory experiences in the other. But many philosophers find the possibility of successfully giving such translations so remote that no philosophical thesis can be supported by them.

Which brings us to rabbitstuff, and to the examples Quine used first in connection with the claim of indeterminacy of translation, and later in support of the theses of inscrutability and relativity of reference. At first glance these examples seem to offer easy illustration of the claim that linguistic empirical components do not determine referential import. 'This is a rabbit,' 'This is a temporal rabbit-stage,' 'This is an undetached rabbitpart,' and 'Rabbithood there' seem to have the same linguistic empirical components although they differ in reference. A question can be raised, however, given the background epistemic framework. Recall that the linguistic empirical component consists of results of a language theory which state warranting relations between physical/theoretical sentences and evidence sentences. If the physical/theoretical sentences and the evidence sentences are formulated in the same terminology, it may be argued that linguistic empirical components for physical/theoretical sentences determine their referential import, as that of the evidence sentences to which the empirical component relates them. It is argued that if there is no content difference between evidence and physical/theoretical sentences there is no question about the content or reference of the physical/theoretical sentences given the evidence sentences.

This line of argument is incorrect. First, I think there is a difference in content between physical/theoretical and evidence sentences. This is reflected in my description of evidence sentences as sensory sentences. But this is part of a longer epistemological story which is not germane here. The key point is that, even if there is no content difference between physical/theoretical sentences and evidence sentences, this simply means that the information in the empirical component of a language theory also fails to determine the referential import of evidence sentences. There is no reason to think that the sort of warrant conditions and relations essential to establishing epistemic completeness, conditions and relations for whole sentences, sort out the referential import of the sentences. Evidence sentences may have—I think they must have—warrant conditions as well as warrant relations. If we regard 'This is a chair' as an evidence sentence, it will be warranted in certain conditions, when one has certain stimulation, sensory experiences, sense data, or whatever—at least when warranting relations to other sentences do not override the support of the conditions. But there is nothing in the statement of the relevant warrant conditions to fix the referential import of a sentence. Even adding warrant conditions, the epistemic information essential to epistemic completeness does not fix referential import.

This conclusion may seem to rest on specific features of the framework within which it is presented. First I considered epistemic completeness in terms of warrant relations between individual, logically simple physical sentences and evidence sentences. But two "holistic" ways of proceeding were noted. Second, I focused on inductive generalizations, rather than on other forms of nondeductive warrant extension. I think there are better reasons to regard certain forms of inductive generalization as warrant preserving than there are to so regard other forms of nondeductive inference, such as the often-named, seldom-formulated inferences to the best explanation. Be this as it may, short of adopting arbitrary warrant principles, it is doubtful that adding warrant principles or "holizing" a language theory leads to determination of referential import by linguistic empirical components plus other information relevant to epistemic completeness. The reason is that any view that allows coherence among sentences a significant role in determining the warrant of sentences—and plausible epistemic views do grant coherence a role—will also allow that, for sentences whose warrant is significantly determined by coherence, some maximally coherent systems include a certain sentence while other maximally coherent (and otherwise adequate) systems include a contrary of the sentence. This result can be avoided, but only by adopting principles (that the system which I or we accept or prefer is *the* warrant determining system) which have little to recommend them outside of avoiding this result. This result concerning coherence cannot be properly supported without having possible evidence sets and warrant principles from which maximally coherent, otherwise adequate (maximally comprehensive, simple, etc.) systems can be constructed. If you fill in your favorite candidates for these roles, I think you will be able to support the result.[12] This epistemological undetermination suffices for a degree of undetermination of reference (with respect to sentences having contraries in equicoherent systems)—roughly proportional to the extent to which it is possible for equicoherent systems to be incompatible (to include contraries). This argument from epistemic coherence does not presuppose tolerance of epistemic incompleteness. In cases where contrary sentences belong to distinct equicoherent, otherwise adequate systems, it is not obvious that either sentence should count as warranted. Even if we do take one sentence (both sentences?) to be warranted in these cases, the fact that empirical factors do not suffice to distinguish warranted and nonwarranted sentences does not show that the distinction cannot be made. It seems that we do count physical sentences as warranted, even when they have "gappy" contraries, on just the sort of grounds appealed to in pressing the claim that language theories having certain results are epistemically complete. This indicates that the determinateness of results of a language theory with respect to which sentences stand at the center of certain warranting relations is not evidentially based.

The two main themes of this paper are that a holistic view of language is consistent with an epistemology which takes warrant and warranting seriously, as measured by the notion of epistemic completeness, and that everything in a language theory relevant to epistemic completeness, along with factual information outside the theory, does not resolve basic issues concerning reference. Too much has been presupposed at each step to seriously claim to have argued to these themes. I hope that I have at least made these themes more plausible by indicating how an epistemologist—even one who accepts much of traditional empiricism—can begin to swallow, if not wholly digest, some of what Quine says about language and reference.

NOTES

1. William Van Orman Quine, "Two Dogmas of Empiricism," reprinted in *From a Logical Point of View* (New York: Harper and Row, 1953), p. 41.

2. W. V. O. Quine, *Ontological Relativity and Other Essays* (New York: Columbia University Press, 1969), p. 11.

3. From here on I shall be careful to distinguish the proposition(s) expressed by a sentence from the sentence only when context does not make clear whether the sentence or proposition(s) is at issue.

4. In my "A Decision Procedure for Epistemology?" forthcoming in *Philosophical Studies*.

5. These senses are distinguished in my "Counterfactuals in Epistemology," *Synthese* 34 (1977): 479–95. See also Fred Feldman's comments on this paper in the same issue of *Synthese* and my response to Feldman's comments in "Warranting Reconsidered," *Synthese* 37 (1978): 459–64.

6. See my "A Decision Procedure for Epistemology?"

7. In W. V. O. Quine, "Epistemology Naturalized," *Ontological Relativity*, pp. 69–90; and "The Nature of Natural Knowledge," in *Mind and Language*, ed. Samuel Guttenplan (London: Oxford University Press, 1975), pp. 67–81.

8. In my "Meaning and Perception," *Journal of Philosophy* 73 (1976): 572–85.

9. See Nelson Goodman, "The New Riddle of Induction," in *Fact, Fiction, and Forecast* (Indianapolis: Bobbs-Merrill, 1973), pp. 59–83.

10. "Meaning and Perception," pp. 577–80.

11. "Two Dogmas of Empiricism," p. 41.

12. I offer at least part of an argument for this claim in "A Reconstruction of Value," *Canadian Journal of Philosophy* 5 (1975): 375–93; and "Counterfactuals in Epistemology."

Quine and Mathematical Reduction*

MARK STEINER
Hebrew University of Jerusalem

The greatness of a contemporary philosopher can be measured by the extent to which his concerns become those of his generation. Whatever the merit of the following essay, it certainly illustrates this truth.

I

Quine's criterion for reduction in mathematics was well expressed in *Set Theory and Its Logic*:

> We have provided a model of arithmetic in set theory when we have provided a way of so reinterpreting arithmetical notations in set-theoretic terms as to carry the truths of arithmetic into truths of set theory. Now what more than such formal simulation is demanded in actually *reducing* numbers to set theory? Seemingly there is also a question of their application; thus, in the case of the natural numbers, class measurement. But we noticed . . . that for natural numbers this posed no added demand; any version of the natural numbers would be suited to class measurement if it fulfilled the formal laws. Now much the same can be said of the real numbers: when they are applied, say by assignment to sundry continuous magnitudes in the physical world, any model could be applied as well. Modeling again proves tantamount to reduction because all traits relevant to application carry over into the model.[1]

This approach to reduction was later modified by Quine, because the Skolem-Löwenheim Theorem—on this approach—threatened to reduce every (finitely axiomatized) science to number theory.[2] Quine thus imposed stronger criteria: the old ontology was to be embeddable

---

* A version of this paper was read at the American Philosophical Association held in Cincinnati in 1978. My thanks to the National Science Foundation for supporting this research.

in the new by a "proxy function" such that the properties of the old object would be preserved under the embedding. This emendation retains the model-theoretic character of Quine's theory.

My view is that Quine's theory is lacking even as a theory of *mathematical* reduction, where one might indeed think modeling sufficient for reduction. I base this view on another, that *explanation* exists in mathematics just as in the sciences. Two proofs of a theorem may differ in explanatory value. And a mathematical explanation articulated in one theory might be destroyed when the theory is modeled in another. I am therefore inclined not to regard modeling as sufficient for reduction even in mathematics.

In general, when "modeling" one theory in another leads to epistemic loss, abstract "unification of universes" is unscientific. In *Mathematical Knowledge*, I discussed the reduction of arithmetic to set theory, in which a more secure theory is reduced to a less.[3] In what follows, I shall discuss examples in which mathematical explanation is at issue.

II

Mathematicians distinguish between proofs that prove and proofs that explain.[4] Solomon Feferman remarks that "abstraction and generalization are constantly pursued as the means to reach really satisfactory explanations which account for scattered individual results. In particular, extensive developments in algebra and analysis seem necessary to give us real insight into the behavior of the natural numbers."[5] Chang and Keisler, in their book *Model Theory*, explain algebraic facts using syntactical ideas.[6] My impression is that the distinction between explanatory and nonexplanatory proofs is widely accepted; agreement on particular cases, widespread. This despite the absence of reference to the concept of explanation in most published papers in mathematical journals.

A simple illustration: It is well known that the sum of the first n positive integers, $S(n)$, is equal to $n(n+1)/2$. One learns to prove this by induction: the theorem is obvious for $n = 1$, and assuming it for arbitrary n, we argue that

$$S(n+1) = S(n) + (n+1) = n(n+1)/2 + (n+1) =$$
$$n(n+1)/2 + 2(n+1)/2 = (n+1)(n+2)/2, \text{Q.E.D.}$$

No mathematician will regard this as an explanatory proof, however; I believe the reason is that in this proof we do not see what *about* the sum is "responsible" for this theorem, what characteristic property of $S(n)$ (regarded as a *sum*) "implies" the value $n(n+1)/2$.

Gauss as a schoolboy, the story goes, instantly hit upon a different proof:

$$\frac{\begin{array}{l}1 + 2 + 3 + \ldots + n = S(n)\\ n + (n-1) + (n-2) + \ldots + 1 = S(n)\end{array}}{(n+1) + (n+1) + (n+1) + \ldots + (n+1) = n(n+1) = 2S(n).}$$

This strikes mathematicians as an explanatory proof; the reason, I believe, is that the proof turns on a characteristic property of $S(n)$: its symmetry.

Another proof which is intuitively explanatory is geometric:

The sum of the first n integers can be represented as an isosceles right triangle of dots; two such triangles give $n^2 + n$ (because we counted the diagonal twice). The equation $2S(n) = n^2 + n$ is obviously what we are looking for. The geometrical pattern also characterizes $S(n)$, which is why this proof too is explanatory.

To clarify what is meant by saying that a "characteristic property" is "responsible" for a theorem, I introduce two undefined notions. The first is that of a mathematical family. I assume that "natural kinds" exist in mathematics. For instance, the natural numbers form a family; so do the polygons of Euclid. The union of these families, however, is not a family. Now a *characteristic property* picks out an entity from a family of entities.

We would *like* to say that an explanatory proof about e (in which e is mentioned in the theorem) characterizes e, by some property K, from among a family of kindred entities and shows that if e did not have K the theorem would fail. Instead of such nonsense, however, we introduce the concept of *deforming* a proof. Suppose we have a proof P about e, a member of family F. Sometimes we can generate a new proof P' about another member e' of F, simply by replacing—in P—the property K by a characteristic of e', K', and reasoning similarly. This is no simple-minded substitution, since P will have to be adjusted, maintaining the same "proof idea." We now state that P is explanatory if there exist e and F such that P is about e, e is a member of F, and P may be deformed into proofs about other members of F.

For example, the two explanatory proofs that $S(n) = n(n+1)/2$ involve characteristics of $S(n)$: Gauss's proof, the symmetry properties of $S(n)$; the other proof, its geometrical properties. As for deformation, both proofs may be deformed, for example, to obtain proofs that the sum of the first n *odd* integers is n^2:

$$\frac{\begin{array}{c} 1 + 3 + 5 + \ldots + (2n-1) \\ (2n-1) + (2n-3) + (2n-5) + \ldots + 1 \end{array}}{2n + 2n + 2n + \ldots + 2n = 2n^2}$$

Geometrically we can write

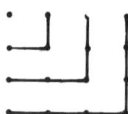

We characterize the new sum either by a different symmetry property or by a different partition of the square. The proof ideas remain the same.

For a final example, consider the Pythagorean theorem. Many of its proofs lack explanatory power: they do not show what about the right triangle compels the theorem. This is not a question simply of the "transparency" of a proof, or its "visualizability." One of the cleverest proofs that $a^2 + b^2 = c^2$ is this:

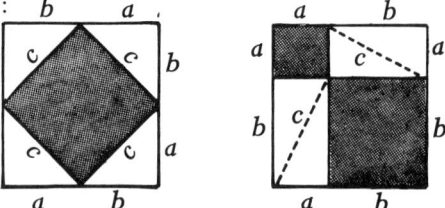

Starting with a square of side $a + b$, we remove four right triangles in two ways, one of which leaves a square of side c, and the other which leaves two squares of sides a and b. Yet this proof is as little explanatory as any of the standard proofs, "transparent" though it be. Though the proof (like all the proofs) *uses* the fact that the triangle is right, it leaves the role of that fact obscure.

An explanatory proof of the Pythagorean theorem is given by Polya:[7]

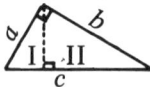

The area of similar figures is proportional to the square of their sides (from the definition of "area"). The areas of any similar figures constructed on sides a, b, and c of a right triangle would thus be given, for some k, by ka^2, kb^2, and kc^2. If the sum of the areas of two of the figures equaled that of the third, we would have

$$ka^2 + kb^2 = kc^2$$

from which the Pythagorean theorem follows. The theorem is therefore equivalent to finding any three similar figures on the sides of a right triangle such that the sum of the first two is the third. But triangle I, triangle II, and the entire right triangle *abc* are three such figures, Q.E.D. *This* proof tells us "what about" the right triangle is "responsible" for the theorem: the right triangle is the only one decomposable into two similar figures similar to the whole. And the proof is "deformable" as well: we can characterize triangles by the area of the remainder when we attempt to cut a nonright triangle into similar, similar triangles:

The coincidence of lines *m* and *n* is what characterizes the right triangle. By calculating the area of the remainder we obtain the following generalization of the Pythagorean theorem:

$$c^2 = a^2 + b^2 - 2ab \cos C$$

the law of cosines, proved without using the Pythagorean theorem itself.

This example teaches us the right relation between explanation and generality. The explanatory proof is not necessarily general, but rather generalizable: we generalize the original proof when we create an array by deformation.

III

In "Mathematics, Explanation, and Scientific Knowledge," I argued that mathematical explanations exist in physics as well.[8] I gave as an example a kinematical theorem that the general motion of a rigid body with a fixed point is a rotation about an axis. Though geometrical proofs of this exist, the modern algebraic proof is explanatory. It turns out that the odd-dimensionality of space is what explains the axis of rotation—if space were four-dimensional, the theorem would fail.

What makes this explanation *mathematical*? It also contains *physical* premises since a physical fact is explained. On the other hand, a "physical" explanation in physics (such as the explanation by Einstein of the photoelectric effect) includes mathematical assumptions. In my opinion the difference is that a "mathematical" explanation of a physical fact is really a mathematical explanation of a *mathematical* fact, with some "bridge principles" thrown in. For example, our kinematic example is really a mathematical theorem about "orthogonal" transformations of abstract Euclidean space with the addition of such premises as that space is Euclidean and that physical rotations under their standard descriptions induce orthogonal transformations. We can detect the difference between the two kinds of explanations if we remove from each all sentences containing a nonmathematical predicate. If the original explanation was "mathematical," a mathematical explanation will remain; if "physical," no kind of explanation will remain.

The peculiar nature of mathematical explanations in physics makes it impossible to use them as evidence for the existence of mathematical entities, unlike the explanation of the photoelectric effect, which establishes the existence of light quanta. The mathematical explanation in physics exhausts its explanatory power, as it were, on the mathematical theorem, leaving none left for the kinematical fact.[9]

A less speculative reason that mathematical explanations in physics are useless to Platonists is grounded in Quine's own argument for the existence of abstract entities: without their assumption we cannot describe the world; consider translating "Jack and Jill went up the hill at the same rate" without referring to numbers.[10] Now an argument for the addition of objects to our "ontology" is that without them we cannot explain a certain phenomenon. But in that case the explanandum cannot already presuppose the existence of those objects. For example, one can describe the photoelectric effect without mentioning light quanta (one need not believe in a fixed "observation language" distinct from a "theoretical language" in which explanations are couched. The boundary may shift with time). But if Quine (and Goodman) are right, almost any explanandum will already be committed to mathematical entities. No explanatory argument, then, can make the existence of mathematical entities any more plausible than Quine's argument has already made it. Our conclusions so far are these: An explanatory proof in mathematics is one which can be generalized in a certain way. Mathematical explanations are offered in the natural sciences—but these are essentially explanatory mathematical proofs with "bridge principles" tacked on. Such mathematical explanations cannot be used to argue for the existence of mathematical objects.

One should not conclude, however, that mathematical explanation is of no relevance to ontology, from the inability of mathematical explanation to decide between nominalism and Platonism. For we shall now show that mathematical explanation has the power to decide "internal" questions such as the reduction of one type of mathematical entity to another.

IV

Quine regards with approval the traditional interpretation of complex numbers $x + yi$ as ordered pairs of reals $<x, y>$; it is a "modeling" and thus a reduction. His only complaint with the traditional modeling is that it distinguishes the real number x from the "complex real number" $<x, \text{o}>$, an unnecessary multiplication of entities: one wants $x + yi$ to be x when $y = \text{o}$; in any case, the field of reals and the subfield $<x, \text{o}>$ are isomorphic.[11] Quine proceeds to provide a different version of the complex numbers which *identifies* the reals with the complex reals; the real numbers become simply a subset of the complex numbers rather than being embedded in them. We shall examine Quine's suggestion later; first, we shall establish that Quine has ignored the point of the traditional reduction.

The interpretation of a kind of number as an ordered pair is standard logical gimmickry.[12] One may interpret the fraction m/n as an ordered pair $<m, n>$—or again as a class of pairs. Quine apparently views the interpretation of the complex numbers as similar, but such a view is misleading. The interpretation of complex numbers as points on a plane or *vectors* opens up new mathematical vistas; the interpretation of fractions as ordered pairs does no such thing.

For example, once we view $x + yi$ as a vector, we can ask for its "length" and for its "direction." We can transform to polar coordinates and obtain the crucial representation of $x + yi$ as $R(\cos\Theta + i\sin\Theta)$, where R is the length of the vector $(x^2 + y^2)^{1/2}$ and Θ, its direction. This opens the way for computing $(x + yi)^n = R^n(\cos n\Theta + i \sin n\Theta)$, for the well-known representation of the nth roots of unity by a regular polygon inscribed in the complex unit circle, and indeed for Euler's theorem which can now be written

$$x + yi = Re^{i\Theta}$$

a form which highlights the relation between the Cartesian and the polar coordinates.

The "vectorial" approach to the complex numbers allows us mathematical explanations of purely number-theoretical results. Take the mysterious (though easily verifiable) fact that the product of two sums of two squares is again the sum of two squares. The mystery vanishes when we realize that a sum of two squares is the norm (square of the length) of a complex number; Euler's theorem immediately implies that the norm of a product of two complex numbers is the product of their norms. This proof is explanatory: it turns on a characteristic property of the sum of two squares—being the norm of a complex number. "Deforming" the proof, by replacing the complex numbers by quaternions, we obtain another theorem of Euler: the product of two sums of four squares is the sum of four squares.

So the reduction of complex numbers (unlike that of the rationals) stimulates mathematical inquiry by formulating new questions. Recall (by way of contrast) Quine's description of mathematical reduction in *Word and Object*: Although reduction renders meaningful a host of new questions—as, in the case of numbers to sets, "Is 3 really a member of 5?"—such questions, labeled "don't cares" by Quine, are to be dismissed.[13] The point of the reduction is not to prove that numbers are sets but to show that sets can "do the work" of numbers. The responses we give to the "don't cares" do not affect the success of the reduction, says Quine. But our example of the complex numbers shows that not all such questions are "don't cares." In the case of the rational numbers the "length" or "direction" of such numbers is as inconsequential after the reduction to ordered pairs as before. But the concept of length and direction when applied to the complex numbers is so fruitful that the reduction in this case seems almost to reveal properties of the complex numbers that were previously hidden—as the atomic explanation of the gas laws reveals properties of gases (degree of interaction among the atoms, etc.) which were previously hidden.

The foregoing argument does not yet prove that reduction requires more than "modeling." There may simply be two kinds of reduction: one with mere "ontic" value; the other which furthers inquiry and fosters explanation. But our discussion of mathematical explanation suggests an even stronger, if speculative, point: that "modeling" is not sufficient for reduction of any sort. The argument hangs on the notion of a "family," used to define mathematical explanation above, and for which we have no good account; still, the argument may have some interest.

V

We mentioned before that Quine is not satisfied by the classical reduction of the complex numbers to ordered pairs of reals; the reduction creates duplication by distinguishing the "old" reals from the isomorphic "complex reals" $<x, o>$. Quine thus proposes a reduction having the "virtue" that $x + yi$ is mapped onto x when $y = o$. Quine describes the procedure:

> We have merely to pick an arbitrary correspondence relating things other than natural numbers to all the natural numbers; then we can explain $x + yi$ as $x \cup w\text{``}y$. Also, as required, the real numbers $x$ and $y$ are each uniquely recoverable from $x \cup w\text{``}y$. For inasmuch as a real number (even when negative) is in our final version of class of natural numbers,

$$x = N \cap (x \cap w``y), \qquad y = w``(x \cup w``y).^{14}$$

But do we *want* to identify the reals with the "complex reals"? The classical reduction, which does not, views the complex field as a *vector space* over the reals—the latter playing the role of a "field of scalars." The vector space is "generated" by the basis <1, o> and <1, o> corresponding to 1 and *i*. The reduction of the complex field to the "complex plane" imposes a natural geometric structure on these numbers. Regarding the reals as just one "axis" of the complex plane, rather than as independent entities to which the imaginaries are subjoined, we can speak of circles, ellipses, indeed a "family" of geometric structures— which is at least a wonderful instrument for *discovering* mathematical theorems. Quine's reduction turns a "circle" into a set with no intrinsic structure; the set of geometric figures is mapped into an artificial set of sets despite the use of the old names. The reduction of Quine (like the Skolem-Löwenheim reduction) would certainly have impeded mathematical discovery had it been adopted.

Quine can certainly protest that he is not interested in the "context of discovery," to which ontology is irrelevant; but our analysis of *explanation* in mathematics links that concept to that of discovery. An explanatory proof, we have seen, is a function from a mathematical family or "natural kind" to an array of proofs related by "deformation." Since the attribute of being a "family" is not necessarily preserved by modeling, neither is the property of being an explanatory proof.

Consider the following example of mathematical explanation which depends heavily on the characterization of the "complex reals" as vectors.[15] The expression $S(x) = 1/(1 - x^2)$, x real, has the expansion $P(x) = 1 - x^2 + x^4 - x^6 + \ldots$ when $x < 1$. As x approaches 1 from below, both $P(x)$ and $S(x)$ approach 1/2. Despite this, $P(x)$ diverges when $x = +1$ (according to the modern definition of convergence) and continues to diverge when $x > 1$. There is nothing in the "behavior" of $S(x)$ which would suggest that its expansion should not be defined for absolute values greater than or equal to 1.

The explanation for the divergence of the expansion of $P(x)$ for $x > 1$ is that 1, regarded as a vector <1, o> is on the same circle as is *i* [= <o, 1>]. According to a theorem of Cauchy, a power series in a complex variable z converges in a circular region of the complex plane centered on the origin. Consider $S(z) = 1/(1 - z^2)$; that is, generalize the analytic expression $S(x)$ to the whole plane. As z approaches $+ i$, $S(z)$ goes to infinity; thus $P(z)$—its expansion—diverges. Thus, convergence of $P(z)$ is precluded outside the circle $|z| = 1$. As for the boundary of the circular region $z \leq 1$ (about which Cauchy's theorem is silent), we have the following theorem: If a function of a complex variable goes to infinity at any point on the circle $|z| = 1$, its expansion as a power series diverges at every point on the circle (proof: the expansion has to go to infinity at some point on the circle; thus the coefficients of the series cannot go to zero, a necessary condition for convergence on the circle $|z| = 1$).[16]

The explanation characterizes $S(x)$ as the projection onto the real axis of an analytic expression with a "pole" at $+i$. Take the points on the circle $|z| = 1$ as our "family." By altering the point and remaining on the circle, we obtain the theorem that the expansion of $1/(1 - x^n)$ does not converge at $x = 1$ for any n. An even more convincing explanation of this type is provided by the divergence of the hyperbolic secant of x, or $2/(e^x + e^{-x})$ for $x > \Pi/2$.[17] Unlike the previous case, in which $P(x)$ had an independent description (we could write the terms of $P(x)$ without actually expanding $S(x)$), there is no obvious way to write down the nth term of the expansion of sech (x), which is obtained by Taylor's theorem by repeated differentiation and summation —rather than by simple long division. Here we are certainly forced to turn to the complex plane, and to the fact that $2/(e^z + e^{-z})$ has a "pole" at $|z| = + \Pi i/2$, for an explanation of why the expansion of sech (x) diverges at $|x| \geqslant \pi/2$. Here we have enlarged the circle from radius unity to $\pi/2$.

Now Quine can surely translate any of these explanatory proofs, indeed an entire explanatory array, into his own system. But the translated array is no longer explanatory, because it is no longer the image of a mathematical family but rather that of an arbitrary collection.

If this argument has any force, it shows that mathematical explanation, though of no value in arguing for the existence of mathematical entities, is of value in deciding "internal" questions of reducing one *type* of mathematical entity to another. Thus mathematical explanation has relevance for ontology.

NOTES

1. W. V. Quine, *Set Theory and Its Logic* (Cambridge, Mass.: Harvard University Press, 1963), p. 135.
2. W. V. Quine, *Ontological Relativity and Other Essays* (New York: Columbia University Press, 1969).
3. M. Steiner, *Mathematical Knowledge* (Ithaca, N.Y.: Cornell University Press, 1975), chap. 2.
4. This section is adapted from my article "Mathematical Explanation," forthcoming in *Philosophical Studies*.
5. S. Feferman, "Systems of Predicative Analysis," in Jaakko Hintikka, ed., *The Philosophy of Mathematics* (London: Oxford University Press, 1969), p. 98.

6. C. C. Chang and H. J. Keisler, *Model Theory* (Amsterdam: North-Holland, 1973), pp. 123–24.

7. G. Polya, *Induction and Analogy in Mathematics* (Princeton: Princeton University Press, 1954), pp. 16–17.

8. Steiner, "Mathematics, Explanation, and Scientific Knowledge," *Nous* 12(1978); 17–28; esp. pp. 17–20.

9. This formulation of my view is due to Paul Benacerraf.

10. N. Goodman and W. V. Quine, "Steps Toward a Constructive Nominalism," *Journal of Symbolic Logic* 12(1947); 105–22.

11. Quine, *Set Theory and Its Logic*, p. 137.

12. Haim Gaifman, in an unpublished paper, gives necessary and sufficient conditions for the definability of the models of a first-order theory as n-tuples of submodels.

13. Quine, *Word and Object* (Cambridge, Mass.: MIT Press, 1960), p. 182.

14. Quine, *Set Theory and Its Logic*, p. 137.

15. From Ellis Kolchin.

16. The mathematics of this example was slightly garbled in "Mathematics, Explanation, and Scientific Knowledge."

17. Thanks to Harry Furstenberg.

De Re Propositional Attitudes Toward Integers*

DIANA ACKERMAN
Brown University

> ... Consider the relational and notional senses of believing in spies:
> (7) (∃ x) (Ralph believes that x is a spy)
> (8) Ralph believes that (∃ x) (x is a spy)
> Both may perhaps be ambiguously phrased as 'Ralph believes that someone is a spy,' but they may be unambiguously phrased respectively as 'There is someone whom Ralph believes to be a spy' and 'Ralph believes that there are spies.' The difference is vast; indeed, if Ralph is like most of us, (8) is true and (7) is false.[1]

This passage from Quine's "Quantifiers and Propositional Attitudes" gives the intuitive basis for the distinction between relational belief, or belief *de re*, and notional belief, or belief *de dicto*. In this paper I discuss conditions for having *de re* propositional attitudes toward numbers, specifically toward integers, since I do not have firm intuitions about *de re* propositional attitudes toward other sorts of numbers. The conditions I suggest for having *de re* propositional attitudes toward integers do not apply to entities in general. That is why it is worthwhile to single out integers for special consideration.

Of course, one paper can seldom discuss every important aspect of an issue. The existence of numbers is a necessary condition for anyone's having *de re* propositional attitudes toward them, since one cannot have *de re* propositional attitudes toward what does not exist. But I will not defend here the view that numbers exist. Instead, I will discuss conditions for *de re* propositional attitudes toward integers, on the supposition that they exist. Quine seems tolerant of numbers. He would take issue with a lot of what I will say, however, since I will use freely such notions as of meaning and proposition. I will not defend these notions here. The basic insight in Quine's above-quoted passage is just as im-

---

* I am very much indebted to Philip Quinn, Ernest Sosa, and James Van Cleve for valuable discussions of the material in this paper.

portant within the philosophical framework I use as within his own, regardless of which framework should be accepted. Another issue I will not discuss is whether the view that we have knowledge of abstract entities conflicts with the causal theory of knowledge and, if so, which view is the loser. I will proceed on the assumption that we do have knowledge of such entities.[2]

Ontological questions about numbers are important here in another way. In another context Chisholm has suggested that

$$(\exists x) \, (J \text{ believes that } x \text{ is } F)$$
$$\text{entails}$$
$$J \text{ believes that } (\exists x) \, (x \text{ is } F).[3]$$

This suggestion is important here, since many people believe that, e.g., 6 is the smallest perfect number without believing that 6 is an entity and hence without believing that $(\exists x)$ (x is the smallest perfect number). (A perfect number is a number that is equal to the sum of all its divisors, excluding itself.) Suppose J is such a person and suppose he is mistaken in his belief that 6 is not an entity. In this situation can 6 be such that he believes it *de re* to be the smallest perfect number? The answer is tied up with many complicated issues that both space limitations and my present philosophical limitations preclude my discussing here, such as whether one can be wrong about the logical form of what he believes, or only about the logical form of something else that provides a sort of analysis of a proposition he believes. For simplicity of exposition I will omit this requirement from my account of *de re* propositional attitudes about integers. It is easy to add for those who want it.

Most philosophical discussions of *de re* propositional attitudes give general conditions that are supposed to apply to such attitudes toward all entities. But Kaplan suggests a special account for abstract entities that exist necessarily.[4] This account relies on his notion of a standard name, which is a name that necessarily denotes a certain entity (assuming that the conventions of our language are held constant). He uses the term 'name' broadly enough to apply to singular terms generally, including definite descriptions; for example, he applies it to 'the least spy' (to be defined below) and to the German description 'die Zahl der Planeten.' I will follow this broad usage. For standard names, he says that "what is at stake is not pure reference in the absence of any descriptive structure but rather reference freed of *empirical* vicissitudes."[5] Moreover, he says that "on certain natural assumptions, '$\triangle n \, (\alpha, y)$' is itself expressed by 'Nec (⌜$\alpha = x$⌝,y)"[6] where 'α' is a variable ranging over expressions, '$\triangle n \, (\alpha, y)$' says that α is a standard name of y, 'Nec (⌜$\alpha = x$⌝,y)', says that ⌜$\alpha = x$⌝ is necessarily (*de re*) true of y, and the boldface letter 'x' is used only as a placeholder to indicate subject position. Kaplan uses the notion of a standard name initially to give an account of quantifying into *modal* contexts, and there it seems adequate. He goes on to say, however, "... the same trick [limiting exportation and existential generalization to standard names] would work for belief contexts if Ralph would confine his cogitations to numbers and expressions."[7] Thus on Kaplan's view if α is any singular term denoting a certain number N, and φ is a predicative expression expressing the property of being F, then if J believes ⌜α is φ⌝, n is such that he believes it *de re* to be F, and hence there is a number such that he believes it *de re* to be F.

This seems wrong. Suppose J believes that the smallest perfect number is the smallest perfect number. On Kaplan's view it follows that 6 is such that J believes it *de re* to be the smallest perfect number and hence that there is something J believes *de re* to be the smallest perfect number. This conclusion suffers from the same defects as other views that Kaplan rejects. For example, consider his expression 'the least spy,' which is defined as follows: Taking advantage of the fact that two persons cannot be born at exactly the same time in exactly the same place (where the place of birth is an interior point of the infant's body), and given any four spatial points a, b, c, d not in a plane, use the relations: t_1 is earlier than t_2, and p_1 is closer to $a(b,c,d)$ than p_2 is, to order all space time points. 'The least spy' is defined as having the same meaning as 'the spy whose spatio-temporal location at birth precedes that of all other spies'.[8] Then Ralph can easily believe that the least spy is a spy. Kaplan reasonably denies that it would follow that there is someone whom Ralph believes *de re* to be a spy. After all, as the Quine passage quoted at the beginning of this paper indicates, if Ralph is like most of us, he lacks the latter belief, which, Kaplan grants, is supposed to be a belief that would interest the FBI. But there is no reason to suppose that 'the smallest perfect number' gets one more *en rapport epistemically* with 6 than 'the least spy' gets one with the person who actually is the least spy. If we rely on the intuitive contrast the quoted Quine passage gives between *de re* and *de dicto* belief, the contrast between the sentences he numbers (7) and (8) seems equally strong if we replace 'is a spy' in each of these sentences with 'is the smallest perfect number'. By contrast, it seems that, if I believe that 6 is the smallest perfect number, then there is a number I believe *de re* to be the smallest perfect number.

It is not surprising that what suffices for exportation and existential generalization in modal contexts does not always suffice for exportation and existential generalization in propositional attitude contexts.

This result parallels (but of course is not entailed by) the fact that a more fine grained approach is also needed in *de dicto* propositional attitude contexts that in *de dicto* modal contexts, since, of course, sentences expressing logically equivalent propositions are not generally interchangeable *salva veritate* in *de dicto* propositional attitude contexts. Quine says that to admit quantified modal logic we need "a frankly inequalitarian attitude toward different ways of specifying [a number]."⁹ The above remarks suggest that for quantification into epistemic contexts we need even more than that. We need a "frankly inequalitarian attitude" toward different *standard names* for a number.

But is this really necessary? This question is highlighted by some theories of *de re* propositional attitudes in general that allow such attitudes even in cases where Kaplan does not. Thus, Sosa proposes that

> S believes about x that it is F (or believes x to be F) if and only if there is a singualr term α such that S believes ⌜α is F⌝ where α denotes x.¹⁰

He would handle my apparent counterexample by distinguishing between what is true and what it is appropriate and not misleading to say.

I think this does not work. To be convincing, such a pragmatic account of why it is misleading to assert p should have the following two features. First, it should say why and how the context makes it misleading to assert p. This should be specific enough to dispel the suspicion that the reason it is misleading to assert p is that p is false. Second, when it is only *misleading* to assert p, the appearance of falsity can be dispelled by specific attention to that fact. For example, Sosa says that it is misleading to say that someone believes a proposition when in fact he knows it because "it is often misleading to say something logically weaker when something stronger is certainly true."¹¹ Furthermore, note that the oddity is dispelled by saying something like, "This proposition is believed; in fact, it's even known." But now suppose that, as a result of mathematical errors, J believes that the smallest perfect number is equal to $\sqrt{64}$. On Sosa's view it follows that 6 and 8 are such that J believes them *de re* to be equal. This seems false, and there is no plausible pragmatic account to dispel the air of falsity. It is inadequate to give a pragmatic account that holds that saying J believes *de re* 6 and 8 to be equal is misleading because it is apt to make listeners think that J believes this of 6 and 8 under some names that are in some sense epistemically closer to 6 and 8 than 'the smallest perfect number' and '$\sqrt{64}$'. This is inadequate because there is no plausible explanation of why listeners would be inclined to think this except that it follows from the proposition that J believes *de re* 6 and 8 to be equal.

Chisholm endorses an account of *de re* belief that is more rigid than Sosa's. Thus Chisholm says:

> S attributes the property of being F to x = Df. There is an individual concept C such that (i) S knows a proposition implying x to have C and (ii) S accepts a proposition which implies x to have the property C and the property of being F.[12]

The key terms in this definition are defined as follows:

> C is an individual concept = Df   C is a property such that (i) it is possible that something has C and (ii) it is not possible that more than one thing has C at a time.[13]

> p implies x to have the property of being F = Df. There is a property G such that: (i) G is an individual concept, (ii) p entails the conjunction of G and the property of being F, and (iii) x has G.[14]

> P entails the property of being F = Df   p is necessarily such that (i) if it obtains then something has the property of being F and (ii) whoever accepts p believes that something is F.[15]

On this view if J knows that there is a smallest perfect number, then there is a number that is known *de re* by J to be the smallest perfect number. Is this acceptable? Chisholm says that philosophers disagree about the answers to such questions (although he does not discuss examples involving numbers) and that it is not obvious how agreement might be reached. He suggests that, if the answer is sought in our linguistic habits, we will find that on some occasions we require quite a lot to say that something is believed by J to have property F and that on other occasions we require very little.[16] There is certainly often such variation. But this seems less plausible with integers, since there are few if any contexts where it seems natural for me to infer that there is a number that is known by me *de re* to be the smallest perfect number simply on the strength of my knowledge that there is a smallest perfect number. If we start with the intuitions reflected in the Quine passage quoted at the beginning of this paper, there certainly seems to be a sharp difference between

(∃ x) (Ralph knows that x is the smallest perfect number)
and
Ralph knows that (∃ x) (x is the smallest perfect number).

The view I will present of *de re* propositional attitudes toward integers is designed to account for such intuitions. I believe that these intuitions are strong and plausible. But Chisholm is certainly right that the issue is not clear-cut, and it would be foolish for me to claim that my account accounts for *all* possible cases (rather than just a sort of central core) and all possible intuitions.

My reservations about Chisholm's view are illustrated by the following objection that he considers. Suppose *J* knows that the tallest spy is a spy and believes that all spies are secretive. Suppose he then infers that the tallest spy is secretive. But this would entail that the tallest spy is then believed *de re* by *J* to be secretive. The objection is that this knowledge that the tallest spy is a spy is much too easily acquired to bring *J* into the requisite relation with the tallest spy for *de re* belief. Chisholm's reply is that the knowledge in question is *not* easily acquired, for it entails knowledge that there is a tallest spy, which is knowledge he claims that probably no one has.[17] But Chisholm's reply can be undercut by replacing 'the tallest spy' in the objection with Kaplan's description 'the least spy.' Very little is required to know that there is a "least spy."

The reason this sort of objection seems forceful is hard to state precisely. Here is an imprecise statement: *J* can come to know that the least spy is a spy without bearing any special epistemic relation of being *en rapport* to the individual who is in fact the least spy; instead, his grounds for this knowledge may be completely general. This formulation is imprecise because of the looseness of its key terms; yet there seems to be something in it. Perhaps views of *de re* propositional attitudes that stress genetic factors in exportable names of concrete objects owe some of their plausibility to this sort of consideration. Similarly, it can be argued that, since one can know that there is a smallest perfect number on grounds that are in some sense purely general, one can know this without being related to 6 in a way that is (in some still unspecified manner) epistemically close enough to the number 6 to make it the case that 6 is such that one knows it *de re* to be the smallest perfect number.

I now suggest the following positive view of *de re* propositional attitudes toward non-negative integers. Suppose n is a non-negative integer. Let A be the set of propositions such that p is a member if and only if, in English or in some extension of English there is a numeral α that designates n and there is a predicative expression Φ that expresses the property of being F and ⌜α is Φ⌝ expresses p. I will argue below that, perhaps surprisingly, A has more than one member. I suggest that n is such that *J* believes it *de re* to be F if and only if he believes at least one member of A.[18] Dictionary definitions of the term 'numeral' seem surprisingly unspecific; e.g., Webster's *New World Dictionary of the American Language* gives "a figure, letter or word, or a group of any of these, expressing a number.[19] But does '8 + 3' "express" a number? Does 'the smallest perfect number'? To avoid misunderstanding, I stipulate that I count as numerals single Arabic, Roman, etc., numerals, such as '5' and 'V', and strings of them such as '523' or 'XII', but not such mathematical expressions as '5 + 8', '10^3', '−2', '⅔', or '$\sqrt{64}$', or descriptions such as 'the smallest perfect number.'

My account is immune to the objections I made to Kaplan, Sosa, and Chisholm, and it seems to accord with most of our (or at least with most of my) central intuitions about when a non-negative integer is such that it is believed *de re* by someone to have a property. For example, if *J* believes that 6 is the smallest perfect number, my account holds that it follows that 6 is believed *de re* by *J* to be the smallest perfect number and hence that there is a number that he believes *de re* to be the smallest perfect numbers. But my account denies that, if *J* believes that the smallest perfect number is the smallest perfect number, it follows that 6 is such that he believes it *de re* to be the smallest perfect number or that there is a number that he believes *de re* to be the smallest perfect number. This provides the required "inequalitarian attitude" toward different standard names for a number.

But what is special about what is expressed by numerals as compared with other standard names? I cannot answer this precisely, but, imprecisely, there seems to be a sense in which a numeral *directly* specifies the position of its referent in the progression of numbers. Of course, a standard name that is a mathematical description such as 'the smallest perfect number' also specifies (in the sense of expressing information that logically determines) the position of its referent. But the position of what a numeral refers to can be known directly simply by understanding the numeral, without having any mathematical knowledge beyond what is necessary to understand the numeral. I do not mean to suggest that one can understand '75' without having the concepts of any other numbers. '75' can be understood only in the context of a system of numbers, and knowing and understanding a system of numerals seems to be a matter of knowing how to generate in order the progression of numerals and knowing how to count transitively (e.g. to count marbles) in accord with the progression.

No account of *de re* propositional attitudes is likely to accord with *all* our intuitions. Some interesting issues are raised by the following possible counterexample to my account. In the binary system '1100' designates the same number that '12' designates in the decimal system. Suppose *J* knows and understands (in the sense I have indicated) both the binary system and the decimal system. A problem may seem to arise from the fact that such understanding of these two systems does not entail knowledge of all cross-system number-identity statements. (To avoid ambiguity, when I use numerals in their binary-system senses, I will follow them with the subscript '2'. I will leave without subscripts numerals used in their decimal-system senses, although it would be more egalitarian to give them a subscript too, such as '10'.) Suppose that J knows that 1100_2 is 1100_2, but does not know that 1100_2 is 12. On my account, 1100_2 is such that he knows it *de re* to be 1100_2. It follows that 12 is such that he knows it *de re* to be 1100_2. This may seem counterintuitive. Accordingly, it may be tempting to argue that this case shows that either my condition for exportation is too weak or my account of what it is to know and understand a system of numerals is too weak, or both. But I think this temptation should be resisted. Even if J has just as much experience and facility with the binary system as he (and the average American adult) has with the decimal system, he may still fail to know cross-system number identities, such as the proposition that $12 = 1100_2$. (This also shows that different numerals for the same number in different base systems do not always have the same sense, assuming a Fregean criterion for the individuation of senses. Hence the proposition that 12 is the number of Apostles and the proposition that 1100_2 is the number of Apostles are different propositions, which proves my contention three paragraphs back.) Blocking exportation in the present case would require exportation conditions that are either unacceptably arbitrary or so strong as to be rarely, if ever, satisfied. An example of the first sort of requirement would be to say there is something special about the decimal system, so that only numerals in that system can be exported. This is preposterous and would invite the tiresomely trendy charge of ethnocentrism. An implausibly strong condition would be to say that a numeral in its base x sense can be exported in contexts ascribing propositional attitudes to J only if, for systems of every base, he knows which numeral in that base system designates the same number that α designates in the base x system.

These remarks are reminiscent of Kaplan's discussion of identity statements involving vivid names.[20] This is not surprising. Any requirement that no identity statement involving exportable names be doubted will require either unreasonably high standards for exportation (either by requiring tremendous amounts of information for exportation or by restricting exportation to logically proper names of objects of acquaintance) or will require arbitrary, ad hoc restrictions on exportation.

This account can be easily adapted to negative integers as follows: Suppose n is a negative integer. Let B be the set of propositions such that p is a member if and only if, in English or in some extension of English, there is a numeral α such that $\ulcorner -\alpha \urcorner$ designates n and there is a predicative expression Φ such that Φ expresses the property of being F, and $\ulcorner -\alpha$ is $\Phi \urcorner$ expresses p. Then negative whole number n is such that J believes it *de re* to be F if and only if he believes at least one member of B.[21] I will not suggest conditions for *de re* propositional attitudes toward other sorts of numbers. My intuitions are not firm enough to support accounts for these cases.

NOTES

1. W. V. O. Quine, "Quantifiers and Propositional Attitudes," in *The Ways of Paradox* (New York: Random House, 1966), p. 184.
2. An interesting defense of this view in the face of the causal theory of knowledge is given by Mark Steiner in "Platonism and the Causal Theory of Knowledge," *Journal of Philosophy* 70 (1973): 57–66. See also Mark Steiner, "Mathematics, Explanation and Scientific Knowledge," *Nous* 12 (1978): 17–28; and Mark Steiner, *Mathematical Knowledge* (Ithaca: Cornell University Press, 1975).
3. R. M. Chisholm, "Believing and Intentionality: A Reply to Mr. Luce and Mr. Sleigh," *Philosophy and Phenomenological Research* (1968): 266–69.
4. David Kaplan, "Quantifying In," in *Words and Objections: Essays on the Work of W. V. Quine*, ed. Donald Davidson and Jaakko Hintikka (Dordrecht, Holland: Reidel, 1969), pp. 206–42.
5. Ibid., p. 223.
6. Ibid., p. 241 n. 22.
7. Ibid., p. 225.
8. Ibid., p. 221.
9. Quine, "Reply to Professor Marcus," in *The Ways of Paradox*, p. 182.
10. Ernest Sosa, "Propositional Attitudes *De Dicto* and *De Re*," *Journal of Philosophy* 67 (1970): 887.
11. Ibid., p. 888.
12. R. M. Chisholm, *Person and Object* (La Salle, Ill.: Open Court, 1976), p. 169.
13. Ibid.
14. Ibid.
15. Ibid.
16. Ibid., p. 168.
17. Ibid., pp. 170–71.
18. I am indebted to Ernest Sosa for advice about how to state this condition.
19. *Webster's New World Dictionary of the American Language*, College Edition (New York: World Publishing Co., 1966) p. 1002.
20. See Kaplan, "Quantifying In," pp. 233–34.
21. See note 18.

Facts of the Matter*

W. V. QUINE
Harvard University

It was emphasized by rationalists and empiricists alike that inquiry should begin with clear ideas. I agree about the clarity, but I balk at ideas. The British empiricists themselves balked at abstract ideas. *Nihil in mente,* they declared in their orotund British measures, *quod non prius in sensu.* They echoed their nominalist ancestors, for whom abstract ideas were *flatus vocis*—words, words, words.

What then about concrete ideas? Even a strictly sensory idea is elusive unless it is reinforced by language. This point was made by Wittgenstein. Unaided by language, we might treat a great lot of sensory events as recurrences of one and the same sensation, simply because of a similarity between each and the next; and yet there can have been a serious cumulative slippage of similarity between the latest of these events and the earliest of them. But if we have learned society's word for the sensation, then social intercourse will arrest the drift and keep us in line. We will be saved by the statistical fact that the speakers have not all drifted in the same direction.

Let us therefore recognize that the whole idea idea, abstract and concrete, is a frail reed indeed. We must seek a firm footing rather in words. The point was urged by John Horne Tooke only shortly after Hume's time, in 1786. Tooke held that Locke's essay could be much improved by substituting the word 'word' everywhere for the word 'idea.' What is thereby gained in firmness is attended by no appreciable loss in scope, since ideas without words would have come to little in any event. We think mostly in words, and we report our thoughts wholly in words. Let us then take one leaf from the old-time philosophy and another from John Horne Tooke. Philosophical inquiry should begin with the clear, yes; but with clear words.

* From *American Philosophy: From Edwards to Quine,* edited and with an Introduction by Robert W. Shahan and Kenneth R. Merrill. Copyright 1977 by the University of Oklahoma Press.

And what words are those? It will not do to say that they are the words that express clear ideas, or the words that clearly express ideas, for we are fleeing the idea idea. For a standard of clarity of language we must look rather to the social character of language and the use of language in communication. Bypassing the idea idea, we can still do something with clarity of communication. The vehicle of communication is the sentence, and one mark of clarity of communication is agreement as to the truth of the sentence. This is a very fallible criterion, but it is a beginning. Let us see what we can do to improve it.

If one party affirms a sentence and the other party assents, this gives little evidence of communication; for a purely random verdict would be affirmative half the time. However, there is some safety in numbers. Instead of relativizing our clarity criterion to two communicants, we may relativize it to increasing sectors of the speech community. We might consider what proportion of the community would be prepared to agree to the truth or falsity of a sentence, and we might take this figure as a measure of the clarity of the sentence.

This is better, but it still will not do. One difficulty is that there are cults, fads, and slogans that can sweep a community, prompting widespread agreement to the truth of sentences that a clear thinker would not rate as clear in the slightest. Another and opposite difficulty is that people can disagree regarding the truth of a sentence even when the sentence would be said to be clear. Now both of these difficulties can be met by appealing once again to numbers: by appealing to what Mill called concomitant variation.

For this purpose we direct our attention to a special sort of sentences, *occasion* sentences. These are the sentences that admit of verdicts and truth values not once for all but from one occasion of utterance to another, depending on what is going on in the neighborhood. They are sentences like 'It's raining', 'This is red', 'That's his uncle', 'He owes me money', 'There goes a rabbit'. Historical truths are not among them, nor are scientific hypotheses, nor credos, nor slogans. Now we might measure the clarity of an occasion sentence by the readiness of witnesses to agree in their verdicts on it from occasion to occasion. By this standard 'It's raining' and 'This is red' rate high; 'There goes a rabbit' not quite so high; 'That's his uncle' rates lower; 'He owes me money' lower still. There are three possible responses—assent, dissent, and abstention—and we may also distinguish degrees of hesitation. The great value of this standard of clarity lies in its linking of language to nonlinguistic reality.

The occasion sentences that pass this clarity test with high marks are what I call observation sentences. They often take the form simply of single nouns or adjectives—'Rabbit', 'Raining'—but for our purposes they are best thought of still as sentences, admitting of assent or dissent in the light of each present local situation. They are expressions that we have learned to associate with publicly observable concurrent circumstances. Previous speakers have taught us some of these expressions by direct conditioning to the circumstances. They are circumstances which, thanks to their public character, can be appreciated jointly by us and our teachers. Some of these observational expressions also are learned indirectly by some of us, through explanations in other words; but all could be learned in the direct way, such is their observational character. They are our introduction to language, for they are the expressions that we can learn to use without learning to use others first. It is through them that language and science imbibe their empirical content. It is back to or toward them, also, that a scientist reverts when he is mustering evidence for a disputed hypothesis; for the distinctive trait of an observation sentence is that present witnesses will usually agree about it on the spot.

Earlier I made Wittgenstein's point: how public language anchors experience, arresting drift. Now we are noting the converse: how public experience anchors language. The observation sentence is the anchor line.

I remarked that the use of an observation sentence often is and always could be acquired directly by conditioning. This process is also called induction. By either name it is the learning process at its simplest. If an event resembles an earlier one, the subject tends to expect its sequel to resemble the sequel of the earlier one. The expectation hinges thus on similarity in some sense—similarity by the subject's own lights. This relation is one of subjective similarity, and no significance need be sought for it apart from the consequent inductive expectations themselves. From a behavioral point of view a subject's expectations are shown by his overt behavior, and his similarity standards are shown by the pattern of his expectations.

Expectations are in large part fulfilled, despite the subjectivity of similarity standards; ours is a fairly friendly world. Evolutionary biology explains this by the fact that those standards are largely innate and thus favored by natural selection according to their survival value.

Primitive inductive learning is evident in the acquisition of various observation sentences. To acquire an observation sentence is to learn when to expect a veteran speaker to approve one's utterance of it, or to assent to it on his own account. This can be learned from sample instances by induction: by extrapolating to further cases along lines of subjective similarity. These linguistic inductions tend to be highly successful—more so still than the general run of inductions in our fairly friendly world. The reason is that, whereas one's inductions regarding nature owe their success only to a rough congruity between one's similarity standards and the trend of events in nature, on the other hand one's inductions regarding the veteran speaker's assent to the observation sentence owe their success to a sharing of similarity standards by the speaker and oneself. Heredity, environment, and social interaction have fostered such sharing of similarity standards to a high degree.

Direct conditioning or simple induction does not suffice for the acquisition of language generally. The learning process has to be more elaborate when we move on to grammatical constructions, to past and future tenses, to conditionals and conjecturals and metaphors, and to theoretical and abstract terms. It is evident that these further linguistic structures are based, however precariously, on the observational vocabulary that was learned by direct confrontation and simple conditioning. The superstructure is cantilevered outward from that foundation by imitation and analogy, by trial and error. In the course of mastering it we may check up now and again by noting the reaction of the listener. But it is in the observational vocabulary that language makes its principal contact with experience. It is this part of language that we first learn to apply, and to which we retreat when a check point is needed.

The situations that command assent to a given observation sentence will not be quite alike. They will be similar by our lights and by the lights of other speakers. But we can count on a curious tolerance of spatial reorientation in these similarity standards. We can see why if we reflect that the language learner and his informant are not situated eye to eye. They see things from unlike angles, receiving somewhat unlike presentations. The learner is thus made to associate with his presentation a word or occasion sentence that was elicited from the informant by a somewhat different presentation. It will have to be a versatile word or sentence indifferently applicable throughout a whole group of presentations.

My talking of observation sentences rather than observation terms is a matter of first things first. We can learn to assent to and dissent from observation sentences as wholes, under appropriate stimulatory conditions, with no thought of what sentences or parts of sentences to count as terms or what objects to count them as referring to. And now what happens when at last we can be said to use some of these sentences or parts of sentences as terms denoting some sort of supposed objects?

The main thing to settle, in the way of fixing the objects, is their individuation: we have to fix standards of sameness and difference. Now it is clear that at this point little or no attention will be paid to differences of perspective; for we saw that such differences are bound to be transcended in the learning of words. What are posited as objects for the terms to refer to will be, primarily, objects that are counted identical under changes of perspective. This explains the primacy of bodies. If clarity can be ascribed to things as well as to words, then bodies are things at their clearest. If inquiry is to begin with what is clear, then let us begin as physicalists.

The move from sentences to terms is already a major step in language learning. On the one hand there is the simple observation sentence 'Rabbit', comparable to 'Red' or 'It's raining'; it commands assent in the presence of rabbits. On the other hand there is the term 'rabbit', which denotes the rabbits. A speaker may be said to have mastered this term, and to have achieved objective reference, only when he has learned to subject the term to all the grammatical apparatus of particles and constructions that go to implement objective reference: the apparatus of singular and plural, of definite and indefinite articles, of pronominal cross reference, of identity and distinctness, and of counting. When he has come this far, he has risen above the primitive base afforded by observation sentences, and has ventured somewhat out onto the cantilevered superstructure. Language learning at this stage is beyond the reach of simple induction; it proceeds by imitation and analogy in more complicated ways.[1]

Various of the one-word observation sentences like 'Rabbit' and 'Apple', which were themselves learned in the simple inductive way, will now spawn terms in their likeness—terms denoting bodies. The terms are already theoretical. A body is conceived as retaining its identity over time between appearances. Whether we encounter the same body the next time around, the same apple, for instance, or only another one like it, is a question not to be settled by simple induction. It is settled, if at all, by inference from a network of hypotheses that we have internalized little by little in the course of acquiring the nonobservational superstructure of our language. These hypotheses are supported only indirectly by past observation: they owe their plausibility to our having inferred other consequences from them that were borne out by observation. Such is the continuing method of science: not simple induction, but the hypothetico-deductive method.

Bodies are basic to our way of thought, as objects go. They are the paradigmatic objects, clearer and more perspicuous than others. Imitation and analogy continue their work, however, not stopping with an ontology of bodies. Grammatical analogy between general terms and singular terms encourages us to treat a general term as if it designated a single object, and thus we come to posit a realm of objects for the general terms to designate: a realm of properties, or sets. What with the nominalizing also of verbs and clauses, a vaguely varied and very untidy ontology grows up.

The common man's ontology is vague and untidy in two ways. It takes in many purported objects that are vaguely or inadequately defined. But also, what is more significant, it is vague in its scope; we cannot even tell in general which of these vague things to ascribe to a man's ontology at all, which things to count him as assuming. Should we regard grammar as decisive? Does every noun demand some array of denotata? Surely not; the nominalizing of verbs is often a mere stylistic variation. But where can we draw the line?

It is a wrong question; there is no line to draw. Bodies are assumed, yes; they are the things, first and foremost. Beyond them there is a succession of dwindling analogies. Various expressions come to be used in ways more or less parallel to the use of the terms for bodies, and it is felt that corresponding objects are more or less posited, *pari passu*; but there is no purpose in trying to mark an ontological limit to the dwindling parallelism.

It is only our somewhat regimented and sophisticated language of science that has evolved in such a way as really to raise ontological questions. It is an object-oriented idiom. Any idiom purports to tell the truth, but this idiom purports, more specifically, to tell about objects. Its referential apparatus, the apparatus for referring to objects, is explicit; there is no question of a dwindling parallelism. Just what those objects are—what else besides bodies—is still as may be; but it becomes a significant question, and it can be variously answered in various scientific systems of the world.

The basic structure of the language of science has been isolated and schematized in a familiar form. It is the predicate calculus: the logic of quantification and truth functions. In representing it thus I do not mean to take issue with those quantum physicists who recommend a different logic of a non-truth-functional kind, but I set them aside in order not to complicate the picture. Also I do not mean to deprecate alternative formulations of standard logic, such as predicate-functor logic; but as long as these are intertranslatable with the classical predicate calculus, we lose nothing in adhering to the latter. For concreteness, then, let us adhere to it; for it is familiar.

Language thus regimented has a simple grammar. There is a lexicon of predicates. Each atomic sentence of the language consists of a predicate, say an n-place predicate, adjoined to n variables. The rest of the sentences are built up of the atomic ones by truth functions and quantification.

Thus the only singular terms are the variables, used for quantification. It would be all right to allow also names as further singular terms and to allow functors for building complex singular terms from the names and the variables. But we can pass over these further conveniences; for there are well-known ways of dispensing with them, however inconveniently, by systematic paraphrasing of contexts.

When language is thus regimented, its ontology comprises just the objects that the variables of quantification admit as values. Some of the turns of phrase in ordinary language that seem to involve novel sorts of objects will disappear under the regimentation. Still we must not expect to end up with bodies as the only values of the variables. Much of the positing of abstract objects that seems to go on in ordinary language proves to be gratuitous and eliminable, but much of it also proves valuable. How *sets* can pay their way is classically illustrated by the definition of the *closed iterate* of a two-place predicate. Ancestor, for instance, is the closed iterate of parent. Neither parenthood nor ancestry has to do with sets, but sets enable us to define ancestor in terms of parent. For every predicate in our language we can express also its closed iterate, if we allow ourselves to quantify over sets as values of our variables.

It must be emphasized that when we reckon the ontology as comprising just the values of the variables, we are assuming the strictly regimented notation: just predicates, variables, quantifiers, and truth functions. Admission of additional linguistic elements can upset this ontological standard. Thus suppose someone adopts outright an operator for forming the closed iterates of predicates, instead of defining it with help of an ontology of sets. Are we to say that he has saved on ontology? I say rather that he has shelved the ontological question by switching to a language that is not explicit on ontology. His ontology is indeterminate, except relative to some agreed translation of his notation into our regimented one.

Another way in which quantification over sets or numbers or other abstract objects can sometimes be avoided is by admitting a modal operator of necessity, if we can see our way to making appropriate sense of this device.[2] Here again we are presented not with an ontological saving but with a question of foreign exchange.

We have just been seeing how the values of the variables may understate the ontology in the presence of some foreign notations. Other foreign notations may work oppositely. If idioms of propositional attitude were admitted, such as 'x believes that p', then the variables might seem to overreach the ontology; for x can believe that $(\exists y)(y$ is a unicorn) without there being any unicorns. The ontological question for such a language, as for ordinary language generally, makes sense only relative to agreed translations into ontologically regimented notation. A language is not necessarily defective in being thus ontologically indecisive; it is just not a language of the object-oriented type.

Translation of ordinary language into the regimented idiom is not determinate. For some sentences there are various acceptable regimentations not equivalent to one another in point of ontology, and for some sentences there is no acceptable regimentation at all. In general this translation venture is significant only when undertaken systematically for a substantial corpus of sentences, a branch of science, rather than for stray sentences in isolation. Many sentences that seem from their grammatical form to talk of abstract objects of various sorts will be translated into regimented sentences that are innocent of those ontic commitments, for the translator will favor ontic economy where he can. Regiment as he will, however, he cannot make do with just bodies. By quantifying over classes he increases the yield of his apparatus, as illustrated by the closed iterates. By quantifying over numbers and functions he is able to make systematic use of measurement and thus to develop his scientific theory along quantitative lines.

These sets, numbers, and functions are posited, as denizens of the universe supplementary to the primordial bodies, in order to strengthen and simplify the over-all theory. To do so is not to repudiate physicalism. The physicalist does not insist on an exclusively corporeal ontology. He is content to declare bodies to be *fundamental* to nature in somewhat this sense: there is no difference *in the world* without a difference in the positions or states of bodies. I say 'in the world' so as not to include differences between abstract objects, as of mathematics.

My qualification 'in the world' may seem to deprive the statement of content, as if to say that there is no difference in the *physical* world without a difference in the positions or states of bodies. I may better phrase the matter in terms of *change*: there is no change without a change in the positions or states of bodies. This serves still to exempt mathematical objects, which are changeless.

One application of this physicalist principle is to dispositions. There is no change even in unactualized dispositions without physical change, no difference in dispositions without physical difference. But the main thrust of the doctrine, of course, is its bearing on mental life. If a man were twice in the same physical state, then, the physicalist holds, he would believe the same things both times, he would have the same thoughts, and he would have all the same unactualized dispositions to thought and action. Where positions and states of bodies do not matter, there is no fact of the matter.

It is not a reductionist doctrine of the sort sometimes imagined. It is not a utopian dream of our being able to specify all mental events in physiological or microbiological terms. It is not a claim that such correlations even exist, in general, to be discovered; the groupings of events in mentalistic terms need not stand in any systematic relation to biological groupings.[3] What it does say about the life of the mind is that there is no mental difference without a physical difference. Most of us nowadays are so ready to agree to this principle that we fail to sense its magnitude. It is a way of saying that the fundamental objects are the physical objects. It accords physics its rightful place as the basic natural science without venturing any dubious hopes of reduction of other disciplines. It has further important implications that we tend not to see.

If there is no mental difference without a physical difference, then there is pointless ontological extravagance in admitting minds as entities over and above bodies; we lose nothing by applying mentalistic predicates directly to persons as bodies, much in the manner of everyday usage. We still have two species of predicates, mental and physical, but both sorts apply to bodies. Thus it is that the physicalist comes out with an ontology of just physical objects, together with the sets or other abstract objects of mathematics; no minds as additional entities.

Note that the situation is not symmetrical. The converse move of dispensing with bodies in favor of minds is not open to us, for we would not allow that there is no physical difference in the world without a mental difference—not unless we were idealists.

I have been talking easily of physical predicates, physical differences, as over against mental ones. Until this notion is better defined or delimited, my formulations of physicalism are inadequate. Thus take the dictum 'no mental difference without a physical difference.' We must not explain 'physical difference' merely as any difference between bodies; this would trivialize the dictum. For, even if we were to recognize minds as entities distinct from bodies and merely associated with them, it would be trivial to say that there is no difference in states of mind without a difference in the associated bodies. The bodies differ at least to the extent of being associated with minds that are in those different states.

Thus the dictum tells us nothing until we define 'physical difference' more narrowly. Similarly for my preceding versions of physicalism: 'no difference in the world without a difference in the positions or states of bodies', 'no change without a change in the positions or states of bodies'. We must say what to count as states of bodies.

One major motivation of physics down the centuries might be said to have been just that: to say what counts as a physical difference, a physical trait, a physical state. The question can be put more explicitly thus: what minimum catalogue of states would be sufficient to justify us in saying that there is no change without a change in positions or states?

Thus take primitive atomic theory. Atoms are posited, small analogues of the primordial bodies. Here, as in the positing of sets or other mathematical objects, one motive is simplification of the over-all system of the world. But here we may recognize also the deeper motive of fixing the notion of a physical difference, a physical state. According to primitive atomic theory with its uniform atoms, any physical difference is a difference in the number or arrangement or trajectories of the component atoms.

Physicalism, on these terms, would say that where there are no such atomic differences there are no differences in matters of fact—and in particular no mental differences. But it would never have held out hope of actually describing mental states or even most gross bodily states in terms of the number, arrangement, and trajectories of atoms.

Atoms have since given way to a bewildering variety of elementary particles. Latter-day physicists have been finding even that the very notion of particle is inappropriate at points; paradoxes of identification and individuation arise. There are indications that the utility of the particle model, the extrapolation of the primordial body into the very small, is now marginal at best. A field theory may be more to the point: a theory in which various states are directly ascribed in varying degrees to various regions of space-time. Thus at last bodies themselves go by the board—bodies that were the primordial posits, the paradigmatic objects most clearly and perspicuously beheld. *Sic transit gloria mundi.*

What then is the brave new ontology? There are the real numbers, needed to measure the intensity of the various states, and there are the space-time regions to which the states are ascribed. By identifying each space-time point with a quadruple of real or complex numbers according to an arbitrary system of coordinates, we can explain the space-time regions as sets of quadruples of numbers. The numbers themselves can be constructed within set theory in known ways, and indeed in pure set theory; that is, set theory with no individuals as ground elements, set theory devoid of concrete objects. The brave new ontology is, in short, the purely abstract ontology of pure set theory, pure mathematics.[4] At first we just tolerated these abstract objects as convenient adjuncts to our central corporeal ontology because of the power and simplification that they contributed. In the end, like the camel who got his nose under the tent, they have taken over.

A lesson to be drawn from this debacle is that ontology is not what mainly matters. When bodies first came into my story I warned that they, even they, were theoretical. All theoretical entities are here strictly on sufferance; and all entities are theoretical. What were observational were not terms but observation sentences. Sentences, in their truth or falsity, are what run deep; ontology is by the way.

The point gains in vividness when we reflect on the multiplicity of possible interpretations of any consistent formal system. For, consider again our standard regimented notation, with a lexicon of interpreted predicates and some fixed range of values for the variables of quantification. The sentences of this language that are true remain true under countless reinterpretations of the predicates and revisions of the range of values of the variables. Indeed any range of the same size can be made to serve by a suitable reinterpretation of the predicates. If the range of values is infinite, any infinite range can be made to serve; this is the Skolem-Löwenheim theorem. The true sentences stay true under all such changes.

Perhaps then our primary concern belongs with the truth of sentences and with their truth conditions, rather than with the reference of terms. If we adopt this attitude, questions of reference and ontology become incidental. Ontological stipulations can play a role in the truth conditions of theoretical sentences, but a role that could be played as well by any number of alternative ontological stipulations. The indecisiveness of ordinary language toward questions of reference is the more readily excused.

What now of physicalism? To profess materialism, after all this, would seem grotesquely inappropriate; but physicalism, reasonably reformulated, retains its vigor and validity. Our last previous formulation came to this: there is no difference in the world without a difference in the number or arrangement or trajectories of atoms. But if we make the drastic ontological move last contemplated, all physical objects go by the board—atoms, particles, all—leaving only pure sets. The principle of physicalism must thereupon be formulated by reference not to physical objects but to physical vocabulary. Let us take stock of the vocabulary.

Our language still has the standard regimented form; there are the truth functions, the quantifiers and their variables, and a lexicon of predicates. The variables now range over the pure sets. The predicates comprise the two-place mathematical predicate 'ε' of set membership and, for the rest, physical predicates. These will serve to ascribe physical states to space-time regions, each region being a set of quadruples of numbers. Presumably regions are always wanted rather than single points—sometimes because of indeterminacy at the quantum level and sometimes for more obvious reasons, as in the case of temperature or entropy. A state may be ascribed outright, for example leftward spin, or quantitatively, for example temperature. In the one case the form of predication is 'Fx', combining a one-place predicate and a variable whose relevant values are sets of quadruples of numbers. In the other case the form is 'Fxy', combining a two-place predicate and two variables. The relevant values of one of the variables are again sets of quadruples of numbers, and those of the other variable are single real numbers measuring the quantitative state. Thus this two-place predicate 'F' might read 'the temperature in degrees Kelvin of the region . . . is . . . .' Also there may by polyadic predicates ascribing relations, absolute or quantitative, to pairs of regions, or to triples, or higher. In any event the lexicon of physical predicates will be finite, such being the way of lexica.

A nice contrast emerges, incidentally, between physical law and physical description. The laws favor no specific space-time regions as values of the variables. Thus they are independent of the parochial specificity that goes into our choice of spatio-temporal coordinates. The specificity shows itself only in more mundane pursuits such as astronomy, geography, and history, where it is welcome.

But this is by the way. What now is the claim of physicalism? Simply that there is no difference in matters of fact without a difference in the fulfillment of the physical-state predicates by space-time regions. Again this is not reductionism in any strong sense. There is no presumption that anyone be in a position to come up with the appropriate state predicates for the pertinent regions in any particular case.

This formulation, 'fulfillment of physical-state predicates by space-time regions,' is decidedly unfinished. The space-time regions are sets of quadruples of numbers, determined according to some system of coordinates that I have not paused over. The physical-state predicates are the predicates of some specific lexicon, which I have only begun to imagine, and which physicists themselves are not ready to enumerate with conviction. Thus I have no choice but to leave my formulation of physicalism incomplete. I suggested before that a major purpose of physics has been to find a minimum catalogue of states—elementary states, let us call them—such that there is no change without a change in respect of them. This is true equally of physics today.

In conclusion I want to relate physicalism to my perennial criticisms of mentalistic semantics. Readers have supposed that my complaint is ontological; it is not. If in general I could make satisfactory sense of declaring two expressions to be synonymous, I would be more than pleased to recognize an abstract object as their common meaning. The method is familiar: I would define the meaning of an expression as the set of its synonyms. Where the trouble lies, rather, is in the two-place predicate of synonymy itself; it is too desperately wanting in clarity and perspicuity.

Translation proceeds, presumably, by interlinguistic equivalence of synonymy of sentences. So, in order to make the problem of synonymy graphic, I developed a thought experiment in radical translation—that is, in the translation of an initially unknown language on the strength of behavioral data.[5] I argued that the translations would be indeterminate, in the case of sentences at any considerable remove from observation sentences. They would be indeterminate in this sense: two translators might develop independent manuals of translation, both of them compatible with all speech behavior and all dispositions to speech behavior, and yet one manual would offer translations that the other translator would reject. My position was that either manual could be useful, but as to which was right and which wrong there was no fact of the matter.

My present purpose is not to defend this doctrine. My purpose is simply to make clear that I speak as a physicalist in saying there is no fact of the matter. I mean that both manuals are compatible with the fulfillment of just the same elementary physical states by space-time regions.

Radical translation proceeds in the light of observed behavior, and behavioral criteria will ordinarily decide in favor of one translation rather than another. When they do, there is emphatically a fact of the matter by microphysical standards; for clearly any difference in overt behavior, vocal or otherwise, reflects extravagant differences in the distribution of elementary physical states. On the other hand my doctrine of indeterminacy had to do with hypothetical manuals of translation both of which fitted all behavior. Since translators do not supplement their behavioral criteria with neurological criteria, much less with telepathy, what excuse could there be for supposing that the one manual conformed to any distribution of elementary physical states better than the other manual? What excuse, in short, for supposing there to be a fact of the matter?

We have here an illustration of what I consider the proper function of behaviorism. Mental states and events do not reduce to behavior, nor are they explained by behavior. They are explained by neurology, when they are explained. But their behavioral adjuncts serve to specify them objectively. When we talk of mental states or events subject to behavioral criteria, we can rest assured that we are not just bandying words; there is a physical fact of the matter, a fact ultimately of elementary physical states.

We learn mentalistic idioms, like other idioms, from elder speakers of our language, in distinctive and intersubjectively observable circumstances. Those circumstances differ from others in respect of the distribution, however inscrutable, of elementary physical states. As long as we use such an idiom in a form and in circumstances closely similar to the original ones, we communicate information; there is a fact of the matter. But our mentalistic idioms, like other idioms, go on growing and stretching by analogy. Factual content becomes meanwhile more tenuous and more elusive and can disappear altogether.

Thus consider the propositional attitudes; consider belief. There are unproblematical attributions of belief—unproblematical attributions even to dumb animals. Observation of behavior would normally prompt us to agree that the dog believes his master is coming, or that he believes the ball is under the sofa. When we attribute a belief about ancient history to someone, on the other hand, we are dependent on what he says—even though we are loath to equate belief with lip service. If the believer is a foreigner, our attribution may be subject also to the vagaries of translation of his testimony into our language. In some cases factual content is lacking; in others it is sparse and ill defined.

I do not advise giving up ordinary language, not even mentalistic language. But I urge awareness of its pitfalls. There is an instructive parallel between questions of reference, on the part of ordinary language, and questions of factuality. Let me recall what I said earlier when discussing ontology. Ordinary language is only loosely referential, and any ontological accounting makes sense only relative to an appropriate regimentation of language. The regimentation is not a matter of eliciting some latent but determinate ontological content of ordinary language. It is a matter rather of freely creating an ontology-oriented language that can supplant ordinary language in serving some particular purposes that one has in mind.

Now factuality is similar. Ordinary language is only loosely factual, and needs to be variously regimented when our purpose is scientific understanding. The regimentation is again not a matter of eliciting a latent content. It again is a free creation. We withdraw to a language which, though not limited to the assigning of elementary physical states to regions, is visibly directed to factual distinctions—distinctions that are unquestionably underlain by differences, however inscrutable, in elementary physical states. This demand is apt to be met by stressing the behavioral and the physiological.

Within these limits there is still much scope, of course, for better and worse. The terms that play a leading role in a good conceptual apparatus are terms that promise to play a leading role in causal explanation; and causal explanation is polarized. Causal explanations of psychology are to be sought in physiology, of physiology in biology, of biology in chemistry, and of chemistry in physics—in the elementary physical states.

NOTES

1. See W. V. O. Quine, *The Roots of Reference* (LaSalle, Ill.: Open Court, 1973), for a speculative account of the steps involved.

2. See Hilary Putnam, "Mathematics without Foundations," *Journal of Philosophy* 64 (1967) 5–22.

3. See Donald Davidson, "Mental Events," Lawrence Foster and J. W. Swanson, eds., *Experience and Theory* (Amherst: University of Massachusetts Press, 1970), pp. 79–101; "The Material Mind," P. Suppes et al., eds., *Logic, Methodology, and Philosophy of Science* 4 (Amsterdam: North-Holland Publishing Co., 1973), pp. 709–22.

4. I develop the point a little more fully in "Whither Physical Objects?" *Boston Studies in the Philosophy of Science* 39 (1976): 303–10.

5. In *Word and Object* (Cambridge: Technology Press of the Massachusetts Institute of Technology, 1960), chap. 2.

Publications of W. V. Quine

BOOKS

1934: *A System of Logistic.* Cambridge: Harvard, xii+204 pp.
1940: *Mathematical Logic.* New York: Norton, xii+344 pp.
    Emended 2d printing: Harvard, 1947.
    Revised edition: 1951.
    Paperback: New York: Harper Torchbook, 1962.
    Translations:
      Spanish by H. Pescador, Madrid: Ocidente, 1972.
      Polish by L. Koj, Warsaw: Panstwowe Wydanictwo, 1974.
    Excerpts reprinted: 1968: pp. 27–33 in Iseminger;[1]
                            1971: pp. 23–33 in Manicas;
                            1974: same in Zabeeh et al.
1941: *Elementary Logic.* Boston: Ginn, vi+170 pp.
    Revised edition: Harvard, 1966.
    Paperback: Harper Torchbook, 1965.
    Translations:
      Italian by F. Gana, Rome: Ubaldini, 1968.
      French by J. Largeault and B. St.-Sermin, Paris: Colin, 1972.
      Japanese by R. Tsueshita, Tokyo: Taishukan, 1972.
1944: *O Sentido da Nova Lógica*, São Paulo: Martins, xii+190 pp.
    Translation: Spanish by M. Bunge, Buenos Aires: Nueva Vision, 1958.
    Excerpts translated: 1943: pp. 140–144, 146–158, 179–183 in "Notes on existence and necessity," below.
1950: *Methods of Logic.* New York: Holt, xxii+272 pp.
    Revised edition: 1959 and London: Routledge, 1962.
    3d edition, revised and enlarged: Holt, 1972, and Routledge, 1974.
    Paperback: Routledge, 1974.
    Translations:

[1] See "Anthologies Where Articles Have Reappeared" below.

      Italian by M. Pacifico, Milan: Feltrinelli, 1960.
      Japanese by S. Nakamura and S. Ohmori, Tokyo: Iwanami, 1962.
      Spanish by M. Sacristán, Barcelona: Ariel, 1963.
      Hungarian by Urban J., Budapest: Akademiai Kiado, 1968.
      German by D. Siefkes, Frankfurt: Suhrkamp, 1969.
      French, 3d ed., by M. Clavelin, Paris: Colin, 1973.

Excerpts reprinted: 1971: Introduction in Manicas;
1973: same in MacKinnon.
1953: *From a Logical Point of View*. Harvard, vii + 184 pp.
Revised edition: 1961.
Paperback: New York: Harper Torchbook, 1963.
Translations:
Spanish by M. Sacristán, Barcelona: Ariel, 1963.
Italian by E. Mistretta, Rome: Astrolabio, 1966.
Polish by B. Stanosz, Panstwowe Wydanictwo, 1970.
Japanese by E. Mochimaru and K. Nakayama, Tokyo: Iwanami, 1972.
German by P. W. Bosch, Berlin: Ullstein, 1978.
Excerpts reprinted: 1961: pp. 47–64 in Saporta;
1964: same in Fodor and Katz;
1969: same in Olshewski;
1971: pp. 139–157 in Linsky;
1974: same in Zabeeh *et al.*
Excerpts translated: 1969: pp. 139–157 in Pasquinelli;
1973: pp. 47–64 in Eisenberg *et al.*;
1975: pp. 102–129, 139–159 in Stegmüller.
1977: pp. 130–138 in Sukale.
(For further excerpting see under component articles.)
1960: *Word and Object*. Cambridge: MIT, xvi + 294 pp.
Paperback: 1964.
Translations:
Spanish by M. Sacristan, Barcelona: Labor, 1968.
Italian by F. Mondadori, Milan: Saggiatore, 1970.
French by P. Gochet, Paris: Flammarian, 1978.
Portuguese by P. Alcoforado, Rio de Janeiro: Alves, 1978. German, Recklam, 1973.
Excerpts reprinted: 1960: pp. 5–8 in Sat. Rev. Lit., Aug. 6.
1964: pp. 170–176, 251–257 in Smart;
1967: pp. 270–276 in Rorty;
1968: pp. 157–161 in Iseminger;
1971: pp. 26–79 in Rosenberg and Travis;
1974: pp. 176–186 in Davidson and Harman.
Excerpts translated: 1973: pp. 214–216 in Simpson.
(For further excerpting see under "Meaning and translation.")
1963: *Set Theory and Its Logic*. Harvard, xvi + 359 pp.
Revised edition: 1969 and Taipeh: Mei Ya, 1969.
Paperback: Harvard, 1971.
Translations:
Japanese by A. Ohe and T. Fujimura, Tokyo: Iwanami, 1968.
German by A. Oberschelp, Brunswick: Vieweg, 1973.
1966: *The Ways of Paradox and Other Essays*. New York: Random House, x + 257 pp.
Paperback: 1968.
Translation: Italian by M. Shantambrogio, Milan: Saggiatore, 1975.
Revised and enlarged edition: Harvard, 1976.
1966: *Selected Logic Papers*. Random House, x + 250 pp.
Paperback: 1968.

1969: *Ontological Relativity and Other Essays.* New York: Columbia, x + 165 pp.
   Paperback: 1977.
   Translations:
   Spanish by M. Garrido, J. L. Blasco, and M. Bunge, Madrid: Tecnos, 1974.
   German, Stuttgart: Reklam, 1975.
   French by J. Largeault, Paris: Aubier, 1977.
   Portuguese, São Paulo: Abril, in preparation.
1970: *The Web of Belief* (with J. S. Ullian). New York: Random House, v + 95 pp.
   Revised edition: 1978.
1970: *Philosophy of Logic.* Englewood Cliff, N.J.: Prentice-Hall, xv + 109 pp.
   Paperback: 1970.
   Translations:
   Portuguese by T. A. Cannabrava, Rio de Janeiro: Zahar, 1972.
   Japanese by M. Yamashita, Tokyo: Iwanami, 1972.
   Spanish by M. Sacristán, Madrid: Alianza, 1973.
   German by H. Vetter, Stuttgart: Kohlhammer, 1973.
   French by J. Largeault, Paris: Aubier, 1975.
   Polish by H. Mortimer, Warsaw: Panstwowe Wydanictwo, 1977.
   Excerpts reprinted: 1972: pp. 35–43, 47–60 in Davidson and Harman
      (*Logic of Grammar*);
      1974: pp. 35–46 in Moravcsik.
   Excerpt translated: 1970: "Sur la tâche de la grammaire," below.
1974: *The Roots of Reference.* La Salle, Ill.: Open Court, xii + 151 pp.
   Translations:
   Spanish, Madrid: Occidente, in preparation.
   German, Frankfurt: Suhrkamp Verlag, 1976.
   Excerpt translated: 1972: "Reflexiones sohre el aprendizaje del lenguaje," below.

ARTICLES

1932: "A note on Nicod's postulate," Mind 41, pp. 345–350.
1933: "The logic of sequences," Summaries of Theses 1932 (Harvard), pp. 335–338.
   "A theorem in the calculus of classes," Jour. London Math. Soc. 8, pp. 89–95.
1934: "Ontological remarks on the propositional calculus," Mind 43, pp. 472–476.
   Reprinted 1966 in *The Ways of Paradox.*
   "A method of generating part of arithmetic without use of intuitive logic," Bull. Amer. Math. Soc. 40, pp. 753–761.
   Reprinted 1966 in *Selected Logic Papers.*
1936: "Concepts of negative degree," Proc. Nat. Acad. Sci. 22, pp. 40–45.
   "A theory of classes presupposing no canons of type," ibid., pp. 320–326.
   "A reinterpretation of Schönfinkel's logical operators," Bull. Amer. Math. Soc. 42, pp. 87–89.
   "Definition of substitution," ibid., pp. 561–569.
   Reprinted 1966 in *Selected Logic Papers.*
   "On the axiom of reducibility," Mind 45, pp. 498–500.

"Toward a calculus of concepts," Journal of Symbolic Logic 1, pp. 2–25.
"Set-theoretic foundations for logic," idid., pp. 45–57.
   Reprinted 1966 in *Selected Logic Papers*.
"Truth by convention," *Philosophical Essays for A. N. Whitehead* (O. H. Lee, ed., New York: Longmans), pp. 90–124.
   Reprinted 1949 in Feigl and Sellars;[1]
      1964 in Benacerraf and Putnam;
      1966 in *The Ways of Paradox*.
   Translated 1969 in Cuadernos de Filosofia (Buenos Aires).

1937: "New foundations for mathematical logic," Amer. Math. Monthly 44, pp. 70–80.
   Reprinted 1953 with additions in *From a Logical Point of View*.
   Translated 1969 in Pasquinelli.
"On derivability," Journal of Symbolic Logic 2, pp. 113–119.
"On Cantor's theorem," ibid., pp. 120–124.
"Logic based on inclusion and abstraction," ibid., pp. 145–152.
   Reprinted 1966 in *Selected Logic Papers*.

1938: "Completeness of the propositional calculus," Jour. Symbolic Logic 3, pp. 37–40.
   Reprinted 1966 in *Selected Logic Papers*.
"On the theory of types," Jour. Symbolic Logic 3, pp. 125–139.
   Reprinted 1970 in Klemke.

1939: "Designation and existence," Jour. Philosophy 36, pp. 701–709.
   Reprinted 1949 in Feigl and Sellars;
      1953 partly in *From a Logical Point of View*;
      1969 in Olshewsky.
   Translated 1972 in Sinnreich.
"Relations and reason," Technology Review 41, pp. 299–301, 324–332.
"A logistical approach to the ontological problem," Jour. Unified Science 9, pp. 84–89 (preprints only).
   Reprinted 1966 in *The Ways of Paradox*

1940: "Elimination of extra-logical postulates" (with Nelson Goodman), Jour. Symbolic Logic 5, pp. 104–109.
   Reprinted 1972 in Goodman.

1941: "Element and number," Jour. Symbolic Logic 6, pp. 135–149.
   Reprinted 1966 in *Selected Logic Papers*.
"Russell's paradox and others," Technology Review 44, pp. 16ff.
"Whitehead and the rise of modern logic," *Philosophy of A. N. Whitehead* (P. A. Schilpp, ed., LaSalle: Open Court), pp. 125–163.
   Reprinted 1966 in *Selected Logic Papers*.

1942: "Reply to Professor Ushenko," Jour. Philosophy 39, pp. 68–71.
"On existence conditions for elements and classes," Jour. Symbolic Logic 7, pp. 157–159.

1943: "Notes on existence and necessity," Jour. Philosophy 40, pp. 113–127. (Translation of part of *O Sentido da Nova Logica*.)
   Reprinted 1952 in Linsky;
      1953 partly in *From a Logical Point of View*.
   Translated 1972 in Sinnreich;
      1973 in Simpson.

1945: "On the logic of quantification," Jour. Symbolic Logic 10, pp. 1–12.

Reprinted 1966 in *Selected Logic Papers*.
"On ordered pairs," Jour. Symbolic Logic 10, pp. 95ff.
Reprinted 1966 in *Selected Logic Papers*, combined with next:
1946: "On relations as coexistence with classes," Jour. Symbolic Logic 11, pp. 71 f.
"Concatenation as a basis for arithmetic," ibid., pp. 105-114.
Reprinted 1966 in *Selected Logic Papers*.
"Os Estados Unidos e o ressurgimento da lógica," *Vida Intellectual nos Estados Unidos* (R. Amorim, ed., São Paulo: U.C.B.E.U.), pp. 267-286.
1947: "The problem of interpreting modal logic," Jour. Symbolic Logic 12, pp. 43-48.
Reprinted 1953 partly in *From a Logical Point of View*;
    1968 in Copi and Gould;
    1973 in Copi and Gould;
    1974 in Zabeeh et al.
Translated 1978 (Hungarian).
"On universals," Jour. Symbolic Logic 12, pp. 74-84.
Reprinted 1953 partly in *From a Logical Point of View*.
Translated 1975 in Stegmüller.
"Steps toward a constructive nominalism" (with Nelson Goodman), Jour. Symbolic Logic 12, pp. 97-122.
Reprinted 1969 in Bobbs-Merrill Reprint Series;
    1972 in Goodman.
Translated 1967 in Cellucci.
1948: "On what there is," Review of Metaphysics 2, pp. 21-38.
Reprinted 1951 in Aristotelian Soc. Suppl. Vol. 25, appendix;
    1952 in Linsky;
    1953 in *From a Logical Point of View*;
    1964 in Benacerraf and Putnam;
    1965 in Nagel and Brandt; partly in Baylis;
    1968 in Copi and Gould; in Iseminger; in Margolis;
        in Bobbs-Merrill Reprint Series;
    1970 in Myers; partly in Loux;
    1971 in Manicas;
    1972 in Landesman; in Feigl, Sellars, and Lehrer;
    1975 partly in Beck;
    1978 in Copi and Gould.
Translated 1958 in Krzywicki;
    1966 in Krishna (Hindi);
    1971 in Bar-On (Hebrew);
    1972 in Pereira;
    1977 in Stegmüller; as pamphlet (São Paulo: Abril); in Jánoska and Kauz;
    1978 (Hungarian).
1949: "On decidability and completeness," Synthese 7, pp. 441-446.
1950: "On natural deduction," Jour. Symbolic Logic 15, pp. 93-102.
"Identity, ostension, and hypostasis," Jour. Philosophy 47, pp. 621-633.
Reprinted 1953 in *From a Logical Point of View*.
Translated 1975 as pamphlet (Abril).
1951: "Ontology and ideology," Philosophical Studies 2, pp. 11-15.
Reprinted 1953 partly in *From a Logical Point of View*;

1972 in Feigl, Sellars, and Lehrer.
"On Carnap's views on ontology," Philosophical Studies 2, pp. 65–72.
Reprinted 1966 in *The Ways of Paradox*;
1972 in Feigl, Sellars, and Lehrer.
"Semantics and abstract objects," Proc. Amer. Acad. Arts and Sci. 80, pp. 90–96.
Reprinted 1953 partly in *From a Logical Point of View*.
Translated 1975 in Stegmüller.
"The ordered pair in number theory," *Structure, Method, and Meaning* (P. Henle et al., eds., New York: Liberal Arts), pp. 84–87.
"[Rejoinder to Mr. Geach] on what there is," Aristotelian Soc. Supp. 25, pp. 149–160.
"A simplification of games in extensive form" (with J. C. C. McKinsey and W. D. Krentel), Duke Mathematical Journal 18, pp. 885–900.
"On the consistency of 'New foundations,'" Proc. Nat. Acad. Sci. 3, pp. 538–540.
"Two dogmas of empiricism," Philosophical Review 60, pp. 20–43.
Reprinted 1951 in small part in "Semantics and abstract objects";
1953 in *From a Logical Point of View*;
1962 in Aiken and Barrett;
1963 in Lewis;
1964 in Ammerman; in Benacerraf and Putnam;
1965 partly in Nagel and Brandt;
1966 in Rorty;
1968 in Tillman, Berofsky, and O'Connor; in Bobbs-Merrill Reprint Series; partly in Margolis;
1969 in Olshewsky;
1970 in Harris and Severens;
1971 in Rosenberg and Travis; partly in Arner; partly in Munsat;
1972 in Morick; in Feigl, Sellars, and Lehrer;
1974 in Berlinski; partly in Fodor, Bever, and Garrett; in Zabeeh et al.;
1976 in Harding.
Translated 1964 in Marc-Wogau;
1966 in Krishna (Hindi);
1972 in Sinnreich;
1974 in Pârvu;
1975 as pamphlet (Abril).

1952: "On an application of Tarski's theory of truth," Proc. Nat. Acad. Sci. 38, pp. 430–433.
Reprinted 1966 in *Selected Logic Papers*.
Preface to Joseph Clark, *Conventional Logic and Modern Logic* (Woodstock), pp. v–vii.
Reprinted 1971 in Bynum.
"The problem of simplifying truth functions," Amer. Math. Monthly 59, pp. 521–531.
Reprinted 1973 in Swartzlander.
"Some theorems on definability and decidability" (with Alonzo Church), Jour. Symbolic Logic 17, pp. 179–187.

"On reduction to a symmetric relation" (with William Craig), ibid., p. 188.
1953: "On w-inconsistency and a so-called axiom of infinity," ibid. 18, pp. 119–124.
Reprinted 1966 in *Selected Logic Papers*.
"On a so-called paradox," Mind 62, pp. 65–67.
Reprinted 1966 in *The Ways of Paradox*.
"Mr. Strawson on logical theory," Mind 62, pp. 433–451.
Reprinted 1966 in *The Ways of Paradox*;
1968 in Copi and Gould.
Translated 1977 (Hungarian).
"On mental entities," Proc. Amer. Acad. Arts and Sci. 80, pp. 198–203.
Reprinted 1966 in *The Ways of Paradox*;
Reprinted 1969 in O'Connor.
"Two theorems about truth functions," Boletín Soc. Matemática Mexicana 10, pp. 64–70.
Translated 1953 ibid.
Reprinted 1966 in *Selected Logic Papers*.
"Three grades of modal involvement," Proc. XI International Congress of Philosophy 14, pp. 65–81.
Reprinted 1966 in *The Ways of Paradox*.
1954: "Interpretations of sets of conditions," Jour. Symbolic Logic 19, pp. 97–102.
Reprinted 1966 in *Selected Logic Papers*.
"Quantification and the empty domain," Jour. Symbolic Logic 19, pp. 177–179.
Reprinted 1966 in *Selected Logic Papers*.
Translated 1976 in Bencivenga.
"Reduction to a dyadic predicate," Jour. Symbolic Logic 19, pp. 180–182.
Reprinted 1966 in *Selected Logic Papers*.
1955: "A proof procedure for quantification theory," Jour. Symbolic Logic 20, pp. 141–149.
Reprinted 1966 in *Selected Logic Papers*.
"A way to simplify truth functions," Amer. Math. Monthly 62, pp. 627–631.
Reprinted 1973 in Swartzlander.
"On Frege's way out," Mind 64, pp. 145–159.
Reprinted 1966 in *Selected Logic Papers*;
1969 in Klemke.
1956: "On formulas with valid cases," Jour. Symbolic Logic 21, p. 148.
"Unification of universes in set theory," ibid., pp. 267–279.
"Quantifiers and propositional attitudes," Jour. Philosophy 53, pp. 177–187.
Reprinted 1966 in *The Ways of Paradox*;
1971 in Linsky;
1972 in Marras;
1974 in Davidson and Harman.
Translated 1973 in Simpson.
1957: "Logic, symbolic," Encyclopedia Americana.
Reprinted 1966 in *Selected Logic Papers*.
"The scope and language of science," Brit. Jour. Phil. of Sci. 8, pp. 1–17.

Preprinted 1955 in Leary with corruption of text.
Reprinted 1966 in *The Ways of Paradox*.
Translated 1969 in Pasquinelli;
1973 in Diánoia (Mexico);
1979 in AMR Info (Vienna).

1958: "Speaking of objects," Proc. and Addresses Amer. Phil. Assn. 31, pp. 5-22.
Reprinted 1959 in Krikorian and Edel;
1960 partly in *Word and Object*;
1964 in Fodor and Katz;
1966 in Kurtz;
1969 in *Ontological Relativity and Other Essays*.
Translated 1960 in Bunge;
1969 in Pasquinelli.
"The philosophical bearing of modern logic," *Philosophy in the Mid-Century* (R. Klibansky, ed.; Florence: Nuova Italia), pp. 3f.
Translated 1969 in Pasquinelli.

1959: "Meaning and translation," *On Translation* (R. A. Brower, ed., Harvard), pp. 148-172.
Reprinted 1960 in large part in *Word and Object*;
1964 in Fodor and Katz;
1969 in Olshewsky;
1971 partly in Rosenberg and Travis;
1972 in Morick;
1974 in Berlinski.
Translated 1973 in Bonomi;
1977 in Sukale.
"On cores and prime implicants of truth functions," Amer. Math. Monthly 66, pp. 755-760.
Reprinted 1966 in *Selected Logic Papers*.

1960: "Posits and reality," *Basis of the Contemporary Philosophy* 5 (S. Uyeda, ed., Tokyo), pp. 391-400.
Translated 1960 ibid.;
1964 in Rivista di Filosofia.
Reprinted 1966 in *The Ways of Paradox*;
1969 in Landesman;
1973 in Grandy.
"Variables explained away," Proc. Amer. Phil. Soc. 104, pp. 343-347.
Reprinted 1966 in *Selected Logic Papers*.
"Carnap and logical truth," Synthese 12, pp. 350-374.
Preprinted 1956 partly in Hook.
Reprinted 1962 in Kazemier and Vuysje;
1963 in Schilpp;
1966 in *The Ways of Paradox*;
1972 in Feigl, Sellars, and Lehrer;
1979 in Bennacerraf and Putnam.
Translated 1957 in Rivista di Filosofia.

1961: "Reply to Professor Marcus," Synthese 13, pp. 323-330.
Reprinted 1963 in Boston Studies in Philosophy of Science;
1966 in *The Ways of Paradox*;
1968 in Copi and Gould;

1978 in Copi and Gould.
"Logic as a source of syntactical insights," Proc. of Symposia in Applied Math, 12, pp. 1-5.
> Reprinted 1966 in *The Ways of Paradox*;
>> 1974 in Davidson and Harman.
> Translated 1966 in Langages (Paris).

"A basis for number theory in finite classes," Bull. Amer. Math. Soc. 67, pp. 391f.

1962: "Paradox," Scientific American 206, no. 4, pp. 84-95.
> Reprinted 1966 in *The Ways of Paradox*;
>> 1968 in Kline.
> Translated 1969 in Pasquinelli.

"Le mythe de la signification," *La Philosophie Analytique* (Cahiers de Royaumont IV, Paris: Minuit), pp. 139-169.

1963: "On simple theories of a complex world," Synthese 15, pp. 107-111.
> Reprinted 1964 in Gregg and Harris;
>> 1966 in *The Ways of Paradox*; in Foster and Martin.

1964: "On ordinals" (with Hao Wang), Bull. Amer. Math. Soc. 70, pp. 297f.

"Implicit definition sustained," Jour. Philosophy 61, pp. 71-74.
> Reprinted 1966 in *The Ways of Paradox*;
>> 1968 in Bobbs-Merrill Reprint Series.
> Translated 1964 in Rivista di Filosofia.

"Ontological reduction and the world of numbers," Jour. Philosophy 61, pp. 209-216.
> Reprinted 1966 in *The Ways of Paradox*.

"Necessary truth," Voice of America Forum Lectures, Philosophy of Science Series, no. 7; 7 pp.
> Reprinted 1966 in *The Ways of Paradox*;
>> 1967 in Morgenbesser.

"The foundations of mathematics," Scientific American 211, no. 3, pp. 113-116, 118, 120, 122, 124, 127.
> Reprinted 1966 in *The Ways of Paradox*;
>> 1968 in Kline.

"Henry Maurice Sheffer," Harvard University Gazette 60, no. 14.
> Reprinted 1965 in Proc. and Addresses of Amer. Phil. Assn.

"Frontières dans la théorie logique," Etudes Philosophiques, pp. 191-208.

1965: "J. L. Austin, comment," Jour. Philosophy 62, pp. 509f. (A résumé; see 1969.)
> Translated 1975 in Muguerza.

1966: "Russell's ontological development," Jour. Philosophy 63, pp. 657, 667.
> Reprinted 1967 in Schoenman;
>> 1968 in Klibansky;
>> 1970 in Klemke;
>> 1972 in Pears.

1967: "On a suggestion of Katz," Jour. Philosophy 64, pp. 52-54.
> Reprinted 1970 in Woods and Sumner.

"Thoughts on reading Father Owens," Proc. VII Inter-Amer. Congress of Philosophy 1, pp. 60-63.

Introductory notes, *From Frege to Gödel* (J. van Heijenoort, ed.; Harvard), pp. 150-152, 216f., 355-357.

1968: Comments, *Problems in the Philosophy of Science* (I. Lakatos and A. Musgrave, eds.; Amsterdam: North-Holland), pp. 161–163, 200f., 223.
Replies, Synthese 19, pp. 264–321.
Reprinted 1969 in Davidson and Hintikka.
Translated 1973 partly in Simpson.
"Ontological relativity," Jour. Philosophy 65, pp. 185–212.
Reprinted 1969 in *Ontological Relativity and Other Essays*;
1971 partly in Steinberg and Jakobovits.
"Propositional objects," Critica 2, no. 5, pp. 3–22.
Reprinted 1969 in *Ontological Relativity and Other Essays*.
"Existence and quantification," L'Âge de la Science 1, pp. 151–164.
Reprinted 1969 in Margolis; in *Ontological Relativity and Other Essays*.

1969: "Natural kinds," *Essays in Honor of Carl G. Hempel* (N. Rescher et al., eds.; Dordrecht: Reidel), pp. 5–23.
Reprinted 1969 in *Ontological Relativity and Other Essays*;
1977 in Schwartz.
"Linguistics and philosophy," *Language and Philosophy* (S. Hook, ed.; N.Y.U. Press), pp. 95–98.
Reprinted 1972 in Morick;
1975 in Stich;
1976 in *Ways of Paradox*.
Translated 1977 in Stanosz.
"Existence," *Physics, Logic, and History* (W. Yourgrau, ed.; New York: Plenum), ca. 15 pp.
Reprinted 1976 partly in *Ways of Paradox*.
Foreword to D. K. Lewis, *Convention* (Harvard), pp. ix–x.
"Stimulus and meaning," *Isenberg Memorial Lecture Series* 1965–66 (East Lansing: Michigan State), pp. 39–61.
Reprinted 1971 partly in "Epistemology naturalized."
"A symposium on Austin's method," *Symposium on J. L. Austin* (K. T. Fann, ed.: Routledge), pp. 86–90.
(For résumé see 1965.)
"The limits of decision," Akten des XIV. Internationalen Kongresses für Philosophie 3, pp. 57–62.

1970: "Philosophical progress in language theory," Metaphilosophy 1, pp. 2–19.
Reprinted 1970 in Kiefer.
Translated 1977 in Stanosz (Polish).
"Methodological reflections on current linguistic theory," Synthese 21, pp. 386–398.
Reprinted 1972 in Davidson and Harman (*Semantics of Natural Language*);
1974 in Moravcsik;
1975 partly in Davis.
Translated 1976 in Dascal;
1977 in Stanosz.
"Sur la tâche de la grammaire," l'Âge de la Science 3, pp. 3–15 (author's translation of part of a draft of *Philosophy of Logic*).
"On the reasons for indeterminacy of translation," Jour. Philosophy 67, pp. 178–183.
Reprinted 1976 in Davis.

"Reply to D. A. Martin," ibid., pp. 247f.
"Grades of theoreticity," *Experience and Theory* (L. Foster and J. W. Swanson, eds.; Amherst: Univ. of Mass.), pp. 1–17.
Reprinted 1976 partly in *Ways of Paradox*.

1971: "Epistemology naturalized," Akten des XIV. Internationalen Kongresses für Philosophie 6, pp. 87–103.
Preprinted 1969 in *Ontological Relativity and Other Essays*.
Reprinted 1972 in Royce and Roozeboom;
1973 in Chisholm and Schwartz.
"Predicate-functor logic," Proc. of II Scandinavian Logic Symposium (North-Holland), pp. 309–315.
"Algebraic logic and predicate functors," pamphlet (Indianapolis: Bobbs-Merrill), 25 pp.
Reprinted 1971 in Rudner and Scheffler;
1976 in *Ways of Paradox*.
Homage to Carnap, Boston Studies in Philosophy of Science 8, pp. xxii–xxv.
Reprinted 1976 in *Ways of Paradox*.

1972: "Remarks for a memorial symposium," *Bertrand Russell* (D. Pears, ed. New York: Doubleday), pp. 1–5.
"Reflexiones sobre el aprendizaje del lenguaje," Teorema 6, pp. 5–23 (author's translation of part of a draft of *The Roots of Reference*).

1973: "Vagaries of definition," Annals N. Y. Acad. of Sci. 211, pp. 247–250.
Reprinted 1976 in *Ways of Paradox*.

1974: "On Popper's negative methodology," *The Philosophy of Karl Popper* (P. A. Schilpp, ed.; La Salle, Ill.: Open Court), pp. 218–220.
"Paradoxes of plenty," Daedalus 103, no. 4, pp. 38–40.
"Truth and disquotation," Proc. 1971 Tarski Symposium (Providence: Amer. Math. Soc.), pp. 373–384.
Reprinted 1976 in *Ways of Paradox*.
"Comment on Donald Davidson," Synthese 27, nos. 3–4, pp. 325–329.
"Comment on Michael Dummett," ibid., p. 399.

1975: "Mind and verbal dispositions," *Mind and Language: Wolfson College Lectures* (Samuel Guttenplan, ed.; Oxford: Clarendon Press), pp. 83–95.
"The nature of natural knowledge," ibid., pp. 67–81.
Translated 1975 in Rivista di Filosofia, by author.
"The variable," Logic Colloquium (Lecture Notes in Mathematics 453, New York: Springer), pp. 155–163.
Reprinted 1976 in *Ways of Paradox*.
Letter of 1964 to Robert Ostermann, *The Owl of Minerva: Philosophers on Philosophy* (C. J. Bontempo and S. J. Odell, eds.; New York: McGraw-Hill), pp. 227–230.
"On the individuation of attributes" *The Logical Enterprise* (R. Martin, ed.; New Haven: Yale), pp. 3–13.
"On empirically equivalent systems of the world," Erkenntnis 9, pp. 313–328.
Respuestas, *Aspectos de la Filosofía de Quine* (M. Garrido, ed.; Valencia: Teorema), pp. 149–168.

1976: "Grades of discriminability," Journal of Philosophy 73, pp. 113–116.
Comments, *Norbert Wiener: Collected Works*, vol. 1 (P. Masani, ed.; MIT), pp. 225, 233.

"Whither physical objects?" *Boston Studies in Philosophy of Science* 39, pp. 497-504.
Preprinted 1976 partly in *Ways of Paradox.*
"Worlds away," *Journal of Philosophy* 73, pp. 859-864.

1977: "A closer look," ibid. 74, pp. 415f.
"Intension revisited," *Midwest Studies in Philosophy*, pp. 5-11.
Reprinted 1978 in French et al.
"Facts of the matter, *American Philosophy: From Edwards to Quine* (R. Shahan, ed.; Norman: University of Oklahoma Press), pp. 176-196.
Reply to Lycan and Pappas," *Philosophia.*

1978: "The ideas of Quine," *Men of Ideas* (B. Magee, ed.; London, Abridged version in Listener, March 23, pp. 367-369).
"On the nature of moral values," *Values and Morals.* (A. I. Goldman and J. Kim, eds.; Reidel), pp. 37-45.
"Postscript on metaphor," *Critical Inquiry.*

1979: "Cognitive Meaning," *Monist.*
"Kurt Gödel," *American Philosophical Society Yearbook.*

At Press: "Symbols," *Oxford Companion of Mind* (R. Gregory, ed.; Oxford: Clarendon).
"Use and its place in meaning," *Erkenntnis.*
Translated 1977 in Δευκαλίων.
The pragmatists' place in empiricism," in proceedings of a symposium (Columbia: University of South Carolina Press).
"Grammar, truth, and logic," in proceedings of a symposium at Uppsala.
"The variable and its place in reference," in a *Festschrift* for Strawson.

ANTHOLOGIES WHERE ARTICLES HAVE REAPPEARED

1949: Feigl and Sellars, *Readings in Philosophical Analysis* (New York: Appleton).
1952: Linsky, *Semantics and the Philosophy of Language* (Urbana).
1955: Leary, *The Unity of Knowledge* (New York: Doubleday).
1956: Hook, *American Philosophers at Work* (New York: Criterion).
1958: Krzywicki, *Filozofia Amerikanska* (Boston Univ.)
1959: Krikorian and Edel, *Contemporary Philosophic Problems* (New York: Macmillan).
1960: Bunge, *Antologia Semantica* (Buenos Aires).
1961: Saporta, *Psycholinguistics* (New York: Holt).
1962: Aiken and Barrett, *Philosophy in the Twentieth Century* (New York: Random House).
Kazemier and Vuysje, *Logic and Language* (Dordrecht: Reidel).
1963: Lewis, *Clarity is Not Enough* (London: Allen and Unwin).
Schilpp, *The Philosophy of Rudolf Carnap* (La Salle: Open Court).
1964: Ammerman, *Classics of American Philosophy* (New York: McGraw-Hill).
Benacerraf and Putnam, *Readings in the Philosophy of Mathematics* (Englewood: Prentice-Hall).
Fodor and Katz, *The Structure of Language* (Prentice-Hall).
Gregg and Harris, *Form and Strategy in Science* (Reidel).
Marc-Wogau, *Filosofia Genom Tiderm, 1900-thalet* (Stockholm).
Smart, *Problems of Space and Time* (Macmillan).

1965: Baylis, *Metaphysics* (Macmillan).
Nagel and Brandt, *Meaning and Knowledge* (New York: Harcourt, Brace).
1966: Foster and Martin, *Probability, Confirmation, and Simplicity* (New York: Odyssey).
Kurtz, *American Philosophy in the Twentieth Century* (Macmillan).
Rorty, *Pragmatic Philosophy* (Doubleday).
1967: Celucci, *La Filosofia della Matematica* (Bari: Laterza).
Morgenbesser, *Philosophy of Science Today* (New York: Basic Books).
Rorty, *The Linguistic Turn* (Cambridge: MIT).
Schoenman, *Bertrand Russell: Philosopher of the Century* (Allen and Unwin).
1968: Copi and Gould, *Contemporary Readings in Logical Theory* (Macmillan).
Iseminger, *Logic and Philosophy* (Appleton).
Klibansky, *Contemporary Philosophy* (Florence: Nuova Italia).
Kline, *Mathematics in the Modern World* (San Francisco: Freeman).
Margolis, *Introduction to Logical Inquiry* (New York: Knopf).
Tillman, Berofsky, and O'Connor, *Introductory Philosophy* (New York: Harper).
1969: Davidson and Hintikka, *Words and Objections* (Reidel).
Klemke, *Essays on Frege* (Urbana).
Landesman, *Readings in the Foundation of Knowledge* (Prentice-Hall).
Margolis, *Fact and Existence* (Oxford: Blackwell).
O'Connor, *Modern Materialism* (Harcourt, Brace).
Olshewsky, *Problems in the Philosophy of Language* (Holt).
Pasquinelli, *Neo-Empirismo* (Turin: UTET).
1970: Harris and Severens, *Analyticity* (Chicago: Quadrangle).
Kiefer, *Contemporary Philosophical Thought* (Albany: State Univ.)
Klemke, *Essays on Bertrand Russell* (Urbana).
Loux, *Universals and Particulars* (Doubleday).
Myers, *The Spirit of Analytical Philosophy* (New York: Putnam).
Woods and Sumner, *Necessary Truth* (Random House).
1971: Arner, *Readings in Epistemology* (New York: Scott Foresman).
Bynum, *Frege* (New York: Oxford).
Linsky, *Reference and Modality* (Oxford: Clarendon).
Manicas, *Logic as Philosophy* (Princeton: Van Nostrand).
Munsat, *The Analytic-Synthetic Distinction* (New York: Wadsworth).
Rosenberg and Travis, *Readings in the Philosophy of Language* (Prentice-Hall).
Rudner and Scheffler, *Logic and Art* (Indianapolis: Bobbs-Merrill)
Steinberg and Jakobovits, *Semantics* (Cambridge Univ.).
1972: Davidson and Harman, *Semantics of Natural Language* (Reidel).
Feigl, Sellars, and Lehrer, *New Readings in Philosophical Analysis* (Appleton).
Goodman, *Problems and Projects* (Bobbs-Merrill).
Landesman, *The Problem of Universals* (Prentice-Hall).
Marras, *Intentionality, Mind, and Language* (Urbana).
Morick, *Challenges to Empiricism* (Wadsworth).
Pears, *Bertrand Russell* (Doubleday).
Pereira, *Significação e Verdade* (São Paulo: Perspectiva).
Royce and Roozeboom, *The Psychology of Knowing* (London: Gordon and Breach).

Sinnreich, *Zur Philosophie der idealen Sprache* (Munich: Deutscher Taschenbuch).

1973: Bleikasten and Birnbaum, *Versions* (Paris: Masson).
Bonomi, *La Struttura Logica del Linguaggio* (Milan: Bompiani).
Chisholm and Schwartz, *Empirical Knowledge* (Prentice-Hall).
Eisenberg, Bense, and Haberland, *Linguistische Reihe* (Munich: Hueber).
Grandy, *Theories and Observation in Science* (Prentice-Hall).
MacKinnon, *The Problem of Scientific Realism* (Appleton).
Simpson, *Semántica Filosófica* (Buenos Aires: Siglo XXI).
Swartzlander, *Computer Design* (New York: Hayden).

1974: Berlinski, *The Cutting Edge* (New York: Alfred).
Davidson and Harman, *The Logic of Grammar* (Encino: Dickenson).
Fodor, Bever, and Garrett, *Psychology of Language* (McGraw-Hill).
Harman, *On Noam Chomsky: Critical Essays* (Doubleday).
Moravcsik, *Logic and Philosophy for Linguists* (Hague: Mouton).
Pârvu, *Epistemologie: Orientari Contemporare* (Bucharest).

1975: Beck, *Perspectives in Philosophy*.
Stich, *Innate Ideas* (Berkeley: California).

1976: Bencivenga, *Logiche Libere* (Turin: Boringhere).
Dascal, *Metologia da Linguistica* (Sao Paulo: Atica).
Davis, *Philosophy of Language* (Bobbs-Merrill).
Harding, *Can Theories Be Refuted? Essays on the Duhem-Quine Thesis* (Reidel).

1977: Jánoska and Kauz, *Metaphysik* (Darmstadt: Wissenschaftliche Buchges).
Muguerza, *Lecturas de Filosofia* (Madrid: Alianza).
Schwartz, *Naming, Necessity, and Natural Kinds* (Ithaca: Cornell).
Stanosz, *Lingwistyka a Filozofia* (Warsaw: Panstwowe Wydanictwo).
Stegmüller, *Das Universalienproblem* (Wissenschaftliche Buchges).
Sukale, *Moderne Sprachphilosophie* (Hamburg: Hoffman).
Zabeeh, Klemke, and Jacobson, *Readings in Semantics* (Urbana).

1978: Copi and Gould, *Contemporary Philosophical Logic* (New York: St. Martin's).
French et al., *Contemporary Perspectives in the Philosophy of Language* (Minneapolis: University of Minnesota Press).

1979: Benacerraf and Putnam 1964, 2d ed.
Tucker, *The Critical Temper* (New York: Ungar).

ABSTRACTS

1935: "A unified calculus of propositions, classes, and relations," Bull. Amer. Math. Soc. 41, p. 338.
1937: "Is logic a matter of words?" Journal of Philosophy 34, p. 674.
1940: *Mathematical Logic*, Year Book of Amer. Phil. Soc., pp. 230f.
1947: "On the problem of universals," Journal of Symbolic Logic 12, p. 31.
1950: "Information patterns for games in extensive form" (with W. D. Krentel and J. C. C. McKinsey), Proc. Internat. Cong. of Math. 1.
1951: "Some theorems on definability and decidability" (with Alonzo Church), Journal of Symbolic Logic 16, pp. 239f.
1952: "The problem of simplifying truth functions," ibid. 17, p. 156.
1956: "Unification of universes in set theory," ibid. 21, p. 216.

1959: "Eliminating variables without applying functions to functions," ibid. 24, pp. 324f.
1970: Comments on Belnap, Nous 4, p. 12.
1971: "Predicate-functor logic," Journal of Symbolic Logic 36, p. 382.

MISCELLANEOUS

1934: Report on Whitehead, "Logical definitions of extension, class, and number," Amer. Math. Monthly 41, pp. 129–131.
1946: Translation (with introduction) of Löwenheim's MS "On making indirect proofs direct," Script and Mathematica 12, pp. 125–134.
1947: Letter in Carnap, *Meaning and Necessity* (Chicago), pp. 196f.
1951: "It tastes like chicken," Furioso 6, pp. 37–39.
1954: Letter on Griggs, Atlantic Monthly 194, p. 21.
1970: Reply to Mr. Flexner, New York Review of Books 13, no. 12, p. 38.
1976: Letter to Grünbaum in Harding (above, p. 132.) Comment on Croddy in *Erkenntnis* 10, p. 103.

BOOK REVIEWS

1930: Of Nicod, *Foundations of Geometry and Induction*, Amer. Math. Monthly 37, pp. 305–307.
1933: Of Peirce, *Collected Papers*, vol. 2; Isis 19, pp. 220–229.
1935: Of same, vols. 3–4; Isis 22, pp. 285–297, 551–553.
Of Carnap, *Logische Syntax der Sprache*: Philosophical Review 44, pp. 394–397.
1936: Of Garcia Baca, *Introductión a la Lógica Moderna*; Journal of Symbolic Logic 1, pp. 112f.
1937: Of Weinberg, *Examination of Logical Positivism*; ibid. 2, pp. 89f.
Of Jeffreys, *Scientific Inference*; Science 86, p. 590.
1938: Of Tarski, *Einführung in die mathematische Logik*; Bull. Amer. Math. Soc. 44, pp. 317f.
Of Ushenko, *Theory of Logic*; Philosophical Review 47, p. 94.
Of Hilbert and Ackermann, *Grundzüge der theoretischen Logik*; Journal of Symbolic Logic 3, pp. 83f.
1941: Of Russell, *Inquiry into Meaning and Truth*; ibid. 6, pp. 29f.
Of Serrus, *Essai sur la Signification de la Logique*; ibid., pp. 62f.
Of da Silva, *Elementos de Lógica Matemática*; ibid., pp. 109f.
1946: Of Godinho, *Esboços sobre Alguns Problemas da Lógica*; ibid., 11, p. 126.
1947: Of Toranzos, *Introducción a la Epistemologia y la Fundamentación de la Matemática*; ibid. 12, pp. 20f.
1948: Of Reichenbach, *Elements of Symbolic Logic*; Journal of Philosophy 45, pp. 161–166.
1951: Of Goodman, *Structure of Appearance*; ibid. 48, pp. 556–563.
1952: Of Ferrater Mora, *Diccionario de Filosofia*; Journal of Symbolic Logic 17, pp. 129f.
1963: Of *National Geographic Atlas*; New York Review of Books 1, no. 3, p. 8.
1964: Of Mencken, *American Language*; ibid., no. 9, p. 7.
Of *Atlas of Britain*; ibid. 2, no. 2, p. 17.
Of Smart, *Philosophy and Scientific Realism*; ibid., no. 11, p. 3.
Of Geach, *Reference and Generality*; Philosophical Review 73, pp. 100–104.

1965: Of Bagrow, *History of Cartography*; New York Review of Books 5, no. 4, pp. 18f.
1967: Of Russell, *Autobiography*, vol. 1; Boston Globe, April 9, p. B43.
1968: Of *Times Atlas of the World*; Book World (in Washington Post and Chicago Tribune), May 5, p. 7.
1969: Of *American Heritage Dictionary* and *Random House Dictionary*, College Edition; New York Review of Books 13, no. 10, pp. 3f.; see also no. 12, p. 38; and vol. 14, no. 102, p. 54.
1972: Of Munitz (ed.), *Identity and Individuation*; Journal of Philosophy 69, pp. 488–497.
1977: Of Evans and McDowell (eds.), *Truth and Meaning*: ibid. 74, pp. 225–241. Of Lakatos, *Proofs and Refutations*; British Journal for Philosophy of Science 28, pp. 81–95.
Of Lewis Carroll, *Symbolic Logic*; Times Literary Supplement, pp. 1018f. Reprinted in 1979 in part in Tucker.
1978: Of Smullyan, *What Is the Name of This Book?* New York Times Review, May 28, pp. 6, 17.

REVIEWS OF ARTICLES

1936: Of Tarski, "Grundzüge des Systemenkalküls"; Journal of Symbolic Logic I, pp. 71f.
Of Russell, "On order in time"; ibid., pp. 73f.
Short ones (under 400 words): ibid., pp. 43, 68, 113.
1937: Of Saarnio, "Zur heterologischen Paradoxie"; ibid. 2, p. 138.
Of Stone, "Note on formal logic"; ibid., pp. 174f.
Short ones: ibid., pp. 37, 46f., 59, 83f.
1938: Of Chwistek and Hetper, "New foundation of formal metamathematics"; ibid. 3, pp. 120f.
Short ones: ibid., pp. 47–49, 56, 94, 121f.
1939: Of Hermes, "Semiotik"; ibid. 4, pp. 87f.
Short ones: ibid., pp. 102, 125.
1940: Of Bröcker, "Antinomien und Paradoxien"; ibid. 5, p. 79.
Of Lesniewski, "Einleitende Bemerkungen"; ibid., pp. 83f.
Of Church, "Formulation of theory of types"; ibid., pp. 114f.
Short ones: ibid., pp. 30, 71, 84, 157, 168f.
1941: Of Rosser, "Independence of Quine's axioms"; ibid. 6, p. 163.
1942: Short one: ibid. 7, pp. 44f.
1946: Of Barcan, "Functional calculus based on strict implication"; ibid. 11, pp 96f.
1947: Of Nelson, "Contradiction and existence"; ibid. 12, pp. 52–55.
Of Barcan, "Identity of individuals"; ibid., pp. 95f. [Correction in 23 (1958), p. 342.]
Of Schröter, "Was ist eine mathematische Theorie?"; ibid., pp. 136f.
Short ones: ibid., pp. 55, 95.
1948: Short ones: ibid. 13, pp. 122, 158.
1949: Of Fraenkel, "Relation of equality"; ibid. 14, p. 130.
Of Saarnio, "Der Begriff der Hierarchie"; ibid., p. 131.
Short ones: ibid., pp. 59f., 64, 257.
1950: Of Feys, "Simple notation for relations"; ibid. 15, pp. 71f.
Short ones: ibid., pp. 139, 149f., 215.

1951: Of Myhill, "Complete theory of numbers"; ibid. 16, pp. 65–67.
Of Geach, "Subject and predicate"; ibid., p. 138.
Of Myhill, "Report of investigations"; ibid., pp. 217f.
Short ones: ibid., pp. 138f., 214, 273.
1952: Of Ajdukiewicz, "On the notion of existence"; ibid. 17, pp. 144f.
1958: Short one: ibid. 23, p. 41.

Notes on Contributors

DIANA ACKERMAN (Ph.D., University of Michigan) is Assistant Professor of Philosophy in Brown University. Her publications include "Plantinga, Proper Names and Propositions," *Philosophical Studies* (1976); "Critical Notes on Jonathan Bennett's Linguistic Behavior," *Canadian Journal of Philosophy* (1978); "Proper Names, Essences and Intuitive Beliefs," to appear in *Theory and Decision*, a special issue of invited papers in the *Philosophy of Language* (forthcoming); "Proper Names, Propositional Attitudes and Non-Descriptive Connotations," *Philosophical Studies* (forthcoming); and "Recent Work on the Theory of Reference," *American Philosophical Quarterly* (forthcoming).

MAXWELL JOHN CRESSWELL (Ph.D., University of Manchester; Litt.D., Victoria University of Wellington) is Professor of Philosophy in Victoria University of Wellington and a British Commonwealth Scholar (1961–63). His publications include *An Introduction to Modal Logic* (with G. E. Hughes, 1968), *Logics and Languages* (1973), and over sixty articles on logic, philosophy of language, and the history of philosophy.

DALE GOTTLIEB (Ph.D., Brandeis University) is Associate Professor of Philosophy in the Johns Hopkins University. He received a National Science Foundation Sabbatical Grant in 1974. He is the author of *Ontological Economy: Method and Application* (forthcoming), and his other publications include "Reference and Ontology," *Journal of Philosophy* (1974); "A Method for Ontology, with Applications to Numbers and Events," *Journal of Philosophy* (1976); and "The Truth About Arithmetic," *American Philosophical Quarterly* (1978).

RICHARD E. GRANDY (Ph.D., Princeton University) is Associate Professor of Philosophy in the University of North Carolina at Chapel

Hill. He is the recipient of a National Science Foundation Postdoctoral Fellowship and an American Council of Learned Societies Study Fellowship, and he is the author of *Advanced Logic for Applications* (1977) and many other publications.

GILBERT HARMAN (Ph.D., Harvard University) is Professor of Philosophy in Princeton University and holds a 1978–79 John Simon Guggenheim Memorial Foundation Fellowship. He is the author of *Thought* (1973) and *The Nature of Morality* (1977) and is coeditor, with Donald Davidson, of three anthologies. His major interest is the nature of reasoning.

STEPHEN LEEDS (Ph.D., Massachusetts Institute of Technology) is Associate Professor of Philosophy in the University of Colorado. His special interests are philosophy of language, logic, inductive logic, and epistemology, and he has published articles on them in several journals.

MICHAEL E. LEVIN (Ph.D., Columbia University) is Associate Professor of Philosophy in City College, City University of New York. A Woodrow Wilson Fellow, he is the author of *Metaphysics and the Mind-Body Problem* (1979), as well as many articles on ethics, philosophy of science, foundations of mathematics, and philosophy of language. He is now writing a book on problems of social philosophy.

J. N. MOHANTY (Ph.D., Göttingen University) is George Lynn Cross Research Professor of Philosophy in the University of Oklahoma. He is a director of the Husserl Archives, a member of the executive committee of the Society for Phenomenology, a lifetime member of the Indian Academy of Philosophy, and a board member of several philosophy journals. His books include *Nicolai Hartmann and A. N. Whitehead: A Study in Recent Platonism* (1957); *Edmund Husserl's Theory of Meaning* (1964), *Gaṅgeśa's Theory of Truth* (1966), *Phenomenology and Ontology* (1970), *The Concept of Intentionality* (1972), and *Readings on Husserl's Logical Investigations* (1977), and he is the author of many articles.

MARK PASTIN (Ph.D., Harvard University) is Associate Professor of Philosophy in Indiana University. He is a member of the Philosophy of Science Association, the Hastings Center, and the Harvard Graduate Society. He has been a National Science Foundation Graduate Fellow and has been the recipient of a National Endowment for the Humanities Summer Grant and Fellowship (1976–77). He has published articles on epistemology, ethics, and metaphysics. He is now writing a book offering a systematic epistemic theory. He is also a devoted marathon runner.

WILLARD V. QUINE (Ph.D., Harvard University; Litt.D., Oberlin College; LL.D., Ohio State University; Dr., University of Lille; Litt.D., University of Akron; Litt.D., Washington University; L.H.D., University of Chicago; Litt.D., Temple University; Litt.D., Oxford University; Litt.D., Cambridge University) is Edgar Pierce Professor of Philosophy, Emeritus, in Harvard University. He is a member of the American Academy of Arts and Sciences, the National Academy of Sciences, the Association for Symbolic Logic (President, 1953–56), and the American Philosophical Society. His more recent awards include the Sir Henry Saville Fellowship, Merton College, Oxford University (1973–74), and awards from the Center of Advanced Studies, Wesleyan University (1965); and the Center for Advanced Study in Behavioral Sciences (1958–59). A bibliography of Quine's works appears elsewhere in this book.

MARK STEINER (Ph.D., Princeton University) is Senior Lecturer in the Department of Philosophy at the Hebrew University of Jerusalem. He has received awards from the National Science Foundation and the National Endowment for the Humanities and has been a Danforth Graduate Fellow. He is the author of *Mathematical Knowledge* (1975).

INDEX

Absolute: 114
Abstract entities: 138, 146
Abstraction: 134
Acquaintance: 99–100, 102
Affection: 39
Alternation: 60
Analogy: 158–59, 168
Analytic hypotheses of translation: 25
Analyticity: 104
Anaphora: 17
Appearance: 113–14
Aristotle: 60
Arithmetic: 45, 54, 57, 74, 82, 107, 133–34
Assenting: 101, 158
Assertion: 35, 39
Association: 36
Atomic theory: 164
Attitudes, propositional: *see* propositional attitudes
Attribute: 104
Autodescriptive system: 50, 65n.
Axiomatization, finite: 53, 133
Axiom of choice: 53, 78n.

Bach, E.: 20n.
Begriffe: 98
Behaviorism: 167
Belief: 168; *de dicto*, 145, 147; *de re*, 98, 145–52; justified, 85; network of, 101, 103; warranted, 120
Benacerraf, P.: 143n.
Bernays, P.: 70; lemma, 76–77
Biology: 169
Birkhoff, G.: 60
Boolean algebra: 55, 61
Bradley, F. H.: 113–16, 117n.
Brentano, F.: 25–26, 30, 39

Brouwer, L.: 47
Brown, R.: 43n.

Carnap, R.: 97, 99, 104, 107n.
Cartesian coordinates: 139
Categories: 26
Cauchy's theorem: 141
Causation: 99
Chang, C. C.: 134
Change: 162
Chemistry: 169
Chisholm, R.: 146, 149–51
Chomsky, N.: 17, 21
Church, A.: 98–99, 102, 104
Class measurement: 133
Coherence: 131
Commutativity: 61
Competence, linguistic: *see* linguistic competence
Completeness: 53; epistemic, 121–28, 131–32
Complex numbers: 138–42, 164; norm of, 139
Concept, individual: *see* individual concept
Concomitant variation: 156
Conditional assent: 101–102
Conditioning: 157–58
Confirmation: 86, 119, 127
Conjunction: 29, 40, 49
Connotation: 103
Consistency: 49
Constants: individual, 110; logical, 46, 57, 61, 74
Constructive deduction: 34
Context of discovery: 141
Conventionalism: 46, 48, 51–53, 62–63
Convergence (in mathematics): 141–42
Counterfactuals: 99, 127

193

Craig, W.: 15
Crucial conditional: 62–64

Davidson, D.: 94–95, 169n.
Deduction: 86
Definite descriptions: 146
Definition: 100, 102
Deformation (of a mathematical proof): 135–37, 139, 141
De Morgan's law: 57
Denotation: 74, 99, 101, 103, 106
Determinacy, epistemic: 85–86, 88–89, 91–93
Determinations, relative: 36–37
Disjunction: 40
Dispositions: 162
Distinctness, criterion of: 82
Distributive laws of logic: 54–55, 57
Duhem, P.: 9
Dummett, M.: 63–65, 119

Egocentric spaces: 33
Eidetic structure: 24
Embedding: 133–34, 139
Empirical component (of theory of language): 128–30
Empirical equivalence: 9–19; potential, 14–15, 18
Empiricism: 46, 119, 126–27, 132, 155
Entailment, logical: *see* logical entailment
"Entrenchment": 125
Epistemology: 79, 90, 109, 117, 119, 124, 132; naturalizing of, 109–17, 124
Epoché: 35
Equivalence class: 71–72
Essentialism: 24, 105
Euler's theorem: 139
Events: 94–95
Evidence: observational, 10–12; theory of, 119, 121
Evidential core: 85–86
Excluded middle, law of: 58
Existence: 31
Existential generalization: 147
Existential import: 22
Experience: preobjective, 27; prepredicative, 36, 38–41; sensory, 126, 129
Explanation: 86; causal, 168–69; mathematical, 134–42

Exportation: 147, 152
Extension: 98–99, 105–107

Fact: 112–13
Factuality: 168
Family resemblance: 51, 60–61
Fan theorem: 65
Feferman, S.: 134
Feldman, F.: 132n.
Fermat's theorem: 87
Field theory: 164
Flavele, J. H.: 43n.
Foundationalism: 85
Frege, G.: 70, 77, 98–99, 103–105, 107n., 152
Friedman, M.: 66n.
Function: 65; predicate, 122–23

Gaifman, H.: 143n.
Gardiner, M.: 60
Gauss, K. F.: 135
Geach, P.: 81–82, 84
Generalization: 134, 137
Glymour, C.: 20n.
Gödel, G.: 102, 110
Goodman, N.: 132n., 138
Grice, H. P.: 65n.

Haack, S.: 66n.
Habit: 39
Hallucination: 129
Harman, G.: 20n., 31
Hartmann, N.: 42n.
Hempel, C.: 102
Holism: 113–14
"Holizing": 127–28, 131–32
Horizon, internal: 36
Hume, D.: 52, 155
Humphries, B.: 11
Husserl, E.: 24, 27, 35–42
Hypothetico-deductive method: 159

Ideas: abstract, 155; clear, 155–56; concrete, 155
Identification: 164
Identity: 22–24, 31, 33, 37–39, 83–84, 87–90, 92–95, 104, 152, 159; criterion of, 80–82, 84, 89–90, 93, 95, 107; of events, 94–95; substitutivity of, 39–40, 93

Imitation: 158–59
Immanence: 60, 62, 66n.
Indeterminacy: 56, 165; epistemic, 86–88; of translation: *see* translation, indeterminacy of
Individual concept: 149
Individuation: 28, 152, 158, 164
Induction: 86, 157–59
Inductive generalization: 131
Inference to the best explanation: 131
Integers: 145–52
Intension: 99, 103, 105–107
Intentional acts: 41
Intentionality: 39, 42
Intentions: 36
Interchangeability *salva veritate*: 148
Interpretation: 56, 66n., 69–71, 74–76, 110, 139, 165; isomorphic, 75; relative, 70, 77
Intersubjectivity: 27
Intuitionism: 54, 58–59, 64–65, 66n., 82

Judgment, predicative: 35–38, 40–41

Kamp, J. A. W.: 118n.
Kant, I.: 24–26, 30
Kaplan, D.: 146–48, 150–52
Keisler, H. J.: 134
Kleene, S.: 45, 59, 77n.
Knowledge: causal theory of, 146, 153n.; holistic conception of, 46; necessary condition of, 84; objective, 90–93
Kripke, S.: 22, 104

Lakatos, I.: 46
Language: 69–71; holistic view of, 119, 126, 132; interpreted, 70; observational, 138; social character of, 156; theoretical, 138; theory of, 119–21, 123–32
Language learning: 21, 32, 34, 40–41, 65n., 93, 91, 158–59
Law of cosines: 137
Laws, logical: *see* logical laws
Leibniz's law: 93
Lewis, C. I.: 129
Lewis, D.: 65n., 111–12, 114, 116, 117n.

Linguistic competence: 83–84
Locke, J.: 155
Logic: classical, 54, 56–57, 59–63, 66n., 160; deviant, 60–61; empirical view of, 47, 51–52; propositional, 45, 53–56; predicate, 45
Logical atomism: 99, 112–13
Logical entailment: 122
Logical incompatibility: 9, 12–13, 15–16
Logical laws: 46–47, 50–53, 57, 59, 63, 65n., 67n.
Lowenheim-Skolem theorem: 70–71, 76, 133, 141, 165

Materialism: 165
Material mode: 104
Mathematical family: 135, 140–42
Mathematical reduction: 133–42
Mathematics: 45, 64, 85, 162
Maximal consistent set of sentences: 76
McNeill, D.: 35
Meaning: 97–106, 119, 145, 166; change of, 57, 61–63; operational, 57; theory of, 9, 64–65, 100, 102–104
Mentalism: 26
Merleau-Ponty, M.: 27
Metaphysics: 110–11, 114, 117
Mill, J. S.: 156
Mistranslation: 47–49, 51, 54, 58, 60, 62
Modal context: 147; *de dicto*, 148
Modalities: 97, 112; *de re*, 105
Modalization: 36, 38
Modal logic, quantified: 148
Models: 69–77, 78n., 112–13, 115, 117n., 133–34, 139–40; finite, 71–74; isomorphic, 71–72, 74–75, 78n.; of same cardinality, 71, 74–76; preferred, 71–72
Moore, G. E.: 82
Morton, A.: 66n.
Murphy, J.: 59

Names: 22, 32, 73–74, 83, 100, 103, 106, 122, 161; proper, 81–82, 89; standard, 146–48; vivid, 152
Naturalism: 117n.
Natural kinds: 135, 141
Necessity: 62, 64, 65n., 104–105, 161; *de re*, 105, 146

195

Negation: 29, 40, 49, 60
Nerlich, G.: 64
Newton, I.: 55
Noema: 39–40
Noetic-noematic structure: 41
Nominalism: 138, 155
Noncontradiction, law of: 48–51
Nondenumerable set: 110
Number theory: 70, 72, 76, 77n., 133
Numeral: 150–53

Objectivity, genesis of: 35
Observation: 109
Obviousness: 51–53
Omnitemporality: 37
Ontological commitment: 72–73, 75, 77n.
Ontological reduction: 69–77
Ontological relativity: 77, 113, 115
Ontology: 23, 28, 40–41, 45, 74, 76, 78n., 79, 84, 91, 133, 138, 141–42, 159–66, 168
Orthogonal transformations: 137–38

Peano, G.: 45
Peirce, C. S.: 9, 10, 60
Phenomenology: 40–42
Phrase-structure grammar: 17
Physicalism: 162–68
Physics: 169
Physiology: 169
Piaget, J.: 27, 32–34, 39
Plato: 69
Platonism: 138
Pleasure: 27–28, 34, 39
Poincaré, H.: 19
Point mass: 54–56
Polar coordinates: 139
Polya, G.: 136
Possible worlds: 65n., 87, 91, 105–106, 111–12, 114
Predicate functors: 105, 160–61
Predicates: 79–80, 97, 101–103, 107, 110, 125, 160–61, 165–66
Predication: 29, 35, 82–83; *see also* divided reference
Pregivenness: 35
Principle of charity: 47
Prior, A. N.: 117n.
Probability: 10, 52
Projectibility: 125

Properties: 97, 99–107, 113, 147, 149–51, 160; characteristic, 135
Propositional attitudes: 112, 147, 161, 168; *de dicto*, 148; *de re*, 145–46, 148–50
Propositions: 105–107, 120, 132n., 145–46, 148–50
Proxy function: 69–71, 75, 77n., 133
Psychologism: 41
Psychology: 109–11, 117, 169
Putnam, H.: 55–57, 60–61, 63, 66n., 102, 104, 169n.
Pythagorean theorem: 136–37

Quantification: 22–24, 26, 28, 30–32, 73, 79, 160–61, 165; into modal contexts, 147–48; substitutional, 71–74
Quantifiers: 79–80, 165
"Quantum logic": 54, 56–57, 60–62
Quantum mechanics: 46, 54–57, 62
Quasi-truth functions: 50
Quaternions: 139

Rationalism: 155
Reality: 112–16
Recursive realizability: 59
Reduction, mathematical: *see* mathematical reduction
Reductionism: 41, 119, 163, 166
Reeves, A. L.: 118n.
Reference: 21–42, 45, 79–85, 89–94, 101, 119, 128–30, 132, 146, 160, 165, 168; divided, 80, 83; inscrutability of, 23, 30–32, 69, 76, 107, 119, 130; objective, 23–32, 34–35, 39, 159; opaque, 22, 25, 41; psychogenesis of, 22–25, 39–42; relativity of, 130; transparent, 22, 31–32, 41
Reidentification, criterion of: 82
Relations-in-intension: 97
Relations of sentences: 120–28, 130–32
Relativity theory: 46
Representation: 98
Rescher, N.: 50, 65n.
Routley, F. R.: 118n.
Rules, syntactical transformation: 17
Russell, B.: 22, 45, 99–100, 102–104

Salience: 27–29, 34
Schema: 33

Self-reference: 115
Sellars, W.: 116
Semantics: 79, 82, 90–92, 101, 105, 107, 111; mentalistic, 166; model-theoretic, 117n.; of 'now', 117n.
Sensory-motor stage: 33
Sensory receptors: 27
Sentences: analytic, 53, 99; as vehicles of communication, 156; atomic, 160; basic v. nonbasic, 124; closed, 105; contingent, 126; eternal, 29; evidence, 130–32; modal, 106; observation, 156–59, 165; occasion, 29–30, 91, 156; open, 70, 93; physical, 130–32; sensory, 128, 130; standing, 29; theoretical, 165
Sets: 160–62; *see also* set theory
Set theory: 70, 76, 110, 133–34, 164; *see also* sets
Similarity: 36; perceptual, 27–28
Sinn: 39, 98–99
Skepticism: 125
Smart, J. J. C.: 115
Smokovich, R.: 66n.
Sortal universal: 82
Sosa, E.: 148–49, 151
Space-time: 64, 66n.; regions, 164–67
Spatio-temporal coincidence: 89–90, 94
Standard names: 146–48, 151
Statements: 120
Steiner, M.: 153n.
Stimulation conditions: 128
Stimulus: 36
Strawson, P. F.: 82–84
Substantivization: 38
Substitutional transformation: 29
Substrate: 36
Successor relation: 76
Syncategorematic expressions: 60
Synonymy: 45, 80, 98, 101, 102, 104, 106, 166–67
Synthesis: active, 37
Synthesis: passive, 37

Tautology: barest, 63, 65n.
Taylor's theorem: 142
Temporality: 38
Terms: individuating, 28–31; mass, 28, 31, 83; observation, 158; singular, 79
Theoretical entities: 165
Theory: 69–71, 109–11, 116–17

Tooke, J. H.: 155
Trace: 27, 29, 34, 39
"Trace theory": 17
Transcendence: 60, 62, 66n.
Translation: deviant, 47, 51–53, 62, 66n.; heterophonic, 59; homophonic, 13, 47, 49, 59, 66n.; indeterminacy of, 9, 30–31, 62, 64, 69, 106–107, 113, 130, 167; manual of, 23; normal, 58; of ordinary language, 162; radical, 50, 53, 62, 167; weakly deviant, 58–59, 66n., 61–62
Translation argument: 47, 51, 53–55, 57, 59
Truth: analytic, 124; coherence theory of, 116; conceptual, 124; contingent, 45; disappearance theory of, 117; logical, 45–65; mathematical, 46; necessary, 45, 63, 124
Truth conditions: *see* truth-functions
Truth-functions: 29, 50–51, 61, 65n., 71–72, 74–75, 84, 86, 106, 125–26, 156, 160–61, 165
Truth values: *see* truth-functions

Undecidability: 87
Under-determination: 9, 15–19, 131
Understanding: 98–99, 101, 103, 120
Unity of self-consciousness: 26
Univalence: 50
Universal categorical: 29–31
Unrevisability: 104

Variables: 160–61, 165–66
Vectors: 139, 141–42
Vector space: 141
Verdict function: 29
Verdict logic: 40–41
Verificationism, holistic: 9–10
Vivid names: 152
Vocabulary: 165–66
Von Neumann, J.: 60, 70
Vurpillot, E.: 43n.

Warrant: 119–32; *prima facie*, 122
Warrant conditions: 120–28, 130–31
Warrant principles: 121–24
Warrant sentence: 122–23
Wilson, N.: 96n.
Wittgenstein, L.: 63–64, 155, 157

Zermelo, E.: 70

LIBRARY OF DAVIDSON COLLEGE

NOV.